AI Innovations in Public Services

Ines Mergel • Carsten Schmidt
Editors

AI Innovations in Public Services

The Case of National Libraries

Springer

Editors
Ines Mergel
Department of Politics and Public Administration
University of Konstanz
Konstanz, Germany

Carsten Schmidt
Department of Politics and Public Administration
University of Konstanz
Konstanz, Germany

ISBN 978-3-032-01343-9 ISBN 978-3-032-01344-6 (eBook)
https://doi.org/10.1007/978-3-032-01344-6

This book is funded by the European Union under grant agreement ID 101061516. The information and views set out in this book are those of the author(s) only and do not necessarily reflect those of the European Union or the European Research Executive Agency (REA). Neither the European Union nor the granting authority can be held responsible for them. The book was made possible through the financial support of LibrarIN project partners Athens Technology Center S.A. and The Lisbon Council.

This Springer imprint is published by the registered company Springer Nature Switzerland AG
The registered company address is: Gewerbestrasse 11, 6330 Cham, Switzerland

Foreword

Artificial intelligence (AI) is no longer a distant concept, it is actively reshaping the way individuals interact with knowledge, access information, and navigate public services. In the public sector, AI is driving innovation, improving efficiency, and transforming service delivery. Libraries, as fundamental cultural and educational institutions, are part of this evolution, embracing AI to improve the management, organisation, and dissemination of knowledge. By integrating AI, libraries are not only streamlining internal processes but also redefining their role as dynamic and future-oriented knowledge hubs in the digital age.

This book is the result of the LibrarIN project [1], a Horizon Europe initiative focused on reimagining library services through social innovation and the co-creation of public value. The project explores how libraries can integrate co-creation strategies, providing actionable insights and recommendations for policymakers and library managers to help shape the future of libraries. Through extensive research and collaboration with library professionals, policymakers, and communities, LibrarIN examines, among other aspects, the role of AI in transforming library services, ensuring they remain accessible, engaging, and responsive to societal needs. The project underscores the importance of human-centred AI implementation, emphasising that technological advancements should complement rather than replace the expertise and essential roles of librarians.

Libraries worldwide are already incorporating AI-driven technologies to enhance both user experience and operational efficiency. For instance, AI-powered search tools utilising natural language processing (NLP) facilitate more intuitive and precise research by delivering highly relevant search results [2, 3]. Automated cataloguing and metadata generation reduce the manual workload of librarians while enhancing the consistency of classification and digital archiving [4, 5]. AI-driven chatbots and virtual assistants provide continuous user support, handling routine inquiries and assisting with research navigation [5]. Personalised recommendation systems enhance user engagement by suggesting books and resources tailored to individual preferences, thereby fostering deeper interaction with library collections [6, 7]. Additionally, AI-based predictive analytics enable libraries to better anticipate user needs, optimise resource allocation, and curate collections in a more strategic and data-informed manner.

Despite these benefits, the integration of AI in libraries presents several challenges. Data privacy and security remain primary concerns, as AI relies on extensive datasets, necessitating strict adherence to privacy regulations and ethical guidelines [6]. Algorithmic bias is a critical concern, as AI systems can unintentionally reproduce biases present in their training data, potentially narrowing the scope of search results and limiting the diversity of recommendations. To address this, libraries must implement rigorous auditing mechanisms and ensure continuous refinement of AI models, prioritising fairness, inclusivity, and equitable access to knowledge. Equally important is the need for transparency in AI-driven decision-making processes to maintain public trust.

Financial and technical constraints also pose substantial barriers. Many AI solutions require significant investment, which may be prohibitive for libraries operating with limited budgets [8]. Furthermore, the successful deployment of AI-driven systems necessitates specialised expertise, underscoring the importance of ongoing professional development and AI literacy training for library staff. Building internal capacity and fostering interdisciplinary collaboration will be key to ensuring that AI is implemented in a way that aligns with libraries' fundamental values of openness, equity, and accessibility [9].

As AI continues to advance, its role in public services will be shaped by evolving regulatory frameworks, ethical considerations, and technological progress. The EU Artificial Intelligence Act [10, 11] establishes key guidelines emphasising transparency, risk management, and accountability. Given their long-standing expertise in data management and commitment to inclusivity, libraries are well-positioned to lead the responsible and ethical adoption of AI within public institutions.

Furthermore, libraries have a unique opportunity to collaborate with public service agencies to ensure that AI applications are designed to meet real community needs, positioning AI as a tool for empowerment rather than exclusion. Looking ahead, libraries may find themselves at the crossroads of technology and knowledge, serving as vital bridges between innovation and public service.

Beyond the technological advancements, the integration of AI in libraries is ultimately about enhancing human experiences, facilitating access to knowledge, supporting library professionals, and empowering diverse communities. AI should not be viewed as a substitute for human expertise but as a powerful tool that enhances the role of libraries as facilitators of learning, discovery, and cultural preservation.

This book is designed for a diverse audience, including library managers, policymakers, researchers, and practitioners, offering both strategic insights and practical case studies on how AI can shape the future of libraries. Our goal is to provide a comprehensive resource that supports the responsible and effective adoption of AI within library ecosystems.

The motivation for this book stems from a growing recognition that libraries stand at a pivotal moment, one where tradition and innovation must converge. The future of libraries will not be defined by technology alone but by how well we harness AI to support libraries' enduring mission as inclusive, accessible, and community-driven institutions.

This publication is the result of extensive collaboration within the LibrarIN project. We sincerely thank all LibrarIN partners, researchers, and professionals whose expertise and contributions made this work possible. Special appreciation goes to Athens Technology Center (ATC)[1] and The Lisbon Council[2] (LC) for their contributions, as well as to our colleagues at University of Konstanz for their exceptional efforts in coordinating and editing this book. Finally, we extend our gratitude to the European Commission for its support through the Horizon Europe Programme, recognising the evolving role of libraries in the digital era.

Acknowledgements This project is funded by the European Union under grant agreement ID 101061516. The information and views set out in this publication are those of the author(s) only and do not necessarily reflect those of the European Union or the European Research Executive Agency (REA). Neither the European Union nor the granting authority can be held responsible for them.

References

1. More information available at https://librarin.eu/
2. A.M. Cox, S. Pinfield, S. Rutter, The intelligent library. Library Hi Tech. **37**(3): 418–435 (2019)
3. K. Steiger, Artificial intelligence in higher education and academic libraries: a literature review. Endnotes. **12**(1): 25–36 (2024)
4. M. Sanji, H. Behzadi, G. Gomroki, Chatbot: an intelligent tool for libraries. Library Hi Tech News **39**(3): 17–20 (2022)
5. British Library, *Foundations of the Future: The British Library's Collection Metadata Strategy 2019–2023* (2019)
6. D. Gunter, *AI challenges for librarians* (2024), https://www.researchinformation.info/analysis-opinion/ai-challenges-librarians/. Accessed 24 Mar 2025
7. *Practical, responsible and human-centered: the future of AI in libraries* (2023). https://blog.pressreader.com/libraries-institutions/practical-responsible-and-human-centered-the-future-of-ai-in-libraries. Accessed 31 Mar 2025
8. *60% of libraries evaluating or planning for AI integration—report* (2024). https://www.researchinformation.info/news/60-libraries-evaluating-or-planning-ai-integration-report/. Accessed 24 Mar 2025
9. FAIFE; IFLA, IFLA statement on libraries and artificial intelligence (2020)

---

[1] **Athens Technology Center (ATC)** (www.atc.gr) is a Greek IT company with a strong presence in Europe, specialising in innovative solutions for media, banking, retail, utilities, and the public sector. With over 30 years of R&D experience (www.ilab.atc.gr), ATC continuously evolves its products and services by integrating emerging technologies such as Generative AI and machine learning. Actively participating in European initiatives, the company contributes to the development of secure and intelligent systems that facilitate digital transformation. ATC is responsible for the project coordination of LibrarIN Horizon project.

[2] **The Lisbon Council for Economic Competitiveness and Social Renewal (LC)** is a Brussels-based think tank and policy network established in 2003 in Belgium as a non-profit, non-partisan association (https://lisboncouncil.net/). The group is dedicated to making a positive contribution through cutting-edge research and by building and mobilising large coalitions capable of ambitiously analysing key issues, sharing experience, and delivering cutting-edge solutions for improved governance and change for the better.

10. European Parliament and European Council, Regulation (EU) 2024/1689 of the European Parliament and of the Council of 13 June 2024 laying down harmonised rules on artificial intelligence and amending June 13, 2024, European Parliament and European Council
11. European Parliament, *EU AI Act: first regulation on artificial intelligence* (2023), https://www.europarl.europa.eu/topics/en/article/20230601STO93804/eu-ai-act-first-regulation-on-artificial-intelligence. Accessed 31 Mar 2025

Athens Technology Center S.A.
Athens, Greece

Anna Triantafillou
a.triantafillou@atc.gr

The Lisbon Council for Economic Competitiveness and Social Renewal asbl.
Francesco Mureddufrancesco.mureddu@lisboncouncil.net,

Brussels, Belgium

Preface: LibrarIN: AI and Innovation in European Libraries and Beyond

Artificial intelligence (AI) is an emerging topic and a continuously evolving technology that contributes to and influences all aspects of our society. It has an impact on the economy, culture, and various other elements of the internal market of the European Union. AI or probably better an artificial intelligence system can be defined as a machine-based system that is designed to operate with varying levels of autonomy and that may exhibit adaptiveness after deployment, and that, for explicit or implicit objectives, infers, from the input it receives, how to generate outputs such as predictions, content, recommendations, or decisions that can influence physical or virtual environments [1]. AI can be seen as an additional catalyst for the digital transformation of the services offered by public institutions across all Member States, associated countries, and beyond.

AI's importance is well recognised by the European Union by the implementation of the Artificial Intelligence Act [1], the first international law that regulates the legal framework for the development, the placing on the market, the implementation into public services, and the use of artificial intelligence systems within the European Union.

The EU LibrarIN project, co-financed by the European Commission, aims to provide new avenues for participatory management and sustainable finance for European libraries as key cultural institutions. It examines ways that libraries can develop new functions, services, and engagement with the individuals, organisations, and communities they serve [2]. This overarching approach fits perfectly into these emerging aspects around the usage of AI in different sectors. One work package of the LibrarIN project focuses on the digital transformation of library services and specifically conducts research on the implementation of AI in European National Libraries. National Libraries can be seen as a centre of development and implementation of new services for their patrons to support the digital transformation of their artefacts in order to fulfil their mission of national heritage preservation. The duty of National Libraries is not only to store books but also to preserve their nation's cultural heritage and provide all available information to their patrons in accessible ways.

This book aims to build a bridge between research, practice, and policy. The goal is to empower library professionals, stakeholders, and policymakers in their AI implementation efforts by providing insights and real-world experiences from organisations that are already well underway in tackling this challenge. The case studies demonstrate these implementation efforts by providing an overview of 12 case studies. The case studies demonstrate how National Libraries co-created the digital transformation of their services by including their stakeholders in the AI implementation efforts to preserve the national values and heritage.

The book is based on a collective effort of leading researchers, practitioners, policy analysts, and stakeholders from various institutions, such as The Lisbon Council, the University of Alcala, the University of Lille, Roskilde University, LIBER, and the University of Konstanz.

The book itself is comprised of three different parts. The first part focuses on the introduction, research design, and description of expectations. The second part consists of 12 in-depth case illustrations of AI projects in national libraries of the European Union, associated countries, and the Library of Congress, United States. The third part includes the recommendations for implementation and provides insights into a "toolkit" for policymakers and innovators in libraries.

From a methodological point of view, the underlying research combines different aspects, such as theoretical modelling, systematic reviews, (semi-structured) expert interviews, and case studies (see Chapter "Studying the Co-production of AI Implementation in National Public Libraries"). Co-creation and co-production models are used to develop and understand the implementation of AI and to reflect on the implementation processes in the different National Libraries.

The book highlights that AI is not simply a technical tool. On the one hand, it explains and showcases that AI is a catalyst for transforming services. On the other hand, it also highlights that new governance models are needed, as well as sustainable funding, a sound ethical framework, and a human-centred design. Related to the implementation, the cases show that an inclusive and interdisciplinary approach is needed to adequately address the different kinds of challenges, such as bias in data, transparency, workforce adaptation, and intellectual property rights issues. For the future and the ongoing developments, it will be explained that it is essential to incorporate community-driven innovations and technology development responsibly. Therefore, this book can be seen as a starting point for follow-up publications based on extended datasets and continued developments based on the outcomes of the LibrarIN project.

The editors want to use the opportunity to gratefully acknowledge the support of the European Union's Horizon Europe Programme and its programme officers, all contributors and research partners, our interview partners, reviewers of the book chapters, and institutions involved in the realisation of this book, especially The Lisbon Council and Athens Technology Center (ATC). Furthermore, a special thank you goes to the LibrarIN Stakeholder Panel, composed of 36 experts from 19 European countries, whose feedback informed the development of the toolkit and policy recommendations. We would also like to thank Giulia Maragno, Anna-Lea

Schumann, and Justus Kühler for their research assistance during the data collection and analysis steps.

References

1. European Union, Regulation (EU) 2024/1689 of the European Parliament and of the Council of 13 June 2024 laying down harmonised rules on artificial intelligence and amending Regulations (EC) No 300/2008, (EU) No 167/2013, (EU) No 168/2013, (EU) 2018/858, (EU) 2018/1139 and (EU) 2019/2144 and Directives 2014/90/EU, (EU) 2016/797 and (EU) 2020/1828 (Artificial Intelligence Act) (2024)
2. https://librarin.eu/. Accessed 8 June 2025

Konstanz, Germany; Berlin, Germany — Ines Mergel
Konstanz, Germany — Carsten Schmidt

Acknowledgements

The work for this book was supported by the European Union's Horizon Europe Research and Innovation Programme under Grant Agreement ID 101061516.

Contents

Introduction, Research Design, Expectations

Studying the Co-production of AI Implementation in National Public Libraries 3
Ines Mergel

In-Depth Case Illustrations of 12 AI Projects in National Libraries

Applying AI to Increase Cultural Accessibility: The Postcard Project at the Royal Danish Library 13
Ada Scupola

Automated Subject Cataloguing at the German National Library 25
Ines Mergel, Justus Kühler, Anna-Lea Schumann, and Corinna Nitsch

AI-Supported Automated Subject Indexing and Metadata Management with Annif and Finto AI at the National Library of Finland 43
Anna-Lea Schumann and Ines Mergel

Visual Discovery Through AI: Unlocking the Postcard Archive at the National Library of Sweden 59
Ada Scupola

From Data to AI-Based Discovery: The Maken Project at the National Library of Norway 71
Ada Scupola

The Retrocatalography Project: Combining AI with the Microsoft Power Platform at the Royal National Library of Belgium 83
Anna-Lea Schumann and Ines Mergel

AI for Access: Strategic Innovation at the Dutch National Library 95
Barbara van der Vaart and Carsten Schmidt

How to Make Millions of Documents Accessible Through AI and a Digital Library? The Case of Gallica, French National Library 109
Antoine Henry

From Metadata to Meaning: Applying AI in the National Library of Estonia 121
Carsten Schmidt

Implementing AI in the National Library of Spain: The ETSO Project and Stylometric Analysis of Golden Age Theatre 135
Alberto Peralta

Assessing Nineteenth-Century Library Collections with the "Living with Machines" Project at the British Library, United Kingdom 151
Justus Kühler and Ines Mergel

Exploring Computational Descriptions for Metadata Creation for E-Books at the Library of Congress, United States of America 163
Anna-Lea Schumann, Justus Kühler, and Ines Mergel

Recommendations

Recommendations for the AI Implementation in Libraries 181
Ines Mergel, Justus Kühler, Anna-Lea Schumann, and Carsten Schmidt

Innovating Libraries: The LibrarIN Toolkit for Policy and Practice 199
Marieke Willems, Marta Anducas, and Elena Silvestrini

Introduction, Research Design, Expectations

Studying the Co-production of AI Implementation in National Public Libraries

Ines Mergel

Abstract AI implementation in National Libraries is a multi-actor endeavour that includes many internal as well as external contributors. The literature on the subject is, however, sparse and still developing. In this chapter, I provide the theoretical framework and the research design for the EU LibrarIN project that is built on the co-production literature in the public management field. The resulting theoretical framework of digital co-production has guided the case study selection and inquiry and set the foundation for the empirical data analysis of the 12 case studies on AI implementation in National Libraries.

Keywords Artificial intelligence (AI) · Co-production · National Libraries · Digital transformation · Stakeholder engagement

1 Introduction

The study of AI implementation in the public sector is still in its infancy. While there are first steps towards understanding how artificial intelligence (AI) approaches in their wide varieties can be adopted in publicly funded organisations, there is still little empirical evidence of their actual implementation steps [1]. The general assumption is that new technologies, such as AI, will have a positive impact on how organisations are working—be it that the general expectation is that they become more efficient and effective by replacing more costly human labour with automated processes or that AI can process data to the extent that other types of (combinations

I. Mergel (✉)
Department of Politics and Public Administration, University of Konstanz, Konstanz, Germany

Fraunhofer FOKUS, Fraunhofer Institute for Open Communication Systems, Berlin, Germany

School of Management, Public Management, University of Vaasa, Vaasa, Finland
e-mail: ines.mergel@uni-konstanz.de

I. Mergel, C. Schmidt (eds.), *AI Innovations in Public Services*,
https://doi.org/10.1007/978-3-032-01344-6_1

of) technologies or humans with the support of technology cannot process (see, for example, [2]).

Despite the growing interest in AI adoption across all disciplines, there is little evidence on how organisations are going about its implementation. As part of the EU LibrarIN grant, we therefore set out to understand how National Libraries implement AI. National Libraries are responsible for collecting, cataloguing, preserving, and storing the cultural heritage of their country. As part of their tasks, they collect and preserve a country's literature, publications, manuscripts, and other documents, both in digital and analogue forms. They publish national bibliographies and make the collected artefacts available to researchers and the general public.

In the big data world, this task has become especially humongous, given that the national heritage includes not only formal publications going through a publication process with the support of publishers or dissertations that are reviewed and accepted by universities and published through official agreements. The task has expanded to the digital sphere now: cultural heritage now also includes social media expressions, such as blog posts or videos, that must be preserved and passed down through generations. AI tools are therefore not only used for the existing formal published artefacts but also help National Libraries to expand the scope of their preservation work to include other digital artefacts, such as social media posts in the form of audio, text, and visual expressions.

A specific challenge emerges for National Libraries: They cannot rely on existing AI tools, mostly created in the Anglo-Saxon hemisphere—instead, they need to develop their language models so that the technologies can process the artefacts in their local languages. Given the size of the countries, this is a very expensive task because National Libraries can rarely buy AI technologies off-the-shelf, instead, they have to invest in developing local solutions in their native languages.

However, National Libraries cannot tackle this task alone—they elicit input from citizens, publishers, researchers, and authors to co-implement the AI tools to preserve their country's national heritage. Given the extent of the task, engage in so-called digital co-production processes [3, 4]—otherwise, they won't be able to create the public value they are tasked with.

In the following, I will outline the theoretical foundations of co-production, its research design that guided the data generation and analysis steps and will provide a theoretical framework for the study of AI implementation in publicly funded National Libraries.

2 Theoretical Foundation: Co-production Framework for the Study of AI Implementation

Since the beginning of the renewed AI revolution in November 2023 and its publicly available GPTs, AI has also caught the attention of many researchers interested in how new technologies are applied in publicly funded organisations. However, most of the literature so far focuses on challenges and barriers, such as algorithmic governance [5], ethical aspects [6], or legal requirements to protect individual knowledge, copyright, privacy, etc. [7].

What has been neglected or not yet reported in the literature is the way that publicly funded organisations are implementing AI in their organisations, what the necessary steps are, and how they engage different actors (external or internal) to support these processes [1]. The reasons might be that researchers can't get access to these otherwise black boxes of decision-making that are made in-house or the still rather experimental nature of most of the AI projects that go beyond the installation of chatbots that are mostly operating based on an existing thesaurus but are not able to learn and expand their interaction base.

To study the implementation of AI, we selected a specific theoretical lens: the co-production of digital public services. So far, co-production—the process of engaging different types of stakeholders in the process steps of creating and then delivering a public service for their recipients—has been predominantly studied in the context of the delivery of social services [8–10]. Citizens or service recipients are seen as co-producers of the service when they, for example, recycle their trash into the right trash bins and bring them to the curb on pick-up day. The service in the designed form cannot be performed without the explicit actions of citizens who are willing or are forced by law to separate their trash into recyclable plastic packaging, glass, paper, or biodegradable trash.

More recently, the notion of co-production has been expanded beyond this value-in-use phase (the phase where citizens actually separate and carry out the trash). Strokosch and Osborne [11] proposed that there is a vast ecosystem of experiences necessary which creates opportunities for different types of actors to be involved. Similarly, Osborne et al. [12] urged their readers to move beyond co-production steps to include also co-value production phase and consider co-value production.

Other authors have started to emphasise the role of digital co-production, but specifically look at the types of technologies that can be used to support co-production processes [4, 13, 14], not the co-production of digital public services. Here, however, we are interested in understanding how a new technology (AI) is implemented and how the National Libraries are engaging in co-production steps to include different types of stakeholders along the way.

Therefore, the inquiries described in the following case studies focus on the co-production steps outlined in Mergel et al. [3], who separate the overall process of co-producing digital public services into the following four steps and six phases (Table 1):

2.1 Initiation

The initiation phase includes two co-production phases: *(1) The co-commissioning phase*, in which the initiation of an AI project is started. An AI project can either be initiated by in-house units who are interested in innovating with AI, such as the

Table 1 Implementation phases and co-production phases

Implementation phases	Co-production phases
I. Initiation	*(1) Co-commissioning phase* *(2) Co-design phase*
II. Implementation	*(3) Co-implementation*
III. Use	*(4) Co-delivery phase* *(5) Co-assessment phase*
IV. Outcome	*(6) Public value creation*

Chief Information Officer or the Chief Innovation Officer. Or, it might also be triggered by external funding opportunities or pressure from society to upgrade to new technologies. In this phase, the overall outcome is decided, the necessary budget is defined, and potentially, the necessary competencies are decided. In this phase, a lot of co-envisioning of a future with AI is conducted to understand where the project might go. *The co-design phase (2)*, as part of the initiation, is focused on involving potential service users in the first round of design of new services. A lot of responsibility is given to current and future users to envision what they might be interested in doing in co-creative processes with AI.

2.2 Implementation

The implementation phase focuses on *(3) the co-implementation* of AI services. This is the phase where, oftentimes, National Libraries have to either reach out to their already established IT service providers to support their implementation efforts. Others might have to involve other libraries that are willing to share established IT solutions and make them available also for use in other languages. In this phase it is also important to work across organisational silos to include the IT department—in case the AI project was initiated outside, for example, in an innovation office. They must also include the legal department, information specialists for testing, and factual knowledge of the previous analogue processes.

2.3 Use

The use phase includes the *(4) co-delivery* phase, which can be labelled the value-in-use phase: The phase in which users start to use the AI tools, and the hope is that it supports them in their interactions with the National Libraries. This is the phase in which both service users and internal information specialists use the newly developed AI tools by contributing their knowledge, input, and the way that they use the outputs. Think, for example, about a PhD student who uploads their dissertation, the

AI tools automatically suggest how to catalogue the entry, and an information specialist approves the output to prevent any hallucinations or faulty entries.

The use phase also includes the *(5) co-assessment* phase, which helps to create feedback during the use of a new digital service while users are engaging with it. This can be simple frequencies of use and the reduction of analogue services as an indicator of the usefulness of a new digital service. It can also be feedback on the quality of the service, for example, is the output mostly faulty, and information specialists need to intervene manually. The assessment results can be iteratively fed back and incorporated into the design to improve the outcomes.

2.4 Outcome

The outcome of the co-production phases can be seen in two dimensions. *(6) Public value creation* can either happen in each of the phases by including the right stakeholders to support the digital transformation of digital public services with AI, or, it can be evaluated at the end of the co-production phases in terms of increased efficiency and effectiveness, or as an increased range and quality of service delivery—which both might lead to greater acceptance and support for the tools and processes.

In summary, the overall theoretical framework derived from the above-described theoretical phases of co-production is displayed in Fig. 1:

3 Research Design

The research design to understand how National Libraries are co-producing AI implementation and how they generate public value is based on the theoretical framework (Fig. 1). It is guiding the data generation for the EU LibrarIN research project.

The research design includes three phases: (1) systematic review and computational analysis of the existing literature on digital public library services, (2) expert interviews with the directors of the international library associations, and (3)

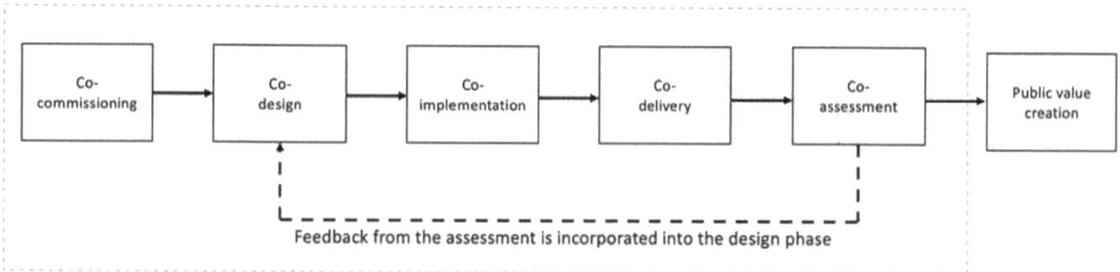

Fig. 1 Co-production framework for the implementation of AI based on Mergel 2025 et al. [3]

country-level case studies to understand the implementation of AI in National Libraries.

With the knowledge of the literature, we identified the most important international library associations and conducted expert interviews with their executive directors to derive the most pressing issues when it comes to current societal challenges that libraries are facing, as well as the digital transformation issues that are currently being discussed. The interviews then led to the identification of issues and cases, which we present here in this book. The executive directors identified the implementation of AI as the most pressing issue. However, they also highlighted that the adoption and implementation should be studied in National Libraries where funding and the necessary expertise are available.

With the help of the experts, we then identified National Libraries that are at the forefront of AI implementation. In each of the cases, we asked a series of questions that were derived from the theoretical framework on co-value creation and the general literature on digital transformation of public services. As we followed along, we noticed that many of the EU-based National Libraries pointed us to two other National Libraries outside of the EU, which they frequently look at as best practice cases. We therefore also included the British National Library (UK) and the Library of Congress (USA).

4 Overview of the Book

The main part of the book (Chapters "Automated Subject Cataloguing at the German National Library, Germany" to "Exploring Computational Descriptions for Meta-Data Creation for E-Books at the Library of Congress, United States of America") consists of 12 case studies of National Libraries describing their AI implementation processes and outcomes. The European Union's National Libraries featured here include:

- Koninklijke Bibliotheek van België, BE
- Deutsche Nationalbibliothek, DE
- Det Kongelige Bibliotek, DK
- Eesti Rahvusraamatukogu, EE
- Biblioteca Nacional de España, ES
- Kansalliskirjasto, FI
- Bibliothèque nationale de France, FR
- Koninklijke Bibliotheek, NL
- Nasjonalbiblioteket, NO
- Kungliga biblioteket, SE

In addition, we included

- British Library (UK) and
- The Library of Congress (US)

because they were frequently mentioned by the interviewees during our data generation phases.

The closing part of the book (Chapter "Recommendations for the AI Implementation in Libraries") provides an overview of the implementation challenges that National Libraries are encountering when they are implementing AI in their countries, authored by Mergel et al. The authors then highlight policy and implementation recommendations for libraries that are embarking on the journey to implement AI tools in their own libraries.

In addition, Willems et al. provide an outlook of a case databank in which the EU LibrarIN consortium has collected their cases of libraries that are engaging in the co-value production activities (Chapter "Innovating Libraries: The LibrarIN Toolkit for Policy and Practice").

Acknowledgements The work for this chapter was supported by the European Union's Horizon Europe Research and Innovation Programme under Grant Agreement ID 101061516.

References

1. I. Mergel et al., Implementing AI in the public sector. Public Manag. Rev., 1–14 (2024)
2. S.N. Giest, B. Klievink, More than a digital system: how AI is changing the role of bureaucrats in different organizational contexts. Public Manag. Rev. **26**(2), 379–398 (2024)
3. I. Mergel, N. Edelmann, N. Haug, Co-production phases in the development and implementation of digital public services. Perspect. Public Manag. Govern. **8**, 93 (2025)
4. S. Perikangas, S. Tuurnas, Design for inclusive digital co-production. Public Manag. Rev. **26**(6), 1731–1751 (2024)
5. A. Meijer, L. Lorenz, M. Wessels, Algorithmization of bureaucratic organizations: using a practice lens to study how context shapes predictive policing systems. Public Adm. Rev. **81**(5), 837–846 (2021)
6. P. Henman, Improving public services using artificial intelligence: possibilities, pitfalls, governance. Asia Pac. J. Public Adm. **42**(4), 209–221 (2020)
7. J. Willems et al., AI-driven public services and the privacy paradox: do citizens really care about their privacy? Public Manag. Rev. **25**(11), 2116–2134 (2023)
8. T. Brandsen, M. Honingh, Definitions of co-production and co-creation, in *Co-production and Co-creation*, (Routledge, 2018), pp. 9–17
9. S.S. Flemig, S. Osborne, The dynamics of co-production in the context of social care personalisation: testing theory and practice in a Scottish context. J. Soc. Policy **48**(4), 671–697 (2019)
10. W.H. Voorberg, V.J. Bekkers, L.G. Tummers, A systematic review of co-creation and co-production: embarking on the social innovation journey. Public Manag. Rev. **17**(9), 1333–1357 (2015)
11. K. Strokosch, S.P. Osborne, Co-experience, co-production and co-governance: an ecosystem approach to the analysis of value creation. Policy Polit. **48**(3), 425–442 (2020)
12. S.P. Osborne, G. Nasi, M. Powell, Beyond co-production: value creation and public services. Public Adm. **99**(4), 641–657 (2021)
13. K.K. Larsson, T. Skjølsvik, Making sense of the digital co-production of welfare services: using digital technology to simplify or tailor the co-production of services. Public Manag. Rev. **25**(6), 1169–1186 (2023)
14. V. Lember, B. Taco, P. Tõnurist, The potential impacts of digital technologies on co-production and co-creation. Public Manag. Rev. **21**(11), 1665–1686 (2019)

Ines Mergel is a University Professor of Public Administration in the Department of Politics and Public Administration at the University of Konstanz and a Fellow of the National Academy of Public Administration (Class of 2018). After holding positions at the Harvard Kennedy School of Government as a Doctoral Fellow and Postdoctoral Fellow (2002–2008), Professor Mergel was awarded tenure at the Maxwell School of Citizenship and Public Affairs (Syracuse University, NY) in 2014 (2008–2014) and then served as Associate Professor with tenure (2014–2016). Professor Mergel is a member of the supervisory board of the e-Governance Academy (Estonia). Other board memberships can be found here. Professor Mergel is a founding member of the international initiative Teaching Public Service in the Digital Age, which aims to integrate digital skills into the teaching and training of public managers. As part of this initiative, Professor Mergel was appointed a Schmidt Futures Innovation Fellow in 2022.

In-Depth Case Illustrations of 12 AI Projects in National Libraries

Applying AI to Increase Cultural Accessibility: The Postcard Project at the Royal Danish Library

Ada Scupola

Abstract This chapter provides an overview of the Danish Royal Library as well as an overview of AI adoption and implementation initiatives taking place at the library. Finally, the chapter presents details of a specific AI project, the postcard project. The Postcard project comprises the digitalisation of the postcard collection of the Danish Royal Library. It includes the digitalisation of approx. 350,000 topographical postcards from the period 1887 to the 1990s from all parts of Denmark and making them accessible to the broader public by using AI. The chapter provides insights into the needs of the project, the actors involved in the implementation and the challenges encountered on the way. Finally, the chapter provides insights into the value that such a project generates for different stakeholders, as well as the lessons learned in the implementation phase.

Keywords National Library · Artificial intelligence · AI · Value creation · Royal Danish Library · Metadata generation · Google Vision AI · Co-production · Digital transformation

1 Introduction

The Royal Danish Library (RDL) [1] is an institution under the Danish Ministry of Culture. The library provides services and communication of knowledge and preserves the Danish cultural heritage. The services include collecting and returning materials to public libraries, digitising material from the extensive collection, guided tours, Danish books on demand and services to professionals. The Royal Danish Library (RDL) was founded in 1648 by King Frederik III in Denmark. In 1697 the Legal Deposit Act was introduced, establishing that all printers in the country must submit copies of the writings and books they print to the Royal Danish Library. This act still applies today in an updated version.

A. Scupola (✉)
Department of Social Science and Business, Roskilde University, Roskilde, Denmark
e-mail: ada@ruc.dk

I. Mergel, C. Schmidt (eds.), *AI Innovations in Public Services*,
https://doi.org/10.1007/978-3-032-01344-6_2

Since its establishment, the Royal Danish Library has undergone several organisational changes and mergers with other libraries, including the merger with the State and University Library of Denmark in 2017. Today, the Royal Danish Library is the national library of Denmark; the university library of the University of Copenhagen, Roskilde University, Århus University and the IT University in Copenhagen; and the loan centre for all the Danish public libraries. The core tasks of the Royal Danish Library are digital material management, physical material management, library service, cultural information and research [1].

According to RDL's Web site, RDL has four focus areas:

- As a university library, the Royal Danish Library provides services that support research and education at Aarhus University, the IT University of Copenhagen, the University of Copenhagen and Roskilde University.
- As a national library, the Royal Danish Library collects, preserves and provides access to cultural heritage via texts, images and audio in both physical and digital forms.
- As a loan centre for the Danish public libraries, the Royal Danish Library provides services that supplement the public libraries' service offerings to citizens.
- As a research institution, the Royal Danish Library increases knowledge and awareness of the Danish cultural heritage [1].

RDL has about 650 employees and about 250 students. About 80 are employed in the division called digital transformation, which in turn comprises 5 different departments. About 60 employees in the digital transformation division deal with classical IT development and maintenance. Twenty employees comprise the communication department of the entire library (Head of Data, Interview 1, January 2024).

1.1 AI Applications in RDL

According to a section leader (Interview 7, March 2024), there are three main application areas in which AI is used in RDL:

1. Data for internal and research use (Data Lab)
2. AI used on collections
3. KB Labs experiment [2]

Within these three areas, RDL is experimenting with different AI projects, and different AI solutions are applied to the context of these projects. It is mostly machine learning embedded in handwritten text recognition (HRT) technology, optical character recognition (OCR) technology, and, more recently, Generative AI. However, most of these technologies are still at the experimental level and have not been taken into full production mode yet. In addition, AI technologies have been applied in the context of specific experimental projects. Recently, RDL has been trying to centralise all the AI-related activities and get an overview of what is going on concerning AI in the RDL.

1. The data labs are labs that provide collection data to researchers and students at the universities. For example, it can be data scientists who teach Python or R that ask for access to collection data. In addition, there are researchers, especially in the digital humanities areas, who use their RDL's collections to train and develop Large Language Models to be applied in research projects.
2. RDL has been experimenting with and applying AI in different special collections and has developed a few main projects. The specific technologies used in these experimental projects are Machine Learning, Google Vision AI Platform, and Transkribus. Google Vision is a technology for recognising things in images and is mainly an Optical Character Recognition (OCR) technology. The most relevant projects are (a) the digitalisation of the Elfelt Negative Collection, where Transkribus, a handwritten recognition program originated by an EU project, had been used to read the handwritten text on the postcards [3]. (b) The application of Google Vision technology to recognise images and text in a special collection of topographical postcards. The postcards have an image on the front side, and the back side has a small text to the recipient. Usually, they are sent by mail. (c) The application of Machine Learning Technology for the preservation of material [4].
3. The KB lab experiments [2] were born from an innovation week, where "all the developers had one week where they worked on a project, and then at some point, they had developed a lot of small projects that were put on the website" (Section leader, Interview 7, March 2024). This is a concept that RDL ran for 3–4 years. Presently, the project has been set on pause due to other priorities, mostly dictated by the Ministry. The AI technology used in these experiments is mostly Machine Learning, for example as in "Fake News Portlet", "Word2vec" and "SoundSearch".

This chapter investigates how the Royal Danish Library developed and implemented AI to make a special collection of topographical postcards available to the wider public. The chapter first introduces the postcard project, including needs for developing and implementing the project and the internal and external actors involved. Then the chapter provides insights into the value (co-) created with the project, the challenges faced, and the lessons learned. Finally, the chapter provides some concluding remarks.

2 Description of the Project

The Postcard project comprises the digitalisation of the collection of topographical postcards at RDL. The collection of topographical postcards includes about 350,000 postcards from the period 1887 to the 1990s from all parts of Denmark. It is part of a larger collection of prints and photographs at RDL, which has over 18 million physical images. The collection of prints and photographs is divided into three main parts:

1. The portrait collection with portraits of Danish men and women
2. The topographical collection with pictures of places
3. The chronological collection with pictures of events

In addition, there are several special collections such as the collection of Danish cartoon art, an album collection and collections donated by photographers, publishers, theatres and other companies [5].

The topographical postcard collection has been built partly through donations from private individuals and partly through compulsory delivery from Danish printers. Railway and local historians often use the collection.

The Postcard project started in 2018, and its main idea was to generate keywords and metadata about the topographical collection of postcards to be able to make them available online to the wider public. The project was initiated by a senior researcher at one of the "Special Collections" of the RDL. Presently, it is on the way to being put into production as a service for the users of the RDL library. The project objectives are mainly cost-effective digitisation and cost-effective generation of metadata. Through the project, however, RDL aims to get experience with and an overview of the opportunities and barriers of automated generation of metadata through the use of commercial AI services or machine learning services such as Google Vision [6] for use in later projects.

2.1 Need(s) Behind the Implementation

The main drivers behind the implementation of the project were the new strategy for broader dissemination of the Royal Danish Library's collections. Such drivers include dissemination to wider target groups; increased accessibility to library collections; the user demands; and the need to generate as many metadata as possible to make it easy for users to retrieve the library material. In addition, the project is addressing indirect and observed needs of the library users to have online access to all the library collections as well as to be able to easily find out what there is in these collections and what possibilities they offer.

Thus, the project aligns with the general RDL's mission of making RDL's collection easily accessible, retrievable and searchable by the public. In fact, the postcard project was initiated to generate better metadata for library users as well as to make it easy to access, use and search the RDL's collections. As a department manager says:

> As I said before, the user demand, we have a reading room downstairs here where we bring down the physical material for the users who come here. But that's not how people use material any longer. They go online and if it's not online, they find something else. Fewer and fewer people come here to use the material in the reading room. So, we can sense that, we can feel that, and we need to react to that. Of course, it's also our task. (Department manager, interview 14, March 2024)

2.2 Actors Involved

The project was started by a senior researcher in the special collection of historical cards and photographs at the RDL. He already had experience with dissemination of topographical material from the aerial photography project "Denmark seen from the air" [1].

The main groups of employees directly involved were the curators, who are historians or experts in the field, the employees at the digitisation department that had to put the postcard into digital format, and a big number of student assistants. There were a number of co-production phases and activities in which different stakeholders were involved. Here, the co-production activities are summarised in Table 1 by following Mergel et al.'s [7] phases of the co-production process.

2.3 Organisational Level

The project received support from the RDL in various ways. The head of the division where the postcard project was anchored directly supported the project. The top management of the RDL indirectly supported the project by providing a general policy of experimentation with AI in the library that functions as an institutional framework for "playing with AI" at RDL. As a senior researcher says:

> I think our AI policy is actually a good first step because that gives some institutional framework, but it also needs to be facilitated. I think the idea of doing this sandbox for the AI is actually a good idea, but also—yeah, we'll probably do it anyway. (Senior researcher, interview 14, March 2024)

Table 1 Co-production activities in the postcard project at the Royal Danish Library

Co-commissioning	*Prospective co-production phase*	The project was started by a curator (senior researcher) in the special collection of historical postcards, but he got support from the head of the division and library management
Co-design	*Concurrent co-production phases*	The project was envisioned by the curators but co-designed with employees from the digitalisation department that specialised in preservation of material
Co-implementation		The project was co-implemented by the digitalisation department, the curators and Google Vision
Co-delivery		The service is co-delivered by RDL, Google Vision and Users
Co-assessment	*Retrospective co-production phase*	Curators, Google Vision, users

2.4 External Actors

The project involved two main external actors: Google Vision Cloud Service and the government attorney. In fact, RDL had made an agreement with Google Vision Cloud Service to send them the digitalised version of the postcards to Google Vision, and Google Vision returns metadata in the form of tags, OCR and Handwritten Text Recognition (HCR) to the library. This service was provided by Google Vision upon a fee paid by RDL. In addition, RDL is also collaborating with the government attorney to find out possibilities to work with collection data in relation to General Data Protection Regulation (GDPR) and copyright issues.

2.5 Challenges

In the implementation of the postcard project, RDL has encountered a number of challenges. The most important challenges were related to copyrights and GDPR issues in using external commercial service providers such as Google Vision to generate metadata on the library postcard collection. In fact, there is a need for a data agreement between the library institution and the service provider if the service provider has to handle copyrighted data. This is illustrated by the following quotes:

> Well, very much copyright and GDPR I think. (Vice director for Digital Transformation, Interview 4, March 2024)

> At the same time, there was also this whole complete question about GDPR and all that regulation. …We did some handheld experiments with some data, which we were confident didn't hold any sensitive information, but we couldn't go through that for the 380,000 postcards. So, we had to limit it. (Senior Researcher, Interview 5, March 2024)

Another important technological challenge was related to the accuracy and quality of the metadata generated by Google Vision. Google Vision not only generated descriptive keywords of the postcards' content but also generated a lot of redundant descriptive keywords, which generated "noise" in understanding the metadata (Senior Researcher, Interview 5, March 2024). Another technological challenge was data bias. This was important as there was a clear American bias in the metadata generated by Google Vision. For example, Danish places displayed in some postcards were interpreted as located in the USA by Google Vision.

The cost of generating sufficient metadata for postcards also represented a challenge. In fact, while it is not expensive to create digital files of cultural heritage material, it is instead very expensive to generate metadata. Two final challenges are the lack of time for library employees to experiment with this type of AI and the accuracy and quality of the metadata provided to the library users.

3 Results

3.1 Organisational Level

The application of Google Vision AI technology in the postcard project has generated a number of important organisational values for RDL. These can be summarised as follows: production of more metadata about the topographical postcard collections; unlocking some of the data which are locked in the handwritten statements on the postcards; better and more precise library search services allowing the public to find whatever they search for precisely; the potential for doing large-scale OCR or handwriting text recognition; freeing resources for other tasks or potentially also translating some of the material making it easier to search in the collections; increasing cost-efficiency by using AI instead of student assistants to generate metadata about the collections (Department manager, interview 14, march 2024); and increasing the potential for the library to understand the data they have in their own collections because the vast part of the collections are still unknown to the library due to the fact that it takes many years of manpower to go through the collections (Research Librarian, Interview 14, March 2024).

3.2 Lessons Learned

The respondents highlighted several lessons they had learned from the postcard projects at an organisational level. One of the main lessons learned in the initiation and co-production of the postcard project is that it is best to start on a small scale and then scale it up to a more considerable quantity of data. Another important lesson is that it is important to make sure to jump on the AI wagon *if, when and how* it is the right thing to do for each specific library. Finally, one other lesson concerns the ethical, sustainability and data bias issues related to using AI, as using AI can be very costly, and we should be aware of copyrights and GDPR issues as well as we should be well aware of how to use AI and for what.

3.3 Value Created and Co-created

According to the respondents, there are different public values that using Google Vision AI in the postcard project has generated or has the potential to generate for society. The first is the important cultural value of making available to the general public both existing collections and new services for library search. In fact, even though the RDL has many student assistants, it would have been impossible to make the postcard collection available to the general public without Google Vision technology, as it would have taken about 80 years of work for a person to generate the metadata generated by Google Vision. That would have not been possible for the library. Another public value is the increase in user satisfaction with the library services, as users are very happy about getting access to old photographs and thus acquiring knowledge about how places looked from a historical perspective. As stated by a Senior Researcher:

> That's a very surplus value that somebody has kept all this data, and we have scanned it and made it available for free. I think we need to do more of that. In order to do that, we need to use AI. (Senior Researcher, Interview 5, March 2024)

The democratic value of increasing access to cultural heritage and making everybody access it from close or far away is another significant public value. In fact, presently, the postcard collection and most of the national collection of heritage materials are located in central Copenhagen. This implies that it is more difficult to access these collections for users located outside the Copenhagen area than for those located in the area.

> Yes, it's a democratisation but it's also a way to make the collections in use, which we have not thought about. (Senior Researcher, Interview 5, March 2024)

The above quote also points out another type of value: the value of using the collections in different ways and for different purposes if there are no copyright restrictions, the metadata are better, and the access is made easier. This implies a broader application and use of the collection data by other stakeholders than the general public. For example, at present, municipalities, regions and private consultants are using the postcard collection for pollution assessment:

> So, I think by putting this digital data online, it's also creating a possibility for reusing almost in a lot of different ways, which you potentially can't even think of. (Senior Researcher, Interview 5, March 2024)

3.4 New Skills

The study points out the need for new skills if AI adoption succeeds in national libraries. Important skills are data science and computer science. As a team leader in the digitalisation department states:

> If we are making AI or making new models or training models, we need the computer science skills or data science skills. (Team Leader, Interview 6, February 2024)

In addition, it is important that the employees working with the library collections (e.g. the curators) have some computational skills and vice versa the computational experts have an understanding of the library collection. As a research librarian states:

> So, you need a lot of computational skills. Still, you need to understand the content. That's why I have emphasised many times that neither the organisation nor the individual employee

> can be divided into in-groups like digital and non-digital. We all have to have the skill—some of the skills; we cannot be expert in both parts but the content people need some computational skills at least, and the computational experts need to understand a bit of the concept.... That is crossover skills. (Research Librarian, Interview 13, March 2024)

4 Conclusions

This chapter has provided an overview of the Royal Danish Library and has investigated RDL's AI initiatives. The findings show that the Royal Danish Library has started experimenting with AI in several ways and has initiated several initiatives, including the data labs that provide collection data to researchers and students at the universities; application of AI on special collections; and the KB lab experiments [2], which are the results of an innovation week, during which all the developers could work on an idea that had.

The chapter provides insights on an important project that has almost been put into production, the postcard project. This project started in 2018 with the main idea of generating keywords and metadata about the topographical collection of postcards in order to make them available online to the wider public.

There were several needs behind the project, including changing user demands, but it generally aligned with the RDL's mission of making the collection easily accessible, retrievable and searchable by the general public. The postcard project was initiated to generate better metadata for the library users as well as to make it easy to access, use and search the RDL's collections. A few actors were involved, including the project initiator, the curators in the postcard collection department, Google Vision and the government attorney to sort out copyright and GDPR issues.

The implementation of the postcard project presented a lot of challenges in applying AI to a library collection. These challenges included copyrights, GDPR issues, metadata quality and data bias.

The project has created organisational and public value. At the organisational level, the project has, for example, increased cost-efficiency by using AI instead of student assistants to generate metadata about the collections as well as providing the opportunity for the library to understand better the data they have in their own collections because the vast part of the collections are still unexplored as it takes many years of manpower to go through the collections. Examples of public value include the cultural value of making available to the general public both existing collections and new search services as well as the democratic value of increasing access to cultural heritage and making it equally possible to access it to users located in any part of Denmark.

Finally, RDL pointed out the need for a convergence of skills for those dealing with this kind of project in the future: the collection specialists need computational skills, and the IT employees need knowledge of the collection.

Acknowledgements The work for this chapter was supported by the European Union's Horizon Europe Research and Innovation Programme under Grant Agreement ID 101061516.

Appendix

See Tables 2 and 3.

Table 2 Overview of the postcard project at the Royal Danish Library

Case and project name			
Royal Danish Library/The digitalisation of postcards collection project			
Country	**Number of employees**	**Type of AI solution**	**Year and maturity level**
Denmark	650	OCR/HRT recognition/Google Vision	Started in 2028/On the way to production
Project description			
Digitalisation of approx. 350,000 topographical postcards from the period 1887 to the 1990s from all parts of Denmark			
Need(s) behind implementation	**Actors involved**	**Challenges**	
The new strategy for wider dissemination of the Royal Danish Library's collections—both in relation to target groups and accessibility; the user demands; need to generate as many metadata as possible	Curators in Special Collections, library management, digitalisation department, Google Vision	Copyright, GDPR, technological challenges, data bias, quality of the generated metadata, lack of time to experiment with technologies, accuracy of metadata provided to library users, high cost associated with generating sufficient metadata	
Results			
Organisational level	**Value created and co-created**	**Lesson learned**	
The value of AI at organisational level includes production of more metadata unlocking of data locked in handwriting text; better and increased precision of search services; potential for large-scale OCR or handwriting text recognition; freeing resources for other tasks; increasing cost-efficiency in generating metadata; better possibility to understand own collection data because	The cultural value of making existing collections available to the public; democratic value of increasing access to cultural heritage; the value of providing new search services and cleaner metadata to the public; potential of using data collection in new ways and different stakeholder groups than the wider public	(1) Start in small scale and later scale it up to a bigger quantity of data; (2) make sure to jump on the AI wagon if and how it is the right thing to do; employee's competences, e.g. employee in library collections need computation skills and vice versa computational experts need an understanding of the collections; awareness of the ethical, sustainability and bias issues in using AI	

Table 3 Overview of the interviews

Interview number	Position	Interview date	Interview length
1	Head of Data	12-01-2024	45 min
2	Head of Data	17-01-2024	1 h and 15 min
3	Head of Data	24-01-2024	45 min
4	Vice Director for Digital Transformation	08-03-2024	1 h
5	Senior Researcher	27-02-2024	1.5 h
6	Team Leader	28-02-2024	1 h
7	Section Leader	08-03-2024	1 h + 15 min
8	Conservator/Senior Researcher	06-03-2024	1 h
9	Head of Section	15-03-2024	1.5 h
10	Head of Department	14-03-2024	1.5 h
11	Centre Director	04-04-2024	1 h
12	Head of Department	Spring 2023	1 h
13	Research Librarian	18-03-2024	45 min
14	Department Manager + Senior Researcher + Research Librarian	18-03-2024	1 h

References

1. https://www.kb.dk. Accessed 1 June 2024
2. http://www.labs.kb.dk. Accessed 12 June 2024
3. https://www.kb.dk/en/inspiration/17000-photos-come-out-transcriptorium. Accessed 7 June 2024
4. https://pure.kb.dk/da/projects/maskinl%C3%A6ring-til-varsling-af-skadeligt-bevaringsmilj%C3%B8-p%C3%A5-arkiver. Accessed 3 June 2024
5. https://www.kb.dk/en/find-materials/collections/collection-prints-and-photographs
6. S.R. Svenningsen, M. Colding Dahl, Hvordan digitaliserer man postkort? PPT presentation (2024)
7. I. Mergel, N. Edelmann, N. Haug, Co-production phases in the development and implementation of digital public services. Perspect. Public Manag. Govern. (2025). https://doi.org/10.1093/ppmgov/gvaf002

Ada Scupola, Ada Skopula is a university professor in the Department of Social Science and Businesses at Roskilde University, Denmark. Her main research interests are at the intersection between digitalisation, innovation, and the service sector and include value (co-)creation, digital transformation, user involvement in innovation, digital innovation, adoption, and diffusion of information and communication technologies (ICT) with a special focus on small and medium-sized enterprises (SMEs). Recently, she has been investigating the role of Artificial Intelligence in organisations with a focus on service organisations.

Automated Subject Cataloguing at the German National Library

Ines Mergel, Justus Kühler, Anna-Lea Schumann, and Corinna Nitsch

Abstract The German National Library (DNB), as mandated by the German National Library Act of 2006, is responsible for collecting all German cultural artefacts, including digital and non-physical resources. To meet this requirement, DNB engaged in a Machine Learning (ML) project to improve metadata generation. After a while the project transitioned to a completely automated approach called subject cataloguing machine using Annif, an AI tool from the National Library of Finland, incorporating ML or subject indexing and metadata creation. This AI development relies heavily on the expertise of librarians, as AI tools are at times not fully accurate. While AI enhances efficiency, librarians and cataloguing specialists remain essential to ensure quality. The transition faced challenges, including limited resources, ethical issues, a diversified workforce's attitude towards AI, and the complexities of copyright laws. Despite these challenges, the integration of EMa has improved the generation and accessibility of metadata within DNB services. While AI can enrich librarians' skills, it cannot replace them. Mistakes encountered along the way should be viewed as learning opportunities, and future advancements should involve collaborative, diverse teams to continue refining the integration of AI in metadata management.

I. Mergel (✉)
Department of Politics and Public Administration, University of Konstanz, Konstanz, Germany

Fraunhofer FOKUS, Fraunhofer Institute for Open Communication Systems, Berlin, Germany

School of Management, Public Management, University of Vaasa, Vaasa, Finland
e-mail: ines.mergel@uni-konstanz.de

J. Kühler · A.-L. Schumann
Department of Politics and Public Administration, University of Konstanz, Konstanz, Germany
e-mail: justus.kuehler@uni-konstanz.de; anna-lea.schumann@uni-konstanz.de

C. Nitsch
Ministry for the Environment, Climate and Energy Sector of Baden-Württemberg, Stuttgart, Germany

I. Mergel, C. Schmidt (eds.), *AI Innovations in Public Services*,
https://doi.org/10.1007/978-3-032-01344-6_3

Keywords German National Library · DNB · AI · Metadata · Cataloguing · Machine learning · Annif · EMa · Generative AI · Library innovation · Digital governance

1 Introduction

The German National Library (DNB) was founded in Leipzig in 1912 and expanded in 1947 with an additional location in Frankfurt [1]. As the central archive and information centre in Germany, the DNB provides access to knowledge and at the same time drives technological innovation, particularly in the field of artificial intelligence (AI). The tasks of the DNB are defined in the German National Library Act (DNBG) [2]. This law provides for the collection, cataloguing, and public accessibility of all media works published in Germany since 1913 in digital and printed form and media works published in German abroad. The DNB employs 617 civil servants and employees under collective agreements [3].

This case study shows that the DNB uses AI in projects to create added value for society in terms of inclusiveness and accessibility of resources and to optimise internal workflows. Two critical AI solutions were developed in succession: PETRUS, a software-based platform for automated subject indexing launched in 2009, formed the basis. The providing company could no longer efficiently provide a working application, and both sides decided to discontinue PETRUS in 2018: "*Over the course of the years, we had always made new requirements with them, and they continued to develop it for us. And the people who programmed and developed it, the first specialists, have all gradually migrated to Silicon Valley in the USA. In other words, we always had new people who had to learn the ropes, who had to understand what we wanted again.*"

For further development, the DNB decided to develop the project on their own to even further customise it to the DNB's needs. This was the starting point for EMa. In alignment with the German National Strategy for AI, this AI model for cataloguing was implemented in 2021/2022 and adapted the National Library of Finland's open-source Annif to the DNB's needs. This is a cataloguing engine for the automatic generation of descriptive metadata.

2 Description of the Main Project

The German National Library is testing and incorporating more than one AI project in its organisation. Next to the PETRUS and its successor, Project EMa, there is the so-called German Exile Archive 1933–1945 that allows visitors to interact with prerecorded interviews of holocaust survivors. Here, the German National Library created an interactive exhibition with documents from authors in exile during *National Socialism* in Germany, as well as pre-recorded interviews with survivors of the Holocaust. Visitors can ask questions, and the AI searches through the more than 900 interviews and identifies matching responses by topic area. The library tested this application on a smaller scale to see how visitors react to this type of communication and interaction [4].

However, this chapter mainly focuses on the subject cataloguing machine EMa, ("Erschließungsmaschine"). The German National Library, in general, distinguishes between automated content indexing and automated formal indexing of records. Automated content indexing involves the generation of metadata that supports information retrieval in the DNB holdings. The application's core task, therefore, is to open "*the possibility of classifying or verbally indexing publications that would otherwise not be indexed at all or only partially*" [5]. The DNB usually receives the formal indexing data from the publishers or the German Publishers and Booksellers Association. However, one interviewee emphasised: "*But the topic [formal indexing] is not off the table because there are also access points where we have no formal data. And that's why we're also looking at ways of extracting the formal data from the digital copy of the title page, for example, and assigning it correctly.*"

The first experiments with automated indexing started with the PETRUS project in 2009. The goal was to improve library operations through process-supporting software. They implemented four main scenarios: *automatic subject classification*, *keyword assignment*, *automatic linking of personal names*, and *parallel matching for print and online publications* [6]. Over the years, challenges arose, including personnel turnover and the need for modular solutions. In addition, the DNB worked closely with an external company that developed the software for them. In 2018, the company decided not to develop the software further. One interviewee stated: "*And that was no longer lucrative for the company, so they discontinued it, and we then had to see how we could do it with the next AI project we started. We then called it the cataloguing machine EMa and relaunched the entire process, so to speak. We've learned a lot over the 10 years and realised that this was actually our original goal, but we had strayed from it a little. We wanted a modular system that we could develop further and add to.*"

In 2018, the DNB initiated a new project called EMa, translated as "subject cataloguing machine". The project aimed to redesign the indexing system using the open-source toolkit Annif from the National Library of Finland, interdisciplinary expertise, and different in-house produced AI processes. EMa was enrolled in April 2022 and generated descriptive metadata to enrich the records in the catalogue [7].

EMa generates DDC subject categories (Dewey Decimal Classification, which identifies a numerical designation for the resource at its specific content location [8]), subject headings from GND ("Gemeinsame Normdatei" (German Integrated Authority File) can be used in the DNB and other libraries to index resources and describes entities, i.e. persons, bodies, subject areas, etc. [9]). Therefore, EMa creates text data by using ML.

A key advantage of the introduction of these machine approaches may be beneficial is the challenge of a lack of skilled labour force in libraries, which will enhance in the future. An interviewee stated that the use of AI in cataloguing systems might also mitigate the consequences of skilled labour force shortage in the library sector: "*A quantitative perspective would be that we will have to manage with fewer people.... If there are simply not as many people entering the industry.*"

2.1 Need(s) Behind the Implementation

The DNB has the legal obligation to collect copies of almost all media published in Germany since 1913, which has led to an enormous accumulation of data. This is also the result of new legislation that came into force in 2006, the German National Library Act (DNBG). This law distinguishes between media works in physical form and non-physical form. Media in physical form are all representations on paper, electronic data carriers, and other media; non-physical form is all representations in public digital networks. This results in a huge amount of resources that need to be indexed, which is why collection habits have changed, together with the distribution between occurrences in printed and digital media, e.g. one-third printed and two-thirds digital media in 2022 [10].

To handle this huge amount of data and gain comprehensive access to its collections, DNB improved the content-related cataloguing and generated bibliographic data. By using ML to capture the semantic context, searchability is facilitated. In general, with the EMa application, it is now possible to extend to further data records, as one interviewee describes: "*And that means we can no longer just open up on a book basis as before, but we can extend to journal articles for articles. And that is a tremendous added value created by these automated processes, so to speak, and offers completely new possibilities.*"

Moreover, the top-level library management must drive and support the introduction of changes brought about by AI: "*This development only exists at the German National Library because it was initiated by the Directorate General. It was also strongly supported despite personnel changes. It wouldn't work without them because it has a bit to do with structural changes.*" Another interviewee stated: "*I would say that the drive mainly comes from within at the moment. We simply want to make better use of what we do and what we have.*" Therefore, the projects respond to the need for faster and more efficient library processes. The aim is to develop or acquire complex systems, e.g. EMa, to enhance these operations, aligning with the national library's mission to collect and provide accessible information.

2.2 Actors Involved in Co-producing EMa

The project is supported by a multidisciplinary team, including experts in mathematics, computer science, and data science and librarians with domain expertise. Collaboration with external vendors, universities, and other (scientific) libraries enhances knowledge exchange and provides additional resources. Top-level support ensures funding and distribution of resources and facilitates coordination across departments. Additionally, legal experts contribute to developing policies for responsible AI use within the organisation.

2.3 Internal Actors Involved

The department "Acquisitions and Cataloguing" is responsible for collecting and producing cataloguing data. The domain includes the section "Automated Cataloguing and Online Publications", which collects and manages online publications such as eBooks, eJournals, and Web sites. It is also responsible for developing automatic processes for formal and content indexing. The section is therefore in charge of further developing EMa and consists of a cross-location team of around 30 people: Staff with different professional backgrounds, such as computer linguists, mathematicians, and experienced librarians, are involved in the AI project. The reason behind the broad scope of expertise was summarised by one interviewee: "*But I have to say that you always need a certain level of expertise, professional expertise. So you can't say you can do the whole thing without specialised staff.*" Most of the development and implementation of the AI project is carried out internally by the project staff. However, they are regularly supported by external partners.

The section "General collection management and use issues" is involved in experimenting and working with various types of innovation, from technical to social. This section is part of the "User Services and Preservation" domain and focuses on cutting-edge innovation and its implementation. They do not have any operational tasks regarding the acquisition of media, but they also seek to incorporate perspectives from other parts of the library.

Librarians' critical task regarding EMa is to monitor the AI outputs as described by one interviewee: "*In my view, AI or certain AI applications are very good at processing and structuring large amounts of information. [...] the evaluation, the final assessment, is still a human matter. AI may be able to make recommendations, but I don't think AI can solve ethnic issues.*" Furthermore, this interviewee stated: "*So the AI does something for us, but we look at the results. And we also evaluate these results [...] and use them to feed a cycle, of course. [...] They [librarians] don't look at all the results, but we have a quality assurance system for what is generated with AI support because we have a quality requirement [...] And this has not become superfluous in all these years.*" Finally, another interviewee sums it up: "*And that was important to me right from the start, that you always see the interlocking, i.e., that you interlock the mechanical with the intellectual and make it clear from the beginning that you always need this intellectual [human] input.*"

2.4 External Actors

Further development in the area of AI requires intensive collaboration with external partners who are in possession of relevant expertise. Collaboration with universities, such as TU Darmstadt, Leipzig University, or Dresden University, with other libraries, such as the Technische Informationsbibliothek Hannover or other National Libraries, and with research institutions, such as the Fraunhofer Institutes, plays an important role. The academic institutions play a more central role in guiding the library scientifically in the development and exploration of the possibilities of AI. They provide special input when it comes to data processing, data quality, and the future development of artificial intelligence. One interviewee stated that the exchange of information with external partners is crucial for the library's development, not only in the field of AI: "*And I mean, outside of the AI project, we are always interested in exchanging information, including with other libraries, of course.*"

However, it is not only academic institutions that are involved in providing AI solutions in the German National Library. The DNB has collaborated with a startup from the City of Heidelberg, Aleph Alpha, to experiment on language models such as Aleph Alpha Luminous to improve the already mentioned GND. This language file describes entities in which the respective resource can be contextualised.

Bringing together diverse professional staff backgrounds and the expertise of external partners is known as co-production. According to Mergel et al. (2025), co-production consists of five phases: co-commissioning, co-design, co-implementation, co-delivery, and co-assessment [11]. Table 1 provides an overview of the different co-production phases in the development and implementation of EMa at DNB.

2.5 Skills and Competencies

The development and progress of AI at DNB is largely determined by the attitude towards AI and the error tolerance of employees. It must be noted that AI applications are not 100% accurate. Therefore, the expertise of librarians and resource indexing and cataloguing specialists is key. While expertise is important, motivation

Table 1 Co-production activities in the EMa project at the German National Library

Co-initiation	The DNB initiated the EMa project in the context of the German AI strategy
Co-design	The DNB designed EMa in-house and incorporated the AI application Annif which was developed by the Finnish National Library, to implement a modular AI solution that can be customised to the specific needs of the DNB. The DNB was supported by various external partners such as universities
Co-implementation	For implementing EMa the DNB used diverse professional staff backgrounds and was in exchange with external partners
Co-use/production moment	Librarians monitor the sample outputs of the AI solution
Co-assessment	The co-evaluation process takes place permanently by using samples of ML-Outputs and is benchmarked in-house by the standards of quality management. The interviewees state that there has been some improvement of the application

and willingness to experiment (with AI and in general) are crucial starting points. Above all, library management needs the skill of patience: "*Just saying something is not enough. And things really are more complex than you think.*" One interviewee sums it up by saying: "*In general, I would say that I think we can continue to do the majority of our business with the expertise we have built up. But I think you just have to have a keen eye and take note of things and not accept everything uncritically, including when it comes to AI.*"

The job description of librarians is also changing, as they have to deal more and more intensively with data management in the course of using AI: "*It's less about fulfilling library tasks intellectually, but you have to work much more intensively with the data, process the data in such a way that the methods, which are hopefully the right ones, lead to good results.*" Henceforth, librarians need to acquire some technical skills: "*And that means that librarians need to be tech-savvy. They don't have to be computer scientists, but they do need to be tech-savvy. We need people who can deal with large amounts of data and who have data management skills. And we need an awareness that the goals are different.*" As a consequence of this, an interviewee stated: "*(...) we need to open up the library to other people with other basic skills. But that's not really a new process. I think it started a long time ago with the introduction of information technologies in libraries. And of course, we also need to change the training of librarians themselves. Other priorities need to be set.*"

This is consistent with the "lifelong learning" skill that several interviewees mentioned: "*it's a case of continuous professional development in many places. I don't think it's ever been the case that you can make it to the end of your career with exactly the knowledge you started with.*"

Therefore, it can be summarised that AI-based solutions can enrich the skills and competences of librarians, but cannot replace them. Librarians will still have to make the final decision on the indexing of resources, especially critical and complex resources. The AI solutions already in use are not able to do this, as one interviewee said: "*In my view, the evaluation, the final judgement, is still a human question.*"

3 Challenges to Implementing AI in the DNB

The introduction of AI-based solution in the German National Library also poses challenges. These challenges can be summarised in seven main fields.

The first challenge arises when the data used by AI applications is evaluated. AI tools are never consistently free from biases. At first glance, the access to knowledge is expanded, but the demands on librarians' information literacy increase as the information needs to be assessed: "*Where does this information come from? How is this information labeled? Do I remember where the source was? What was the source? Is the source actually 'clean'?*". In addition, one interviewee emphasised: "*I believe that libraries will face a debate about how we position ourselves as places where you can find reliable information and also information where it is clear how it came about.*"

The second challenge was already mentioned above when it comes to the perceived threat of job loss among librarians. Whereas the interviewee above mentioned that there will be the need of librarians collaborating with the AI application: "*And if this job changes now and disappears, then I can well understand that this is difficult for you (…)*". Related to this kind of challenge is also another aspect. This aspect mitigates the threat of job loss. Still, it stresses the enhancement of a librarian's job portfolio and thereby the need to update their AI literacy and competencies to face less accurate results of AI applications, as already mentioned above: "*the quality is getting worse, and you're embarrassing yourself to the outside world. So that has been a factor because, of course, we also have a lot of mistakes in there, so the processes are not perfect, and especially in the library context, this perfectionism was and is very pronounced, which is also right and important.*"

The third challenge is thereby characterised differently. The limited availability of resources is challenging. Enough funding can be a problem, and the constant battle between personnel and material resources is always a delicate matter. One interviewee stated that there is a lack of enough funding to train the AI models with data that has sufficient quality: "*This means that certain pre-selected training data has a certain quality and is made available. But if so, then it's more of a niche topic and not a broad one, because I don't think that individual libraries at least have enough money to do something all-encompassing.*" Furthermore, public tenders have the potential to complicate project implementation, often resulting in significant delays. There is a growing demand for greater agility within the administration to facilitate more efficient and timely project execution.

The fourth challenge describes the complex task of implementing AI solutions in the whole organisation. When experimenting with the AI solution in only parts of the library, the implementation is not as difficult as implementing it in the whole organisation: "*If we really wanted to implement this, it would affect so many areas and involve so many dependencies, including the publication process itself. That's why I always like to use this comparison: In the lab environment, we have faster and simpler ways to achieve things than if we were to offer something for the DNB as a whole.*" Therefore, it must be addressed that integrating AI into the organisational structure is a multifaceted task.

The fifth challenge describes the transparent handling of the use of AI. The interviewees and experts in the German National Library already see some constraints in the broad use of AI. In the DNB, it is evident which data records were created by machine or intellectually by autopsy. Nevertheless, the question arises as to whether standardised labelling of AI-generated outputs is necessary. An interviewee described it as follows: "*Perhaps even a kind of stamp, a watermark, indicating what kind of information was generated by AI*", could help to make the use of AI more transparent.

The sixth challenge addresses ethical considerations related to the use of AI, especially in the context of language models. The necessity of considering ethical issues in developing and training AI models is emphasised by several interviewees. They address ethical biases, meaning that the resources used to enhance machine learning could contain harmful language or misinformation: "*But we absolutely need the expertise. I mean, if AI does something for me, I don't know. When you ask these ChatGPT things, you can see that some parts are terribly wrong, expressed in the most eloquent language.*" Furthermore, this issue highlights the dilemma institutions such as the DNB face regarding the decision to make their high-quality content available for training AI models. Especially in the German context, the danger of resources created during the time of *National Socialism* poses a substantial threat: "*But libraries, for example, still have collections from the times of National Socialism or colonialism, which means they also hold data that would normally need to be put into context before being made publicly available. If such data were simply released without curation, one would have to carefully consider in what form this could be done. But in some cases, that would certainly be quite challenging.*"

The seventh challenge, again, is related to aspects of training data. In this context, instead of judicial concerns, the organisation is mainly considering ethical challenges of training AI with existing data. The copyright status of most records imposes limitations on the extent to which the DNB can utilise them: "*Most of our collection, yes, is copyright protected, and there are legal, strict legal limits on what you can and cannot do with it.*" Also, when it comes to the internal use of different AI applications, the legal department of the library is worried: "*And if you read through some of the terms and conditions, it says (…) we immediately bag everything you enter and what comes out. And if any copyrights are infringed, which nobody really knows in the end because it hasn't been clarified by the courts yet, then we're out of it. Well, some of these terms and conditions are also written very flippantly. So, I just see a lot of risks because a lot of things haven't been clarified yet.*"

4 Results

4.1 Organisational Level

Four years after its inception, the EMa was implemented. The initial temporary project group has evolved into a whole organisational unit that is collaborating with several other project groups across the library.

The usage of AI in different departments of the DNB leads to new and more effective ways of working. This also includes interdisciplinary work and the breaking down of specialist silos: "*Everything is much more interrelated than it used to be. Even the individual subject areas, from a librarian's perspective, are merging more and more.*" However, it has to be stated that the project is still being improved and monitored. One interviewee states: "*So we are networked with various things and we really do research in that sense. We are really trying to go into depth and understand this in order to find out for ourselves, for our purposes, how we can best proceed in the future and improve productive operations. So we have already improved it enormously.*"

There are still unresolved issues, including how to deal with legal and ethical considerations, but clarification is already being worked on with several stakeholders inside and outside the DNB.

4.2 Value Created and Co-created

The German National Library considers it its duty to uphold democratic values that are closely tied to the thoughtful consideration of information sources. However, AI outputs are not necessarily unbiased and have the potential to compromise these values. Consequently, the DNB aims to serve as a platform through which society can stay informed about various developments in AI. In addition, the DNB is a reliable source of information for AI tools. The DNB's role as a data supplier is closely linked to this, e.g. by providing metadata for other academic and public libraries.

Furthermore, in a changing society, libraries are increasingly evolving into a protected space that is not merely a place of education but also a place to meet and exchange. The vital role of libraries in society is further reinforced by AI adoption, which enhances accessibility, search functionalities, and personalised library services. Nevertheless, it is emphasised: "*[...] we need to make people more aware that we have these skills, materials, content, collections and also this knowledge and that we can communicate it better, that we also have expertise on AI, for example, and that we can also be consulted on questions relating to AI as such.*"

A certain proportion of the DNB staff's attitude has shifted following the introduction of AI-supported methods: "*Younger colleagues have a different attitude to this than many older colleagues, and it very much depends on their personal attitude. Many colleagues are going along with the path, but the big problem is that there are also large areas that are not going along because the results are not yet such that they can be fully satisfied. This problem of acceptance and integration into everyday library work is a much bigger task than many people imagine.*" However, changes in technological approaches might also support the development of new standards for cataloguing within the library community.

4.3 Lesson Learned

The experimentation and implementation of new technologies, such as AI-based solutions like EMa, are always associated with lessons learned. These experiences, which are presented below, help DNB to learn and develop its AI-based solutions further.

The DNB has a reasonably large IT Department, but more developers and AI specialists are needed for the automatic cataloguing unit. Moreover, it is crucial that the IT department stays up to date and has access to training and education to properly support the automatic cataloguing unit.

The team's composition was influenced by an employee with an IT background joining: "*It wasn't planned, but it had a very positive effect on our development. The IT perspective offered new insights into methods and processes, enabling us to set a course that IT, which was too far removed from our specialist topics, could not achieve at the time.*" As the project progressed, highly skilled specialists were intentionally recruited as a result.

Also, the DNB must be aware of AI's inherent complexity, which extends beyond the realms of methods and implementation. One interviewee summarises this: "*Looking back, I would say that it is very important that the institution is aware that this is not a sprint, but a marathon. It's not enough to select a method and implement it. That's a bit of a suggestion because the technology is developing so quickly. The methods are only a small part of the whole.*" No technical applications should be implemented solely based on their current popularity. Instead, only technical applications that provide demonstrable added value for the DNB should be considered for implementation. However, one interviewee elaborated: "*We don't need to adopt technical applications that don't add value for us. We don't have to follow every trend. However, as a national library, we need to be knowledgeable about this environment to have a say. What is effective, what can be effective, and what might.*" Ultimately, a rethinking process towards AI is essential at all levels in the library, which takes time: "*People expect quick results and are not prepared for the fact that it is so time-consuming and that the result will also look different to what they were used to before.*"

When EMa was introduced, there was a debate within the DNB as to whether metadata in the familiar form is still needed at all. Over time, the DNB finally decided that metadata is still necessary but no longer needs to be created according to library rules in the EMa-Project. One interviewee described the discourse: "*This also led to controversial positions because colleagues who are trained accordingly naturally have a completely different relationship to the library rules. And the discussion as to whether the results of the automated processes are good enough was also conducted from the point of view of whether the bibliographic rules are being adhered to. No, they are not adhered to, but the aim of the automated processes was exclusively to find and support.*"

It is crucial to approach AI projects with a fresh and unbiased perspective, recognising the value in embracing mistakes as a part of the learning process. Consequently, top management must foster an environment that embraces experimentation and a culture of failure. It is important to recognise that such projects are iterative processes, necessitating the establishment of effective team dynamics as well. One interviewee summarised the AI experience: "*But because we had the chance to rebuild and redo everything, I would say today that I wouldn't do anything differently. We needed this experience. We worked with an external company, learned a lot, and were able to redo everything. [...] You also need the mistakes to learn from them. And the good thing for us was that we had a managing director at the time who gave us this freedom, who invested money, who invested people, who gave us the freedom to tackle the issues.*"

More than 10 years ago, DNB strategically used the first steps in ML processes, which then led step by step to AI processes. This decision is currently being reviewed to determine whether a semi-automated process would be more advantageous, at least for certain applications. One interviewee commented: "*This is all justified, but experience shows that fully automated processes do not deliver the results that we would like. That's why these feedback processes with intellectual evaluation are more important.*"

Finally, the allocation of more resources towards the AI project by the DNB would have been preferable: "*[...] we should, or we should have put even more resources into it, yes. We should have invested, both in personnel and financially, as well as simply something like hardware, yes, and yes, I think that's what I would do differently.*"

5 Conclusion

The German National Library is Germany's central archive and library institution. The DNB has been using AI in various forms since 2009 to efficiently catalogue and facilitate accessibility of its extensive collection of media. The central projects were *PETRUS, starting in 2009* and *EMa* ("subject cataloguing machine"). *PETRUS* was initiated as a software-supported solution in 2009. The development of *EMa* began in 2018. Based on the National Library of Finland's open-source toolkit *Annif*, *EMa* was launched in 2022. It is a modular tool, meaning that its composition and function can be adjusted to the special needs of the library and create metadata such as DDC subject categories and GND keywords for German and English-language media.

The use of AI became key to efficiently managing the growing number of publications necessitated by the legal obligation. This involved the development of new approaches for modifying publication formats and the establishment of interdisciplinary teams of librarians, IT specialists, and other experts. The biggest challenges encompassed limited resources, ethical issues, and resistance to change processes within the workforce. The legal requirements of copyright and the processing of copyright-protected resources made the implementation even more complex.

Despite these challenges, the projects have influenced the DNB's operational processes. The integration of *EMa* has enabled an efficient generation of metadata, thereby facilitating its accessibility to other libraries via DNB services. This has not only enhanced efficiency but also strengthened the role of the library as a protected space for learning. In addition, the use of AI offers new opportunities for the personalisation of library services and the improvement of search and access processes.

The projects have provided valuable insights, such as the importance of an interdisciplinary and autonomous approach by strengthening internal processes. Mistakes along the way should be regarded as learning opportunities, and the involvement of diverse teams is recommended. The feasibility of semi-automated processes for specific applications is being evaluated. Long-term investment in resources and further development of AI technologies are crucial to ensure that the DNB can meet the demands of the future and fulfil its social obligation as a central source of information in Germany.

Acknowledgements The work for this chapter was supported by the European Union's Horizon Europe Research and Innovation Programme under Grant Agreement ID 101061516.

Appendix

See Table 2.

Table 2 Overview of the EMa project at the German National Library

Case and project name			
EMa (subject cataloguing machine) at the National Library of Germany (DNB)			
Country	**Number of employees**	**Type of AI solution**	**Year and maturity level**
Germany	617 employees located in Frankfurt am Main and Leipzig	EMa (subject cataloguing machine) is the abbreviation for "*Erschließungsmaschine*". EMa is an automatic subject cataloguing machine that generates descriptive metadata to enrich the records in the DNB's catalogue	2009: Project start PETRUS 2019: Project start EMa 2022: EMa went in operation
Project description			
The first experiments with automated indexing started in the Petrus project in 2009. The goal was to improve library operations through process-supporting software. They implemented four main scenarios: automatic subject classification, keyword assignment, automatic linking of personal names, and parallel matching for print and online publications. In 2018, it was decided not to follow the PETRUS application any longer. In 2018, the project called cataloguing machine EMa began to rebuild the indexing system using the open-source Annif from the National Library of Finland, interdisciplinary expertise, and different in-house produced AI processes. EMa was enrolled in April 2022 and generated descriptive metadata to enrich the records in the catalogue. The metadata is available for external applications via the DNB data services and, in general, EMa-generated DDC subject categories, subject headings from GND, and DDC short numbers in the subject categories			
Need(s) behind implementation	**Actors involved**	**Challenges**	
Since 1913 there is a legal obligation that requires the acquisition of a copy of every media published in Germany, which results in the accumulation of vast amounts of data. Moreover, the German National Library Act (DNGB) came into force in 2006 New forms of publications, especially electronic ones, mean that the established procurement channels no longer work Support from the library management behind the introduction of changes brought about by ML and AI	A broad multiprofessional in-house team consisting of librarians, mathematicians, and computer linguists was involved in the process However, it is important to mention that there must be always a close cooperation between AI and librarians to achieve valuable results The in-house team was supported by a broad scope of external actors consisting of, e.g. universities and research organisations	1. Evaluating the AI-Output 2. Fear of losing the job 3. Scarce resources 4. Integration in the organisational structure 5. Labelling of AI-Outputs? 6. Ethical considerations 7. Copyright	

Results		
Organisational level	**Value created and co-created**	**Lesson learned**
The usage of AI leads to interdisciplinary work and the breaking down of specialist silos The risks in the library sector are generally manageable, as they primarily involve the quality of results and the changing nature of the librarian profession	The DNB goal is to serve as a platform where society can stay informed about various media with the help of AI DNB's role as a data supplier is closely linked to this. It provides metadata for other libraries in the academic and public library networks. This means that DNB indexes the publications, and the libraries can obtain the metadata via automated processes and import it into their catalogues	1. Need for more data specialists 2. Teams with diverse professional backgrounds 3. AI is not just a question of method and implementation 4. Debate about whether metadata in the familiar form is still needed at all and whether AI-Output is accurate 5. Projects should be approached with curiosity and a form of naivety 6. Evaluation of trade-offs between fully automated and semi-automated subject cataloguing solutions 7. More investment in resources

References

1. Deutsche Nationalbibliothek, Eine Bibliothek zwei Standorte (2025), https://www.dnb.de/DE/Benutzung/Oeffnungszeiten/oeffnungszeiten_node.html#:~:text=Die%20Deutsche%20Nationalbibliothek%20hat%20zwei,kulturellen%20oder%20fachlichen%20Veranstaltungen%20besuchen
2. Bundesministerium der Justiz (ed.), *Gesetz über die Deutsche Nationalbibliothek (DNBG)* (Bundesministerium der Justiz, Berlin, 2006)
3. Deutsche Nationalbibliothek. ORGANISATION—Beschäftigte (2024), https://www.dnb.de/DE/Ueber-uns/Organisation/organisation_node.html
4. K. Hendinger, DIGITALE ERINNERUNGSKULTUR Deutsche Nationalbibliothek: Wie KI hilft, mit Holocaust-Überlebenden zu reden, in *MDR Kulturdesk*, (2024)
5. C. Poley, U. Sandro, F. Busse, J.-H. Jacobs, M. Kähler, M. Nagelschmidt, M. Schumacher, Automatic subject cataloguing offers the possibility of classifying or verbally indexing publications that would otherwise not be indexed at all or only partially. LIBER Q. **35**, 1–29 (2025)
6. C. Schöning-Walter, PETRUS Prozessunterstützende Software für die digitale Deutsche Nationalbibliothek, in *Dialog mit Bibliotheken 2010/1*, (Deutsche Nationalbibliothek, 2010)
7. Start der Erschliessungmaschine EMa (2023), https://jahresbericht.dnb.de/Webs/jahresbericht/DE/2022/Hoehepunkte/Erschliessungsmaschine/erschliessungsmaschine_node.html
8. B. Lund, D. Agbaji, Use of Dewey decimal classification by academic libraries in the United States. Cat. Classif. Q. **56**(7), 653–661 (2018)
9. Deutsche Nationalbibliothek (ed.), *Kooperationsvereinbarung zur Gemeinsamen Normdatei* (2024)
10. Deutsche Nationalbibliothek, *Jahresbericht 2022* (Deutsche Nationalbibliothek, 2022)
11. I. Mergel, N. Edelmann, N. Haug, Co-production phases in the development and implementation of digital public services. Perspect. Public Manag. Govern. **8**, 93 (2025)

Ines Mergel is a University Professor of Public Administration in the Department of Politics and Public Administration at the University of Konstanz and a Fellow of the National Academy of Public Administration (Class of 2018). After holding positions at the Harvard Kennedy School of Government as a Doctoral Fellow and Postdoctoral Fellow (2002–2008), Professor Mergel was awarded tenure at the Maxwell School of Citizenship and Public Affairs (Syracuse University, NY) in 2014 (2008–2014) and then served as Associate Professor with tenure (2014–2016). Professor Mergel is a member of the supervisory board of the e-Governance Academy (Estonia). Other board memberships can be found here. Professor Mergel is a founding member of the international initiative Teaching Public Service in the Digital Age, which aims to integrate digital skills into the teaching and training of public managers. As part of this initiative, Professor Mergel was appointed a Schmidt Futures Innovation Fellow in 2022.

Justus Kühler is studying for a bachelor's degree in political science and public administration at the University of Konstanz. He is particularly interested in the latest developments in public administration that reflect the trend towards democratisation. He is particularly interested in the application of new forms of participation at the local level. He has already gained initial experience with municipal administration through his involvement in local politics.

Anna-Lea Schumann is currently pursuing a master's degree in politics and public administration at the University of Konstanz. Her research interests focus on applying modern working practices within public administration and their implications for public value creation. In her bachelor's thesis, she explored the use and implementation of design thinking in libraries. She has gained initial practical experience through various internships in public administration, providing her with valuable insights into the operational methods and processes of the public sector.

Corinna Nitsch currently serves as the Chief Information Security Officer in the Baden-Württemberg Ministry for the Environment, Climate and Energy Sector. In both her bachelor's degree in public management and her master's degree in politics and public administration, she concentrated her studies on matters pertaining to digitalisation in public administration. In her theses and part-time roles, she addressed a range of issues and projects, including 5G expansion in municipalities, the integration of artificial intelligence in public libraries, and inequities in online information seeking. She gained experience in several roles at the Kehl Institute for Applied Research and the Cluster of Excellence at the University of Konstanz, among other institutions.

AI-Supported Automated Subject Indexing and Metadata Management with Annif and Finto AI at the National Library of Finland

Anna-Lea Schumann and Ines Mergel

Abstract The National Library of Finland developed and implemented an automated subject indexing and classification tool, Annif, which is now also used by other National Libraries. The tool is integrated into Finto AI, an in-house metadata management system launched in 2020. These two AI-driven solutions were created by the growing volume of digitally collected data, the extensive digitisation of paper archives, inadequate AI support for various Finnish languages, and a lack of transparency in the services offered by external providers on the market. The successful implementation of Annif and Finto AI can be attributed to the strong collaboration between the project team and their external stakeholders, such as other National Libraries or universities, as well as the awareness within the Finnish National Library. Use cases, for example, from the University of Jyväskylä, highlight the value of these AI-driven solutions. However, challenges remain, such as identifying hidden errors in the automatically generated records. Fortunately, the National Library's extensive in-house expertise allows for the immediate detection of mistakes in both the code and the generated records.

Keywords National Library of Finland · National Library · AI · Annif · Finto AI · Automated subject indexing · External stakeholders

---

A.-L. Schumann
Department of Politics and Public Administration, University of Konstanz, Konstanz, Germany
e-mail: anna-lea.schumann@uni-konstanz.de

I. Mergel (✉)
Department of Politics and Public Administration, University of Konstanz, Konstanz, Germany

Fraunhofer FOKUS, Fraunhofer Institute for Open Communication Systems, Berlin, Germany

School of Management, Public Management, University of Vaasa, Vaasa, Finland
e-mail: ines.mergel@uni-konstanz.de

I. Mergel, C. Schmidt (eds.), *AI Innovations in Public Services*,
https://doi.org/10.1007/978-3-032-01344-6_4

1 Introduction

The National Library of Finland, founded in 1640, is affiliated with the University of Helsinki and employs more than 230 experts in different library fields. It includes two branches: the Research Library and the Library Network Service. While the Research Library is responsible for traditional library services, the Library Network Services branch is responsible for developing the National Digital Library's service and work environment. Furthermore, the Library Network Services department provides services to other libraries, museums, and archives in Finland in the form of the open-source library system Koha, which is a system that can be used to manage acquisitions and borrowing [1]. Koha is used by many universities and other special libraries in the country [1]. Furthermore, the National Library of Finland is the administrator and primary developer of Finna (https://finna.fi), an open-source search service that was launched in 2013 [2].

In this chapter, we focus on the open-source toolkit called Annif (https://annif.org) for automated subject indexing and classification [3]. Annif is a multilingual tool that works independently of the indexing vocabulary in a modular fashion and "*integrates many text classification algorithms, including Maui, fastText, Omikuji, and a neural network model based on TensorFlow*" ([3], p. 265). The Annif tool enables user interaction through the command line interface (CLI) or the REST-style API [3]. These options can be utilised to integrate Annif with the Finto AI Web user interface, which is an in-house-produced metadata management system [3]. It applies traditional machine learning and language technology and consists of more lightweight software compared to large language models like ChatGPT. As one interviewee mentioned, "*It's more convenient in some cases, and we've been quite happy with that.*"

This chapter investigates how the National Library of Finland developed and implemented the AI-based solutions Annif and Finto AI. We begin by exploring the National Library's motivations for developing and implementing an automated subject indexing and classification system. Following that, we provide a comprehensive overview of the Annif and Finto AI project itself. Then, we discuss the internal and external actors involved in developing and implementing the AI-based solution. Before addressing the results achieved and the value (co-)created through Annif and Finto AI, we highlight the challenges the National Library of Finland faced. Finally, we present the lessons learned throughout the project.

2 Needs for the Implementation

With the increasing amount of data being collected digitally and the extensive digitisation of paper archives, the National Library of Finland needed to implement automated subject indexing. This minimises manual indexing work and ensures consistency. It also allows for indexing library collections where manual indexing is impractical.

The National Library of Finland created an in-house solution for specific reasons. Finland has two national languages, Finnish and Swedish, and some dialects that most existing AI tools do not support. Additionally, most AI tools are commercial, providing little control over the AI system for the library and its patrons, and often are difficult to integrate into existing systems used for cataloguing and indexing. Consequently, in 2017, the National Library of Finland developed the automated subject indexing tool Annif in-house as an open-source tool.

The Annif project team initiated the first ideas about Annif at a Library Networking Services meeting for the management and the library colleges. They also conducted presentations about Annif outside the library and had previously established a first use case with the University of Jyväskylä, demonstrating its effectiveness to the management: "*I think that helped a lot in showing people that this actually works, this can be used, and they were brave enough to adopt the software full-on in early stages.*"

3 Description of the Project

Annif is an automated tool for subject indexing and classification developed by the National Library of Finland as open-source software. Table 1 provides an overview of the maturity level of Annif's development and implementation.

Annif has a modular architecture and is compatible with various text classification algorithms [3]. It can support regular and fusion backends, which can be added: "*Regular backends work directly on document text and produce a suggestion of possible subjects*", based on lexical and associative approaches ([3], p. 268). The fusion backends, also known as ensemble backends, "*use the suggestions from other backends as input and produce a combined suggestion*" ([3], p. 268).

To evaluate Annif, the National Library of Finland examined manually indexed corpora such as master's and doctoral theses from the University of Jyväskylä covering the years 2010–2017 [4]. They also used non-fiction e-books from 1998 to 2019, which are housed in the National Library and indexed in Fennica as well as a

Table 1 Maturity level of Annif's development and implementation

2014	Start of the Finto project
2017	Start of the first prototype of Annif consisted of "*a loose collection of Python scripts that implemented a minimal REST API and a simple web user interface*" ([4], p. 5).
2018	Begin developing Annif on a more robust technical foundation with the following features: multilingual support, independence from the indexing vocabulary, compatibility with various subject indexing algorithms, a command line interface, a Web user interface, and a REST API suitable for integration with other systems [3]. Additionally, it should be open-source software.
2020	Launch of the Finto AI service that is intended for production use.

database for non-fiction books published between 2000 and 2019 by the book distributor Kirjavälitys Oy [3]. Furthermore, the evaluation incorporated informal questions and answers on various topics collected from public libraries in Finland through the "AskLib" service and digital unindexed documents from the regional newspaper Satakunnan Kansa [4].

The National Library of Finland utilised this data to "*train, validate, and test subsets*" ([3], p. 271). In addition, the library also used humans to evaluate the results of the automatic subject indexing [3]. In 2019, the National Library of Finland organised a workshop where 48 librarians and specialists evaluated indexing created by humans versus by the Annif algorithms [3]. It was not declared to the participants whether the output was created by a human or machine [3]. The results revealed that the participants rated the human indexers slightly higher than the Annif model, with the Annif-assisted semi-automatic indexing falling in between [3]. In addition, the Finnish Public Broadcasting Company Yle, the National Library of the Netherlands, and the German National Library evaluated Annif and decided to implement it in their own libraries [3].

In May 2020, the National Library of Finland finally launched the Finto AI service: "The service offers an easy way for introducing automatic subject indexing into information systems, provided that the vocabularies and language support offered by the API service meet local requirements" ([3], p. 274). It can be used for Finnish, Swedish, and English subjects and can be found at ai.finto.fi [5].

To use Finto AI, the librarian manually inputs text into the tool. The librarian can easily copy and paste the summary into the tool. Then, they read the record summary and consider which subject heading might fit. After that, the librarian uses Finto AI to generate suggestions. Sometimes, Finto AI provides additional information that the librarians can add, but usually, they receive the same information that they have already familiarised themselves with. But there are reasons not to use Finto AI, as one interviewee stated: "*The biggest reason why I don't use it all the time is that it's time-consuming because what I'm getting from Finto AI is obviously guesses. It's not information that I can immediately rely on. I have to check again those subject headings that I do not immediately recognize as valid and that takes time.*"

Despite its early shortcomings, Finto AI is beneficial in the following case: "*I usually use it only when I'm dealing with material that I'm not very good at myself and I want to get some extra feedback a little as if I had a colleague and would ask the colleague whether he has something extra for me.*"

Finto AI has been implemented at the University of Jyväskylä, where students submit their master's thesis online and receive suggestions from Annif on how to tag it with keywords [5]. They can use or discard the suggestions before a final check by a librarian [5]. Moreover, the Finto AI has been piloted at the Osuva repository of the University of Vaasa starting in 2020 and subsequently been implemented in the services of Kirjavältys Oy and the museum collection management programme Collecte [6].

3.1 Actors Involved in Co-producing AI Innovations

A variety of internal and external actors participated in the development and implementation of Annif and Finto AI. The collaboration among these stakeholders is referred to as co-production [7]. Co-production consists of five phases: co-commissioning, co-design, co-implementation, co-delivery, and co-assessment [7].

While co-commissioning is a prospective phase and co-assessment is a retrospective phase in the co-production process, co-design, co-implementation, and co-delivery are simultaneous co-production phases that are mutually dependent [7]. Table 2 gives an overview of the co-production process in the development and implementation of Annif and Finto AI at the National Library of Finland.

3.2 Internal Actors

The National Library of Finland has extensive in-house IT expertise. One employee stated, "*I would say that 30% of the staff of the National Library has some kind of IT title in their work description, and we have really dedicated professional software developers working for those projects.*" The library's substantial IT background benefits the institution by allowing for experimentation and the use of AI. The Interoperability Services team, consisting of three people, is responsible for

Table 2 Co-production process in the development and implementation of Annif and Finto AI at the National Library of Finland

Co-commissioning	*Prospective co-production phase.*	The Annif project team developed the first prototype in 2017 and tested a use case at the University of Jyväskylä. The library management and the public showed interest in it, leading to further work on the project.
Co-design	*Concurrent co-production phases.*	The Annif project team collaborates closely with external stakeholders to develop and enhance Annif by using, testing, and modifying the tool's code.
Co-implementation		Annif is not only implemented in the National Library of Finland but also in other libraries such as the National Library of Germany, universities like the University of Jyväskylä, organisations like Leibniz Information Centre for Economics (ZBW), and companies like the Finnish Broadcasting Company Yle.
Co-delivery		At the University of Jyväskylä, for example, students, librarians, and Annif work together to review master's theses. Students upload their theses to the Finto AI tool, review the suggestions, and then a librarian gives it a final check. This process in Annif is a semi-automated indexing system.
Co-assessment	*Retrospective co-production phase.*	The Annif project team warmly welcomes feedback and suggestions for improvement from external partners such as universities and other libraries that use the tool.

automated cataloguing as part of the Library Network Service department. The team members are either information specialists or software developers/system architects. They described their work atmosphere: "*So, it's a division of labor and all this coordination between how we do things. It's been there from the beginning. It's hardwired into us now....*"

In the Annif project team, different specialists from across the library are involved. The role of the information specialist in the Annif project is mainly content-related. This includes various administrative tasks, testing, and constructing different corpora to test Annif. The software developers primarily focus on Annif's system architecture and technical development. However, the interviewees mentioned: "*... we, are a three-person team, so we are pretty agile by nature. Everybody has to do everything that comes up.*" They hold regular meetings and exchange information on Slack with the Finto working group.

Additionally, the Annif project team introduced various platforms for discussing the open-source tool with other Finnish libraries that use Annif, such as a Google Group Forum or email exchange.

However, using automated subject indexing also requires skills and competencies in manual subject indexing and subject description: "*You would have to have some or quite a lot of experience in working with subject description. I would never recommend that beginners or unprofessional people would be told to use this program...*" Furthermore, "*But if you're not familiar with that [subject indexing] then it's much more difficult and requires more expertise practice.*"

3.3 External Actors

The National Library of Finland aims to create a community around Annif to promote the use of the tool and support its continuous development. On their Web site, institutional users are frequently updated [3]. Additionally, the Annif GitHub project provides technical descriptions and tips for using Annif, as well as reporting bugs and accepting pull requests [3]. They use GitHub to maximise their openness about Annif: "*We try to keep everything public, like the issues, pull requests, all the discussions. ... we try to keep it public what is going on in the development side.*" In addition, one interviewee stated: "*They can give us feedback, and they can submit bug reports and they have also submitted their own pieces of code. For example, Annif uses these algorithms that run in the background, so some of our organizations that also use Annif have also submitted into Annif, for example, these new algorithms.*"

In addition, the Annif team provides a user forum called Annif-users and a hands-on tutorial that the National Library of Finland created with the Leibniz Information Centre for Economics (ZBW) in Germany [3]. The ZBW serves as an important technical resource for the development of Annif: "*ZBW is probably our most important user in terms of cooperation because they have also been able to provide actual code and algorithms.*"

While other collaboration partners often lack extensive programming skills, it is valuable to maintain communication channels with them to understand how Annif is being utilised. This feedback helps the National Library of Finland identify strengths, weaknesses, and opportunities for further development: "*When it's not only used by us but also others, then we can get more and better ideas.*"

According to Suominen et al. ([3], p. 275f) Annif and Finto AI are in use by the following institutions:

- JYX Digital Repository, University of Jyväskylä
- Kirjastot, an e-book platform for public libraries
- Kirjavälitys Oy, a Finnish book distributor
- Osuva, University of Vaasa
- Taju, University of Arts
- Theseus, used by a lot of Finnish universities
- Trepo, University of Tampere

In addition, the following institutions use a standalone Annif installation, which means they can install Annif by themselves and train their own models ([3], p. 277):

- Dissemin.in
- Finnish Broadcasting Company Yle
- Finnish National Audiovisual Institute (KAVI)
- Leibniz Information Centre for Economics ZBW
- National Library of Germany (DNB)
- National Library of the Netherlands
- National Library of Sweden

Future steps may involve intensifying cooperation with universities, as suggested by an interviewee: "*... if there could be some cooperation with maybe the universities that it could be implemented somewhere earlier in the process and perhaps with ... the publishing sector. That's something I would be happy to see happening and also to see it develop towards a more interactive tool that gives more information ....*"

4 Challenges to Implementing AI in the Finnish National Library

During the development and implementation of the AI-based cataloguing solution, the National Library of Finland also faces some challenges, as described in this chapter. Over time, the Annif has become more accurate, with fewer obvious mistakes than before: "*It's more correct with the most basic things that is does and the user interface has also developed in that time.*" Nevertheless, the interviewee stated: "*There has always been hidden mistakes and that's my biggest concern that we inadvertently give incorrect subject headings.*" Therefore, it is important that librarians are still skilled in cataloguing and indexing subject headings: "*If the more inexperience the person using it is in doing this, the more difficult it is probably to spot these subject headings.*"

Furthermore, librarians require sufficient time to use the tool effectively in order to achieve satisfactory results: "*If I have enough time to use it properly, then it can actually make the end result better because I can use my own brain and I can use the extra help.*"

However, some librarians are concerned that the tool may replace human workers and lead to layoffs: "*But what I'm worried about is that it's seen on the upper levels/management level as something that may help reduce staff ... That has, I think been from the very beginning something that many people, in addition to myself, are afraid of that it's been used—that it will be used in this way as an excuse to reduce staff.*" The National Library of Finland has not replaced human workers up to this point.

On the macro level, the development of AI by big commercial companies is a challenge and even a dangerous undertaking: "*[In] the current situation is quite dangerous because the development of the best AIs is basically being done by these big companies in California mostly or in China, and there's not that much transparency into what they are doing.*" Furthermore, the role of libraries is stated as follows by one interviewee: "*So, I see that the role of libraries as well as other public institutions could be to form a counterbalance against this, to try to use AI not to make money, but also for purposes that benefit society in general and also to counter bias, to try to come up with solutions to the ethical issues.*"

Therefore, libraries must constantly keep track of AI development and direction to learn and apply AI in ways that benefit their local interests. In addition, there are challenges to using AI and handling copyright: "*We can do things in-house, usually, but giving out this material to researchers or even to companies, it's not clear if it's allowed. The laws around this are evolving, but it's a little bit of a gray area.*"

5 Results

In the following, we show how the implementation of AI has impacted the operations of the Finnish National Library. We distinguish between the overall organisational impact and the general value that was created respectively co-created with the different stakeholders.

5.1 Overall Organisational Impact

At this time, the National Library of Finland is experimenting with AI tools, but the processes are not yet integrated at the organisational level, as one interviewee mentioned: "*I think it's pretty much the same for all of us that we are experimenting with it, but not really, not really implemented in the general process.*"

Furthermore, another interviewee stated: "*... at the moment, of course, the role of AI is marginal in the library setting. We have the Annif and it's doing its job, but it's of course, behind the scenes and it still needs some human help to give useful results. Where I see AI doing great steps at the moment is actually software development. Our developers use AI quite a lot, for example, in creating tests and also finding bugs and even writing some new code that they can ask the AI, how would you solve this problem, what code you would write.*"

For now, the National Library of Finland has decided against developing an AI department within the library: "*We have decided against treating AI as a new module that we would have an AI unit or anything like that in organisational terms. It needs to be implemented evenly across the organisation because the applications are varied and can be used in different ways, in different contexts. It needs a little bit of knowledge from pretty much everyone in the library, from the customer desk to the software developer.*" Nevertheless, one interviewee emphasised the advantages of opting for an open-source solution and developing an in-house automated subject indexing tool. However, this approach takes some resources: "*Basically, you need to have these people with technical skills working in-house because if you're only relying on companies and consultants, it's not going to work. You'd end up paying a lot of money, and probably the results will not always be what you wanted.*"

The overall organisational strategy towards AI in the National Library of Finland is to invest in their capabilities, which includes the AI competencies of the employees and the necessary technological infrastructure: "*You have to invest in the people, ... you then don't have to pay that much for consultants or other types of external services.*"

5.2 *Value Created and Co-created*

Using Annif and Finto AI benefits the National Library of Finland in several ways. Automated subject indexing can assist manual indexing through semi-automated indexing, where Annif suggests subjects for a new record that are then verified manually. In addition, the National Library of Finland tests Annif for fully automated indexing, where Annif's suggestions are accepted without manual verification.

The interviewees mentioned two benefits of using automated subject indexing tools in the future. First, the tool will become more communicative and, therefore, faster to use. Second, it gives the potential to work with stakeholders together. The interviewee stated, "*But the most useful thing that I have been thinking about for a long time is that it would be much better if the person who is the author of the resource would use it because he would know immediately if there are mistakes. He would also know if something's missing and could add it as a suggestion, and that would really make an immense help, especially with scientific texts.*"

Moreover, one interviewee described: "*AI needs custodianships; someone has to look after it a little bit and keep a watch on it. That's something that libraries, I guess, will be doing in the future, that they are critical also on AI and it's quite okay to use it.*"

Another interviewee mentioned, "*The feedback we receive from end users is usually very positive, which is encouraging. It demonstrates that there is indeed a demand.*"

They also consider use cases, such as when students submit their theses to the repository. Since students typically lack experience with subject indexing, receiving suggestions from Annif through Finto AI really helps them. This also reduces the workload for librarians by minimising the need for checking and adding subject indexing.

5.3 Lesson Learned

Automated subject indexing requires skills and competencies in manual subject indexing and description. For this reason, they advise that beginners or non-professionals avoid using the tool. In addition, some librarian staff are worried that the AI tool is seen as a way to cut off staff and provide quick but inadequate input, which could lead to incorrect information in the library database. Therefore, one interviewee recommended using the tool carefully and thoughtfully to improve metadata but urged more cautious usage: "*I think that if it would be always used in a careful and well thought out manner, then it could actually make a difference or give us better metadata. But we have to or we should maybe be, I think, a bit more cautious than we are now.*" Furthermore, they already started embracing open access, data, and software. Progress has been slow, but there has been a gradual shift towards these principles.

6 Conclusion

In this chapter, we investigated how the National Library of Finland developed and implemented the AI-based solutions Annif and Finto AI.

Due to the increasing volume of digitally collected data and the extensive digitisation of paper archives, the Finnish National Library recognised the need for an application to facilitate automated subject indexing, particularly for library collections where manual indexing proves impractical. Given the insufficient AI support for various Finnish languages and dialects, the National Library of Finland developed an in-house solution. Moreover, the desire for greater control over the AI system—compared to what commercial service providers offer—and the complexities involved in integrating such systems into existing library infrastructures underscored the need for an internal solution. Finally, they started to develop Annif and Finto AI.

Annif is an open-source toolkit for automated subject indexing and classification that was developed in-house. It is multilingual, works independently of the indexing vocabulary, is modular, and integrates different text algorithms [3]. The Finnish National Library uses manually indexed corpora, such as master's and doctoral theses from the University of Jyväskylä, to evaluate the application Annif [4].

Annif is integrated into the Finto AI Web user interface, an in-house—produced metadata management system launched in 2020. Finto AI introduces automatic subject indexing into information systems and understands Finnish, Swedish, and English subjects [5]. This application is, for example, already implemented at the University of Jyväskylä, where students submit their master's theses using the tool and receive suggestions from Annif. The application allows students to use or discard the suggestions before a final check by a professional librarian [5].

The successful collaboration between the project team, the National Library itself, and external stakeholders has contributed significantly to the project's achievements. These stakeholders enhance the AI-based solutions by using, testing, and modifying the tool's code. Use cases from institutions such as the University of Jyväskylä, the Finnish Broadcasting Company Yle, and other National Libraries, including the National Library of Germany, demonstrate that Annif is effective beyond the Finnish National Library. Presentations in-house and outside the library provided an understanding and awareness of AI-based solutions.

However, AI tools have not yet been fully integrated into the general process of the Finnish National Library. Besides, the National Library of Finland decided against developing an AI department and tends to incorporate working with AI across the library. Therefore, due to the in-house developed applications Annif and Finto AI, the National Library has vast knowledge, and staff can immediately identify mistakes in the code or the automated produced records.

Using AI in the Finnish National Library presents challenges, including automated created records with hidden mistakes, time constraints for tool usage, concerns that AI may replace human work, or copyright issues. However, the positive feedback from the users shows how valuable the AI-based solutions are for National Libraries and other stakeholders that use the tools. Moreover, in the future, the tools will become more communicative; therefore, faster and closer collaboration with stakeholders could be possible. Finally, AI requires custodianship and oversight, and the National Library of Finland plays a vital role in this aspect of society.

Acknowledgements The work for this chapter was supported by the European Union's Horizon Europe Research and Innovation Programme under Grant Agreement ID 101061516.

Appendix

Overview of the Annif and Finto AI at the National Library of Finland

Case and project name			
Annif and Finto AI at the National Library of Finland			
Country	**Number of employees**	**Type of AI solution**	**Year and maturity level**
Finland	+230	Open-source toolkit called Annif for automated subject indexing and classification integrated into Finto AI Web user interface, an in-house-produced metadata management system	2014: Start of the Finto project 2017: Start of the first prototype of Annif 2018: Begin developing Annif on a more robust technical foundation 2020: Launch of the Finto AI service that is intended for production use
Project description			
The National Library of Finland has created an open-source Annif toolkit for automated subject indexing and classification. Annif is multilingual, works independently of the indexing vocabulary, is modular, and integrates different text algorithms. Annif can be integrated into the Finto AI Web user interface, an in-house-produced metadata management system. To evaluate Annif, they use manually indexed corpora, such as master's and doctoral theses from the University of Jyväskylä. Additionally, humans evaluate the results of the automated subject indexing. Finally, in May 2020, the National Library launched Finto AI, which introduces automatic subject indexing into information systems and can be used for Finnish, Swedish, and English subjects. Finto AI is, for example, already implemented at the University of Jyväskylä, where students submit their master's thesis using the tool and receive suggestions from Annif. The students can use or discard the suggestions before a final check by librarians.			

Need(s) behind implementation	Actors involved	Challenges
1. Need for automated subject indexing arises due to the growing volume of digitally collected data and the extensive digitisation of paper archives. 2. Allows for indexing library collections where manual indexing is impractical. 3. Need an in-house solution due to the lack of AI support for multiple Finnish languages and dialects. 4. Need an in-house solution due to the lack of control over the AI system from commercial providers and the difficulty of integrating them into existing systems.	• The Annif project team developed the first prototype in 2017 and tested a use case at the University of Jyväskylä. The library management and the public showed interest in it, leading to further work on the project. • The Annif project team collaborates closely with external stakeholders to develop and enhance Annif by using, testing, and modifying the tool's code. The Leibniz Information Centre for Economics (ZBW) is an important collaboration partner, for example, in technical development. • Annif is implemented not only in the National Library of Finland but also in other libraries, such as the National Library of Germany, universities like the University of Jyväskylä, organisations like ZBW, and companies like the Finnish Broadcasting Company Yle. • At the University of Jyväskylä, for example, students, librarians, and Annif work together to review master's theses. Students upload their theses to the Finto AI tool, review the suggestions, and then a librarian gives it a final check. This process in Annif is a semi-automated indexing system. • The Annif project team welcomes feedback and suggestions for improvement, for example, on the GitHub platform, where external partners can report bugs and make pull requests, or in the user forum called Annif-users. Additionally, they provide a hands-on tutorial with the ZBW.	• The model constantly improves its accuracy, but hidden mistakes in, for example, subject headings remain a concern, emphasising the need for skilled librarians in cataloguing. Librarians need adequate time to utilise the tool effectively. There are worries that these tools may replace human jobs. • The development of AI by large companies poses challenges due to a lack of transparency, but libraries can harness AI to promote social good and address bias. Navigating copyright issues with AI is complicated, as the legal landscape constantly changes. • Despite these challenges, investing in library staff and infrastructure is essential for effective AI implementation.

(Continued)

Case and project name		
Annif and Finto AI at the National Library of Finland		
Results		
Organisational level	**Value created and co-created**	**Lesson learned**
Presentations in-house and outside the library provided an understanding and awareness of the development and implementation of the application. A first use case with the University of Jyväskylä demonstrated its effectiveness in the library management. However, one interviewee described that they are experimenting with AI tools but not have fully integrated them organisation-wide, and it has not yet been implemented in the general process. The Finnish National Library decided against developing an AI department. They aim to integrate AI across the organisation and understand its basics from everyone in the library. An in-house solution benefits from the huge amount of knowledge in-house, and staff can immediately identify mistakes in the code or the automated record produced. Annif operates behind the scenes and still requires human assistance to yield valuable results.	1. There is positive feedback about the efficiency of the indexing tools from users, for example, in the use case, where students submit their theses to the repository, which in return encourages the library to work further on it. 2. Automated subject indexing assists manual indexing through semi-automated indexing, where Annif suggests for a new record that is verified manually. Additionally, they test Annif for fully automated indexing. It minimises the need for librarians to check and add subject indexing. 3. In the future, the tools will become more communicative and, therefore, faster. This improvement gives further potential for working with stakeholders.	Automated subject indexing requires skills and competencies in manual subject indexing and description. For this reason, they advise that beginners or non-professionals avoid using the tool. In addition, some library staff are worried that the AI tool is seen as a way to cut off staff and provide quick but inadequate input, which could lead to incorrect information in the library database. Therefore, one interviewee recommended using the tool carefully and thoughtfully to improve metadata but urged more cautious usage. Furthermore, they already started embracing open access, data, and software. Progress has been slow, but there has been a gradual shift towards these principles.

References

1. Library System Service (n.d.), https://www.kansalliskirjasto.fi/en/services/library-system-service
2. Finna (n.d.), https://www.kansalliskirjasto.fi/en/services/finna
3. O. Suominen, J. Inkinen, M. Lehtinen, Annif and Finto AI: developing and implementing automated subject indexing. JLIS.it **13**(1), 265–282 (2022)
4. O. Suominen, Annif: DIY automated subject indexing using multiple algorithms. LIBER Q **29**(1), 1–25 (2019)
5. M. Lehtinen, Finto AI, a service for automated subject indexing (2023), https://www.kiwi.fi/display/Finto/Finto+AI%2C+a+service+for+automated+subject+indexing
6. M. Lehtinen, Annif/Finto AI users (2022), https://www.kiwi.fi/pages/viewpage.action?pageId=175865984
7. I. Mergel, N. Edelmann, N. Haug, Co-production phases in the development and implementation of digital public services. Perspect. Public Manag. Govern. **8**(2), 1–13 (2025)

Anna-Lea Schumann is currently pursuing a master's degree in politics and public administration at the University of Konstanz. Her research interests focus on applying modern working practices within public administration and their implications for public value creation. In her bachelor's thesis, she explored the use and implementation of design thinking in libraries. She has gained initial practical experience through various internships in public administration, providing her with valuable insights into the operational methods and processes of the public sector.

Ines Mergel is a University Professor of Public Administration in the Department of Politics and Public Administration at the University of Konstanz and a Fellow of the National Academy of Public Administration (Class of 2018). After holding positions at the Harvard Kennedy School of Government as a Doctoral Fellow and Postdoctoral Fellow (2002–2008), Professor Mergel was awarded tenure at the Maxwell School of Citizenship and Public Affairs (Syracuse University, NY) in 2014 (2008–2014) and then served as Associate Professor with tenure (2014–2016). Professor Mergel is a member of the supervisory board of the e-Governance Academy (Estonia). Other board memberships can be found here. Professor Mergel is a founding member of the international initiative Teaching Public Service in the Digital Age, which aims to integrate digital skills into the teaching and training of public managers. As part of this initiative, Professor Mergel was appointed a Schmidt Futures Innovation Fellow in 2022.

Visual Discovery Through AI: Unlocking the Postcard Archive at the National Library of Sweden

Ada Scupola

Abstract This chapter provides an overview of the National Library of Sweden (NLS) as well as an overview of AI initiatives taking place at the library. Finally, the chapter presents details of a specific AI solution, Bildsök, a service developed to search the National Library of Sweden's postcard collection. Bildsök is an AI-based service that makes ca. 17,000 digitalised postcards accessible to the broader public by using AI. The chapter provides insights into the needs for the project, the actors involved in the planning and implementation and the challenges encountered on the way. The chapter also provides insights into the value that such a project generates for different stakeholders, the lessons learned and the skills that national libraries need in the era of AI.

Keywords Swedish National Library · Artificial intelligence · AI · Value creation · Digitalisation · Postcard project · Digital transformation

1 Introduction

The National Library of Sweden (NLS), located in Stockholm, Sweden, is a government agency under the Ministry of Education. It collects, preserves and provides access to almost all material that is published in Sweden, from books and newspapers to music, TV programmes and pictures. The library also holds foreign research literature, mainly in the humanities.

The NLS was established in 1661, when Sweden introduced a legal deposit act requiring all printers to deliver one copy of their material to the NLS. In the late 1900s, the act was expanded to include sound, moving images and video games. In 2009, the Swedish National Archive of Recorded Sound and Moving Images became a part of the National Library and ceased to be an independent institution [1].

A. Scupola (✉)
Department of Social Science and Business, Roskilde University, Roskilde, Denmark
e-mail: ada@ruc.dk

I. Mergel, C. Schmidt (eds.), *AI Innovations in Public Services*,
https://doi.org/10.1007/978-3-032-01344-6_5

The NLS is also responsible for coordinating all Swedish libraries, including public libraries and for providing information to higher education and research, which includes obtaining central license agreements for research and university libraries to increase access to various databases [2].

NLS's collections currently include over 18 million items. The library had a budget of 394 Million Swedish Crowns in 2017 and counts about 350 employees [3].

1.1 AI Applications in NLS

In 2019 NLS established an AI lab, the KBLab, that is a national research infrastructure for digital humanities and social science. The KBLab counted about 10 employees in 2024 but planned to employ about the double in 1 or 2 years. The lab experiments with AI technologies to provide access to the library collections in structured and quantitative form, as well as to design, develop and train AI models to analyse the library's collections in innovative ways.

One project where KBLab has used AI to provide access to collections that otherwise would not have been able to be accessed by the public is the postcard project, Bildsök (Bildsök—en demotjänst från Kungliga biblioteket (kb.se)) [4]. In this project, AI supports the library users' interaction with the postcard collection by generating metadata on the fly. As the director of the KBLab states:

> *It's one of the tools from the lab. It's nothing, that's old news now, but it's an example of AI-supported interaction with the collections. It's a small collection of postcards but still, you don't really need metadata. You can create metadata on the fly. (Director of the KBLab, Interview 1)*

This chapter investigates how the National Library of Sweden developed and implemented the AI-based solution Bildsök. The chapter first introduces the KBLab, that is a national research infrastructure for digital humanities and social science established at NLS. Then the chapter goes in depth with Bildsök, which is one of the AI solutions developed at the KBLab. The chapter first provides a description of the project. Then it explores the National Library's motivations for developing and implementing such a solution and discusses the internal and external actors involved in developing and implementing Bildsök. Finally, the chapter provides insights into the value (co-)created through Bildsök, the challenges faced and the lessons learned.

2 Description of the Project

NLS stores and preserves a huge amount of data due to the Swedish legal deposit act that dictates that the national library receives a copy of everything published in Sweden. Therefore, it has been impossible for the NLS to manually catalogue each and every incoming item due to the huge amount of material that the library receives.

The result is that certain types of items get grouped together under collective catalogue entries and detailed information and metadata about each single item is not provided by the library. This has been the case for the postcard collection, which counts a rich and diverse collection of c. 600,000 postcards from the nineteenth and twentieth centuries [5] as Haffenden et al. [6] write on the KBLab blog:

> A pertinent example of a material that, while preserved, lacks description—perhaps due to its perceived ephemerality historically and the limited valuation this has granted in terms of archival resources and attention—is visual heritage collections from the nineteenth and twentieth century. Descriptive cataloguing has long been a central part of KB's making its collections accessible and searchable, but it has been impossible for each and every incoming item to be manually catalogued, given that legal deposit legislation dictates the library receives a copy of everything published in Sweden. Instead, certain items such as postcards or adverts have tended to be grouped together and classified under collective catalogue entries that often preclude the detailing of any specific information about the individual object per se...Although KB has a rich and diverse collection of *c. 600,000 postcards*, the lack of navigability and overview entrenched by scarce metadata has made the material hard for users to access—or even to be aware of its existence. Despite being preserved as part of our shared cultural heritage, such items are thus at risk of disappearing from view altogether. [6]

The library users have had, therefore, difficulties in accessing this collection due to the lack of detailed information about each specific item.

Recently, the KBLab, as part of its wider mission to contribute to wider use and discussion of AI tools for the heritage sector, has applied AI to develop a service, Bildsök, that provides access and makes it possible to search part of the postcard collection. The Bildsök project is still at the experimentation stage, and a demo has been launched on the Web [4]. The project only includes 17,409 postcards because they are the only postcards that have been digitised. To be able to display the postcards, NLS has signed a contractual license agreement with Bildupphovsrätt in Sweden as Haffenden et al. report on the KBLab's blog [6]:

> The Royal Library can display the postcards in this service because we have signed a contractual license with Bildupphovsrätt i Sverige. It is you as the user who is responsible for finding out whether the material is copyrighted and for obtaining approval if you wish to distribute it further. [6]

To make it possible to search in the postcard collection, the KBLab has used the adaptation of the CLIP model, Swe-CLIP 2M, developed by Carlsson et al. [7] to enable free-text search in Swedish. The Swe-CLIP 2M is the Swedish adaptation of the OpenAI model CLIP, which enables free-text search on images in English.in English. The Swe-CLIP 2M AI model, instead, enables free-text search in Swedish. It is possible to search by simple keywords such as "Church", blue sky, etc. As stated on the Web site of the project [4]:

> *Slowly, the model has learned to associate texts in image descriptions with corresponding images. When "church" has appeared in a text, the model has become good at generating a similar numerical representation for the text "church" as well as for images depicting a church. Similarly, it has learned to associate the text "blue sky" with the color blue and horizon and sky-related motifs in images.*

2.1 Need(s) Behind the Implementation

The main need to start Bildsök was the very limited access that the library users had to these kinds of collections or sometimes even the awareness of their existence. Such limited access was a result of the lack of navigability and overview due to scarce metadata. There is therefore the risk that such material may be completely forgotten, even though it is part of Sweden's cultural heritage, as Haffenden et al. [6] state on the KBLab's blog:

> Although KB has a rich and diverse collection of *c. 600,000 postcards*, the lack of navigability and overview entrenched by scarce metadata has made the material hard for users to access—or even to be aware of its existence. Despite being preserved as part of our shared cultural heritage, such items are thus at risk of disappearing from view altogether. [6].

2.2 Actors Involved

The project was initiated and completely developed internally in the library. It is supported directly by the head of the KBLab and indirectly by the library top management, by supporting and financing the KBLab to innovate and experiment with AI solutions in the library context.

The project was started and implemented by a team of KBLab developers. However, the KBLab team has collaborated with other departments at the library including key librarians/archivist experts of the postcard collection. KBLab employees have also involved User Experience (UX) employees at the library and final users of the library in testing the service. In addition, they have collaborated with the copyright agency to get permission to publish the postcards on the Web. As the director of the KBLab states:

> *When it comes to implementation into the library, we work in very close collaborations with the other departments at the library, the librarians basically, or archivists. Sometimes we need to work very close with them and sometimes we don't really need that much because it's collections that we're already familiar with. When it comes to articulating the needs, we do that together with the team around the developers. (Director of the KBLab, Interview 1)*

During the project implementation, several co-production activities with different stakeholders' involvement were identified. Here we follow Mergel et al.'s [8] phases of the co-production process to identify the co-production activities characterising the Bildsök project, which are summarised in Table 1.

2.3 External Actors

The postcard project was initiated and completely developed internally in the NLS. However, the CLIP model applied in the project, Swe-CLIP 2M, was developed and adapted by KBLab data scientists together with scientists employed at

Table 1 Co-production activities in the development and implementation of Bildsök at the National Library of Sweden

Co-commissioning	*Prospective co-production phase*	The developers of the KBLab initiated the project as part of KBLab's wider mission to contribute to wider use and discussion of AI tools for the heritage sector
Co-design	*Concurrent co-production phases*	Bildsök was designed by the KBLab developers together with the librarians (archivist expert of the postcard collection)
Co-implementation		The KBLab developers and the librarians experts of the postcard collection were the main actors involved in the implementation of Bildsök. User experience employees and library users were involved in testing the service. Collaboration with scientists employed at other research institutions and the copyright agency was key to make the service a reality
Co-delivery		Bildsök has presently a demo page on the NLS Web site and can be used and tested by library users and anybody interested in the service
Co-assessment	*Retrospective co-production phase*	The KBLab developers, the librarians/archivists, the library UX employees and the library users are the main actors involved in the co-assessment of the service in the initial implementation phase. Presently, on the Web page of the service, there is a link where it is possible to use and test the service

other research institutions. In addition, the copyright agency has been involved to clear/buy all the needed copyrights of the postcards to make them available online and searchable to the library user.

2.4 Challenges

In developing Bildsök, the NLS and the KBLab have encountered several challenges. One major challenge in the project is related to technical requirements necessary both to scale up the project to all the ca. 600,000 postcards in the collection and to go from the present demo stage to full implementation as a library service. Such technical requirements include developing a public interface which meets the accessibility standards required by the library services and integration of Bildsök into the existing library system. As the research coordinator (Interview 2) points out:

> *There's a difference between just showing something works on one person's laptop to we need to get developers in, we need to think about a public interface, we need to make sure that interface meets the accessibility standards that the libraries website must have. That's a different phase of development work that necessarily also takes time. (Research Coordinator, Interview 2).*

Another important challenge is the copyright issues that need to be cleared to publish the postcards and make them available and retrievable on Bildsök as the research coordinator (Interview 2) points out:

> Another part of that though was the licensing issues to be able to show this material. Technically, they're copyrighted, the postcards, even though we're not always sure who produced them. It's not like a book where we know we have the author of this is X, Y, and Z. (Research Coordinator, Interview 2)

Finally, the lack of resources and lack of strategic leadership to put the demo service into full production is also pointed out as an important challenge by the research coordinator:

> *But once you've come up with something, the next step [is] about how do we go from prototype to something that exists for all of our library users in the real world as it were...They need other type of skills and competences, not least the legal aspect. (Research Coordinator, Interview 2)*

3 Results

3.1 Organisational Level

The postcard project has generated different values for the National Library of Sweden. The main value consists in making library material such as the postcard collection accessible and available to the broader public, therefore contributing to accomplish the library overall mission. As a metadata strategist states:

> *The significance for us is that we can make our collections available and useful through a trained model that other stakeholders can value and use and fine-train for their own. needs. (Metadata strategist, Interview 4)*

Another important value for NLS is the administrative value. In fact, the AI model relieves library employees from eventually having to retrieve the physical postcards and therefore frees resources to conduct other tasks as a metadata strategist states:

> *I think that also goes hand-in-hand with the digitisation and AI to be for the staff within the library that don't need to go and fetch these postcards, go and look for them in boxes, and so on. It makes the material available directly and we could use our resources for other things than getting things in and out of the archives DALL·E and also saving the material from preservation actions through wear. (Metadata strategist, Interview 4)*

Finally, another important value for NLS is the project contribution to innovation processes within the National Library of Sweden:

> *The second point of value from this project is about method development within the library itself. (Research Coordinator, Interview 2)*

3.2 Lessons Learned

There are a few lessons that NLS has learned through the postcard project, many of them related to funding issues. The first is that it is important to have internal AI expertise and competence and not only rely on external providers. The second lesson is the importance of integrating the AI competences within the specific context of libraries and not only having and developing AI competences per se. The third is that the library leaders need to understand the AI use cases and make decisions that support the adoption of AI projects within the library. Fourth, it is important to use AI responsibly and ethically and think carefully about where AI can add value to the library. Fifth, it is important to have cleared all copyright issues related to the material that has to be made available online to the wider public. Some of these lessons are summarised by Haffenden et al. [6] on the KBLab's blog:

> There are certain practical preconditions for the adoption of such technology in a heritage setting, most of which can be related to questions of funding: that the material has been digitized, that there are sufficient resources available for computation, data science and developer expertise, and that there are licensing agreements in place [6].

3.3 Value Created and Co-created

According to the respondents, there are different public values that the postcard project at NLS has generated or has potential to generate for the society. The most important value is the democratic value. Specifically, the postcard demo generates this value by providing accessibility to the postcard collection. Such a collection would otherwise be nearly impossible to access without using AI. As a metadata strategist states:

> *One of the key points that's lifted is to be an effective research infrastructure to raise the quality of Swedish research. And then, the sub-points relating to that is, of course, collecting the cultural heritage as part of our assignment with legal deposits. Not only collecting and preserving, but also making it searchable and available for researchers in appropriate forms, so that they can access it. (Metadata strategist, Interview 4)*

In addition, the postcard project may generate cultural heritage access value for diverse groups of external actors such as journalists, authors, and researchers as a metadata strategist states:

> *But for the library, I think it's in a way broader, the cultural heritage also includes value for the public and professionals, for example journalists, authors and people doing other kinds of research, like genealogy. So, it's a much broader group that could find value in this, especially if we start to see that this pilot works even though we have a very, very small subset of our postcards. (Metadata strategist, Interview 4)*

From a larger perspective, the KBLab generates democratic value at the societal level by building large language models that understand Swedish in all its variants and dialects; increasing access to heritage material; developing open source AI models; and making them available on the Hugging Face open source platform [9] contributing to build an effective research infrastructure to raise the quality of Swedish research. This is illustrated by the following quotes by the director of the KBLab, metadata strategist and research coordinator, respectively:

> *Our languages are underrepresented in the multilingual model. We see that as a democratic task for us that every way that Swedish is spoken or written or otherwise, that should be represented also or mirrored in these models, transform the models, because these are transformative techniques, and we need them to be representative. So, every dialect spoken in Swedish—when we train some models, for example, we based the training on—we try to get as much variation into the underlying data as possible. (Director of the KBLab, Interview 1)*

> *This is important for an open society, for democratic values that it's possible for researchers but also for the general public to be able to access our preserved cultural heritage. (Metadata strategist, Interview 4)*

> *Open-source AI models... we released these AI models on the platform, Hugging Face, that way they're freely available AI-tools. (Research Coordinator, Interview 2)*

Another important value generated at the societal level is the administrative value for external stakeholders. This mainly consists of the application of the AI models produced at KBLab by other stakeholders such as governmental organisations to automate information heavy processes with AI thus increasing efficiency, as a metadata strategist (Interview 4) states:

> We know that the models are used, for example, in the governmental sector to make the information processes more effective. As you know, these processes usually have a resource-heavy manual side to it. If you can support that with automation through AI, that's a good thing for streamlining processes and transparency. (Metadata strategist, Interview 4)

3.4 New Skills

The most important new skills needed in implementing AI at the KBLab are data scientist skills. However, the director also points out the importance of other skills for the implementation of AI projects. These include classical librarian skills, for example, historians, traditional IT skills such as IT architects and IT developers, product managers, product leaders and UX experts:

> *The key competence at the lab is data science...Then, we have all the historians at the library, typically with a PhD.... who know stuff about the collections. We need that....And then, the typical—we have to have IT architects to set up the whole computational environment locally...When it comes to implementing applications into the library, the team that we're building now it's data science, but it's also product management, product leaders, UX people, developers, etc. (Director of the KBLab, Interview 1)*

A research coordinator adds that in addition to pure data scientist skills there is a need for *data generalist skills*, that is employees who can see the connection between AI and library operations and the potential of applying AI specifically to the data that the National Library of Sweden has:

> You also need more generalists that have an understanding of AI and data science, but also see some bigger picture, that see what these things might be able to do within the library and beyond, and also how that affects the other types of the library's operations that aren't going to be rooted in data science. (Research Coordinator, Interview 2)

4 Conclusions

In this chapter, we investigated the use, development and application of AI in the National Library of Sweden.

The National Library of Sweden has established an AI lab, called KBLab, where the library is experimenting with AI to provide improved access to the library collections as well as to design, develop and train AI models that can be used to analyse the library's collections in innovative ways. Recently, the KBLab, as part of its wider mission to contribute to the wider use of AI tools for the heritage sector, has applied AI to part of the NLS's postcard collection and has developed Bildsök. Bildsök is a service that provides access and makes it possible to search part of the NLS's postcard collection. Bildsök *is still at demo stage, but its long-term aim is* to provide access to a digitalised postcard collection that otherwise would not have been able to be accessed by the public. In fact, the main reason why the KBLab has started the project was the very limited access that the users have to these types of items and collections. Even though the main actor responsible for the initiation and implementation of the project was the KBLab, several internal and external actors were essential for the success of the project, including key librarians, experts of the postcard collection, the library users, UX employees and the copyright agency.

Bildsök has generated different values for the NLS. The most important value is the democratic value, which is enacted in the project contribution to the library mission of making the Swedish cultural heritage widely accessible to the broader public.

In conducting the project, NLS has learned several lessons concerning the application of AI in the national library context. They include the importance of developing internal competences such as data science, building AI on a contextual understanding of libraries as a particular type of organisation with specific challenges. Finally, NLS pointed out the need for data generalist skills, that is employees that are able to understand not only AI but also how it can be applied to the specific context of the National Library of Sweden to generate value.

Acknowledgements The work for this chapter was supported by the European Union's Horizon Europe Research and Innovation Programme under Grant Agreement ID 101061516.

Appendix

See Tables 2 and 3.

Table 2 Overview of the postcard project at the National Library of Sweden

Case and project name			
The postcard project at the National Library of Sweden			
Country	**Number of employees**	**Type of AI solution**	**Year and maturity level**
Sweden	350	A multimodal AI system called Swe-CLIP 2M	Experimentation stage; a demo has been launched on the Web
Project description			
Searching in postcard collections of ca. 17,000 digitised postcards			
Need(s) behind implementation	**Actors involved**	**Challenges**	
Very limited access that the users had to this kind of collection; sometimes even the awareness of its existence	KBLab developers/librarians/archivists/user experience designers; library users; copyright agency	Copyright, technical integration and accessibility challenges with the rest of the library system; the lack of resources and lack of strategic leadership to put the demo service into full production	
Results			
Organisational level	**Value created and co-created**	**Lesson learned**	
AI models relieve library employees and free resources for other jobs; KBLab's contribution to library innovation processes	The democratic value of accessibility to a postcard collection	Develop internal competences to use AI responsibly and ethically; AI expertise gets integrated within the library and takes into consideration some of the informational challenges of large-scale collections; building AI on a contextual understanding of libraries as a particular type of organisation with specific challenges; develop AI where it can add value to the library	

Table 3 Overview of interviews at the National Library of Sweden

Interview number	Position of the respondent	Interview length
1	Head of data lab at the Swedish National Library	1 h
2	Research Coordinator	50 min
3	Research Coordinator	30 min
4	Metadata strategist at the National Library of Sweden	1.20 h

References

1. https://en.wikipedia.org/wiki/National_Library_of_Sweden#Audiovisual_media
2. The National Library of Sweden—Kungliga biblioteket—Sveriges nationalbibliotek—kb.se. Accessed 3 July 2024
3. Annual Report 2017 to CENL and CDNL (PDF). The Conference of European National Librarians. Accessed 3 July 2024
4. Bildsök—en demotjänst från Kungliga biblioteket (kb.se). Accessed the 4 July 2024 and 1 Apr 2025
5. Kungliga bibliotekets vykortssamlingar—ARKEN (kb.se)
6. C. Haffenden, F. Rekathati, E. Rende, Unearthing forgotten images with the help of AI (2023), https://kb-labb.github.io/posts/2023-10-20-unearthing-forgotten-images-with-the-help-of-ai/. Accessed 3 July 2024 and 1 Apr 2025
7. F. Carlsson, P. Eisen, F. Rekathati, M. Sahlgren, Cross-lingual and multilingual CLIP, in *Proceedings of the Thirteenth Language Resources and Evaluation Conference*, (European Language Resources Association, Marseille, France, 2022), pp. 6848–6854
8. I. Mergel, N. Edelmann, N. Haug, Co-production phases in the development and implementation of digital public services. Perspect. Public Manag. Govern. **8**(2), 1–13 (2025)
9. https://huggingface.co/. Accessed 3 July 2024

Ada Scupola, Department of Social Sciences and Business, Roskilde University, Denmark. Her main research interests are at the intersection between digitalisation, innovation and the service sector and include value (co-)creation, digital transformation, user involvement in innovation, digital innovation, adoption, and diffusion of information and communication technologies (ICT) with a special focus on small and medium-sized enterprises (SMEs). Recently, she has been investigating the role of Artificial Intelligence in organisations with a focus on service organisations.

From Data to AI-Based Discovery: The Maken Project at the National Library of Norway

Ada Scupola

Abstract This chapter provides an overview of the National Library of Norway as well as an overview of the AI initiatives taking place at the library. The chapter presents details of a specific AI project, Maken. Maken is a discovery engine that finds similar books and images. For example, based on the pixels of a given image, Maken finds related images, or based on the text of a book, Maken finds similar books. The chapter provides insights into the needs for developing Maken, the actors involved in the project implementation and the challenges encountered. Finally, the chapter provides some insights into the value that such a project generates for different stakeholders, the lessons learned in the implementation phase and the skills that the library needs to adopt AI.

Keywords National Library · Norwegian National Library · Artificial intelligence · AI · Value creation

1 Introduction

The National Library of Norway (NLN) as we know it today was opened in 2005. The National Library of Norway counts about 420 employees and about 8.5 million items [1]. The University of Oslo Library functioned as both a university library and a national library from 1813 until 1989 when Norway established a repository in Mo i Rana as part of the national library.

The National Library of Norway has the mandate to preserve everything published within the country in compliance with the Legal Deposition Act [2]. In 1999, a new branch of the National Library was established in Oslo, and in 2005, the national library moved finally into a renovated building also located in Oslo. This marked the beginning of the Norwegian National Library as a new national

A. Scupola (✉)
Department of Social Science and Business, Roskilde University, Roskilde, Denmark
e-mail: ada@ruc.dk

I. Mergel, C. Schmidt (eds.), *AI Innovations in Public Services*,
https://doi.org/10.1007/978-3-032-01344-6_6

institution, being the main source of information about Norway, Norwegians and Norwegian culture with bases in two locations: Oslo and Mo i Rana.

The National Library in Oslo is responsible for library activities aimed at the public, including reading rooms and research workspaces, as well as communication activities such as physical events and permanent and temporary exhibitions. The National Library's Repository Library is located in Mo i Rana where there is also a separate repository for storing archival materials from the National Archives of Norway [3]. The National Library in Mo i Rana has the responsibility of collecting, preserving and making available all material published for the Norwegian public, i.e. all legal deposit materials. In addition, cultural heritage materials from Norwegian archives, libraries and museums are also digitised and stored in Mo I Rana.

The Ministry of Culture and Equality maintains the overall national responsibility for archives, libraries and museums in Norway according to the government of Norway's official Web site "Government.no" [3]. According to such a Web site, one of the main tasks of the National Library is "*to secure and preserve legal deposit materials and other collections, and to encourage interest in and the use of these collections. The National Library also has the task of strengthening libraries as promoters of literature, knowledge and cultural heritage, as well as digitising document-based cultural heritage from Norwegian archives, libraries and museums*" [3].

AI Applications in NLN's AI activities are centred in the AI-lab that was formally established in 2018. The AI-lab at the National Library of Norway explores the potential use of AI in Libraries, including Archives and Museums. The AI-lab is involved in research and development as well as building resources, datasets and models and making them available to the public [4]. According to the director of the AI-lab, the AI-lab deliverables include "experiments, pilots, and demonstrations; support for internal workflows; internal and external knowledge; training datasets based on NLN's collections; fully trained models for free use across modalities; services and APIs; collaboration, networks such as 'ai4lam', 'CENL AI group'; research" [5].

Examples of such deliverables include: (1) Data sets such as the Norwegian Colossal Corpus which is a collection of multiple smaller Norwegian corpora suitable for training large language models; (2) AI models for various purposes that are often based on the combination of NLN's digital collections; an example is NB-Whisper for Norwegian Bokmål and Nynorsk; (3) AI tools tried in real contexts including user experiences/services, components in internal library workflows, or AI services for library services. Examples of applications include Maken, a recommendation system based on the content of books and images and described below and the Sami Bibliography Assistant. The Sami Bibliography holds publications relevant to the Sami community in Norway, and it is maintained by a special office at the National Library of Norway. The Sami Bibliography Assistant is based on a model trained on content and metadata both from inside and outside the existing

Sami Bibliography and has the purpose to assist the workflow in the Sami Bibliography office by suggesting material to be included in the Sami Bibliography based on analysing the content of the digital versions of the items.

This chapter investigates how the National Library of Norway developed and implemented the AI-based solution Maken. The chapter first introduces the project, including needs behind the implementation and actors involved. Then it presents the results, including the challenges faced in implementing the project, the value created and the skills that national libraries need to embark on the AI journey. Finally the last session provides some concluding remarks.

2 Description of the Project

One of the AI-based applications developed by the AI-lab is Maken, a recommendation system based on the content of books and images. Maken is an experimental new service that uses artificial intelligence to find books or images that are similar to each other. Given the immense collection of the NLN, it is sometimes hard for library users to find relevant related content when they navigate through the main site. Maken should help to make the search easier (Maken—AI-lab (nb.no)). As the director of the library and the director of the AI-lab respectively state:

> *Maken, which means "similar", which we put into production, is a vectorising of our digitised books and our digitised images where AI gives you samples of something that is similar to the picture or the book you have chosen. There is no human in this loop. It's only the analysis of the vectorised space that gives you this. If you find a picture of a mountain, you'll find a lot of mountains. If you find a book, you can see what AI thinks the book is to be compared to. This is put into production. (NLN Director, Interview 1)*

> This is not based on metadata at all. There is no metadata supporting this. The way this is done is that we vectorise the content that is producing a numerical mathematical representation of the content, the text itself, and then we have a large numerical space. You can look at this space as your room and the content is spread around in your room. .... This enables navigation in a collection without caring about the description of the content. (Director of AI lab, Interview 3)

The project is still at the experimentation stage, and a demo has been launched on the Web [1].

2.1 *Need(s) Behind the Implementation*

The primary need to start this project was the increasing difficulty in discovering the digital material of the library both due to the increasing amount of material and potential lack or insufficient metadata. The NLN possesses a huge and growing digital collection of every item published in the two official Norwegian Languages,

Norwegian and Sámi, including media, books and TV programmes. As de la Rosa et al. [6] write in a presentation given at the "Fantastic Futures 2021" conference:

> As such collections grow, discoverability becomes harder. Metadata may be missing or insufficient, and it may be difficult to search within the actual content. We wanted to see if AI could help make this experience more useful, interesting, or fun. So, we started building Maken. [6]

It was the NLN top management that started the initiative to look into this issue in 2020. The main idea was that Maken had to apply some of the knowledge that the AI Lab had acquired over several years of experimenting, prototyping and tool-building with AI. As a team leader states:

> *Let's say you go into our digital collection online and you select a book on flowers. You could, in the traditional method, just search for flowers and see what content shows up in your search table. But using this one is more like Spotify or Netflix or other content platforms where you use a bit of content as an entrance to show something to navigate and be presented with other content that is similar in some way. That is an interesting new way to discover digital content on our platform. (Team leader, interview 5)*

2.2 Actors Involved

The director of the library initiated the project. The main actors involved at the beginning of the project were the AI lab and the library's top management. Later, other stakeholders, external to the library (see below), were involved such as the library users.

2.3 Organisational Level

The Maken project was supported directly by the director of the NLN and the AI-lab director. The project aligns with the digitalisation strategy of the NLN [6].

2.4 External Actors

The project was initiated by the NLN, but the AI lab collaborated both with other internal teams, the users/patrons and other external actors in implementing, designing, producing and testing the recommender system. Maken was implemented by the AI-lab in collaboration with an internal team called Digital Outreach and a specialised IT consulting company, Dekode Interaktiv AS [7]. As an AI Lab Research Scientist states:

> We work in projects. Depending on the scope of the project we define who's going to be involved or not. For example, we're now working on language models and we are—the AI Labs is a unit, so we have different units… So, we do this cross-sectional work together. When we built Maken, we work together with a team called digital outreach, and that team already includes a few designers, a few frontend developers because we don't know how to make websites. So, we have to work with other teams if we want to deliver a product that is public-facing… (AI Lab Research Scientist, Interview 4)

The users had an essential role in developing the AI system both directly and indirectly. In fact, in parallel to developing Maken, the AI-lab tried to understand how the digital services were used by diverse types of users through data collection and analytics from the NLN's digital services and user surveys and by involving the users in testing the system:

> In parallel to developing Maken, we worked to understand how of our digital services were being used, in particular The Digital Library. Through data collection and analytics from our digital services, user surveys, and also some user testing, we had a general understanding of our user segments. [6]

Therefore, co-production characterised the development and implementation of Maken, and the co-production activities are summarised in Table 1 by following Mergel et al.'s phases of the co-production process [8].

Table 1 Co-production activities in the development and implementation of Maken at the National Library of Norway

Co-commissioning	*Prospective co-production phase*	The director of the Library initiated the project idea and involved the director of the AI lab
Co-design	*Concurrent co-production phases*	Maken was designed by the AI-lab in collaboration with an internal team called Digital Outreach and an external consulting company called Dekode Interaktiv AS
Co-implementation		The AI-lab, the Digital Outreach Team and Dekode Interaktiv AS implemented Maken by involving also other external actors such as the library users, which were involved, for example, in testing the system
Co-delivery		Maken is presently a library service offered by the library and used by the public to retrieve books online the same way as if the users were in the physical library
Co-assessment	*Retrospective co-production phase*	The AI Lab and the Demo users were the main actors involved in the co-assessment of the service in the initial implementation phase. Presently, on the Web page of the service there is a link where the service users can send messages to the Maken team with feedback about the service

2.5 Challenges

In the implementation of the Maken project, NLN has encountered several challenges. The main challenges were GDPR and privacy issues, Data Protection Impact Assessment and consent for the interviews [6]. In fact, they had to make sure to collect only the data they needed, that they respected the data protection law of the people they interviewed and the future user of the service, get the informed consent to record, store and analyse the data collected through interviews and workshops as well as respect the user rights and privileges.

3 Results

This paragraph depicts the main results of the study. It touches upon the value that AI has generated at the organisational and societal level, the main lesson learned and the new skills that libraries need in the era of AI.

3.1 Organisational Level

The implementation of Maken has generated a number of important organisational values for NLN. The main value generated by Maken consists of making easier to access and retrieve similar kinds of books and images to the broader public, thus contributing to accomplish the library mission. Another important value that Maken has generated for NLN is its contribution to the library strategy of experimenting with AI. Finally, Maken contributes to the administrative value of the library as it makes it unnecessary to generate (certain) metadata of the books and images in order to find the ones that are similar to each other.

3.2 Lessons Learned

The two most important lessons that NLN has learned from the Maken project are the key importance of involving users in the process as early as possible as well as the importance of understanding the digital changes that are affecting libraries. This is pointed out by a team leader and the library director, respectively, for example, in the following two quotes:

For the next AI project, we want to be even more aware of bringing in the people who are eventually going to use it. … So, that is the key thing, I guess. I keep coming back to it. It sounds like a cliché, but it really is true from our experience. The technology is there to serve humans and bring humans along the way. It's always the way to go. (Team leader, interview 5).

So, we need a digital change in libraries, on how you focus. (NLN Director, Interview 1)

3.3 Value Created and Co-created

Experimenting with AI at the AI-lab and specifically the Maken project generates potential and realised value for society. The most important societal value is the democratic value. This is enacted by the easier access to digital books and images for the library users, thus getting new insights into the country's cultural history as shown by the following quotes:

The value, for example… Using this system, they (final users) are able to find related documents that they could be interested in. We run user testing with different user profiles and user stories, and they all found the service really useful. (AI Lab Research Scientist, Interview 4)

We don't want to sell a service and earn cash. We just want to provide value in the form of people getting new insights into the cultural history that we have. (Team leader, interview 5)

3.4 New Skills

There are several skills and competences that are needed to embrace AI in NLN. Some skills are more general; others are more specific to the responsibility/ the role that an employee has in the library. As the director of the AI Lab states, first, everybody in the library needs to have a minimum understanding of AI technology, and then there is the need for more specialised competences.

We have realised that we need to build internal, I would say, capacity in terms of understanding, but also brain muscles to do work in this field. We need to educate a lot of people up to a minimum level. (Director of AI lab, Interview 3)

At a more specific level, AI skills are extremely important as also pointed out by the AI lab director:

Definitely, in our library we need extremely good people on AI to be able to understand AI and the potential of AI. (Director of AI lab, Interview 3)

In addition, it is pointed out that leadership capable of understanding the strategic significance and implications of AI is also important for national libraries in the AI era:

In the other end, we need a director with a good enough knowledge about the potential of both AI and the potential of the digital collection in the library used by AI. That is about strategy. So, it is about the politics, it is about the purpose of the library, the director level. (Director of AI lab, Interview 3)

The skills of the librarians must change from cataloguing skills to be organisers of knowledge in the digital world and being able to generate metadata about the material as the library director states:

The role of the librarian needs to change.... instead of doing what the librarians have been doing in the past couple of centuries, which is based on physical books needing to be found on shelves and a hierarchy of knowledge based on that as Dewey, you need to move into being the best organisers of knowledge in the digital sphere, in your digital collection... (NLN Director, Interview 1)

Another important skill that national libraries need in the future is data analysis skills. These are necessary both to understand the data and to understand how machine learning algorithms use the data.

For finding the good data, if you could choose from a buffet of what knowledge or competence you need, then data analysts will be really, really useful to have because, of course, you need someone who knows the ins and outs of machine learning as a subject. (Team leader, interview 5)

Also design thinking defined as "a human-centred innovation process that emphasizes observation, collaboration, fast learning, visualisation of ideas, rapid concept prototyping, and concurrent business analysis" [9] could be an important skill because it is important to understand the process and what the library users want as a team leader points out:

Design thinking could be useful. There are a lot of ways to facilitate the process, but the process is important. So, someone with a good understanding of what the process looks like is important. (...) From there, it's just testing, testing, testing and have the end user in the loop. (Team leader, interview 5)

4 Conclusions

The National Library of Norway as we know it today opened in 2005. It has the responsibility of collecting, preserving and making available all the material published in Norway, which is all legal deposit material, to the Norwegian public. In addition, the library stores all cultural heritage material from Norwegian archives, libraries and museums.

The National Library of Norway is very advanced in experimenting with AI. The main AI activities are centred on the AI lab, established in 2018, and include (1) data sets such as the Norwegian Colossal Corpus; (2) AI models for various purposes such as NB-Whisper for Norwegian Bokmål and Nynorsk; and (3) AI tools tried in real contexts including user experiences/services, components in internal library workflows, or services for services as Maken. Maken is an experimental new service that uses artificial intelligence to find books or images that are similar to each other.

There were two main needs for starting this project. The first was the increasing difficulty in discovering the digital material of the library both due to the increasing amount of material and potential lack or insufficient metadata. The second was NLN's wish to apply some of the knowledge that the AI Lab had acquired over several years of experimenting, prototyping and tool-building with AI on real-life applications.

Several internal and external actors were involved in the project, including the director of the library who was responsible for starting the project, a team called Digital Outreach as well as the users of the system.

The project was not free from challenges that included GDPR and privacy issues, Data Protection Impact Assessment and consent for the interviews [6].

The project has created several organisational and public values. The main value generated by Maken at organisational level is its contribution to accomplish the library mission, by making it easier to access and retrieve similar kinds of books and images to the broader public. The most important value generated for society is the democratic value. This easier access to the library material also generates democratic value for society as it makes it easier to get new insights into the country's cultural history.

In the process of developing and implementing AI in the library, NLN has also learned some important lessons; the most important are user involvement in projects and the importance of understanding the digital changes that are affecting libraries.

Finally, NLN points out new skills that national libraries need in the era of AI, including general AI knowledge for all employees in the library, good leadership skills, design thinking skills, data analysis skills and librarians' skills on how to generate metadata in the digital world.

Acknowledgements The work for this chapter was supported by the European Union's Horizon Europe Research and Innovation Programme under Grant Agreement ID 101061516.

Appendix

See Tables 2 and 3.

Table 2 Overview of the Maken project at the National Library of Norway

<table>
<tr><td colspan="4">Case and project name</td></tr>
<tr><td colspan="4">National Library of Norway/Maken project</td></tr>
<tr><td>Country</td><td>Number of employees</td><td>Type of AI solution</td><td>Year and maturity level</td></tr>
<tr><td>Norway</td><td>420</td><td>Recommendations system based on the content of books and images</td><td>Experimental stage/demo launched on Web site</td></tr>
<tr><td colspan="4">Project description</td></tr>
<tr><td colspan="4">Maken is a discovery engine to find similar books and similar images. Based on the pixels of the images, Maken finds related images. Based on the text of a book itself, Maken finds books that have some resemblance to each other</td></tr>
<tr><td>Need(s) behind implementation</td><td>Actors involved</td><td colspan="2">Challenges</td></tr>
<tr><td>Increasing difficulty in discovering the digital material; increasing amount of material; potential lack or insufficient metadata</td><td>Top management, AI-lab, users, external digital agency</td><td colspan="2">GDPR and privacy issues, Data Protection Impact Assessment, consent for the interviews</td></tr>
<tr><td colspan="4">Results</td></tr>
<tr><td>Organisational level</td><td>Value created and co-created</td><td colspan="2">Lesson learned</td></tr>
<tr><td>Importance of involving users in the process and the importance of understanding digital change in the libraries</td><td>Democratic value enacted by the easier access to digital books and images for the library users, contribution to the library strategy of experimenting with AI</td><td colspan="2">Importance of involving users in the process and the importance of understanding digital change in the libraries</td></tr>
</table>

Table 3 Overview of interviews at the Norwegian National Library

Number	Position	Interview date	Interview length
1	Director of the Library	13-03-2024	1 h
2	Director of AI lab	22-02-2024	1 h 20 min
3	Director of AI lab	27-02-2024	1 h 30 min
4	AI Lab Research Scientist	06-03-2024	1 h 20 min
5	Team Leader	09-04-2024	1 h 40 min

References

1. https://www.nb.no/maken/. Accessed 8 July 2024 and 14 Jan 2025
2. M. Takle, *Det Nasjonale i Nasjonalbiblioteket—Tilgang for Alle* (Novus Forl, Oslo, 2009) ISBN 978-82-7099-545-5. Det nasjonale i Nasjonalbiblioteket (nb.no). Accessed 6 July 2024
3. Libraries—regjeringen.no. Accessed 9 July 2024
4. AI-lab—Innovations on AI in Libraries. Accessed 14 Jan 2025
5. S.A. Brygfield, Artificial intelligence: the great divider. (NB AI-lab—The National Library of Norway, 2023), https://bit.ly/202311-nbailab-degr. Accessed the 9 of Aug 2024
6. J. de la Rosa, A. Sund, J.A. Schyberg, Maken—a user oriented discovery services to make sense at scale, PDF, 2021-12-28. (Maken—The National Library of Norway presentation Fantastic Futures 2021—sharing version, 2021), bnf.fr. Accessed 9 July 2024
7. National Library of Norway, Nasjonalbiblioteket lanserer AI-tjeneste i Nettbiblioteket (2021), https://www.nb.no/pressemeldinger/nasjonalbiblioteket-lanserer-ai-tjeneste-i-nettbiblioteket/. Accessed 27 Mar 2025
8. I. Mergel, N. Edelmann, N. Haug, Co-production phases in the development and implementation of digital public services. Perspect. Public Manag. Govern. **8**(2), 1–13 (2025)
9. T. Lockwood (ed.), *Design Thinking: Integrating Innovation, Customer Experience, and Brand Value*, 3rd edn. (Allworth Press, New York, NY, 2009)

Ada Scupola, Department of Social Scicnccs and Busincss, Roskilde University, Denmark. Her main research interests are at the intersection between digitalisation, innovation and the service sector and include value (co-)creation, digital transformation, user involvement in innovation, digital innovation, adoption, and diffusion of information and communication technologies (ICT) with a special focus on small and medium-sized enterprises (SMEs). Recently, she has been investigating the role of Artificial Intelligence in organisations with a focus on service organisations.

The Retrocatalography Project: Combining AI with the Microsoft Power Platform at the Royal National Library of Belgium

Anna-Lea Schumann and Ines Mergel

Abstract The Royal National Library of Belgium (KBR) collects all Belgian publications and safeguards the country's cultural and historical heritage. Given the increasing volume of records and the existence of records that are only catalogued on paper cards, there emerged a need for an AI-based solution. In response, KBR initiated a project called Retrocatalography, collaborating with the external service provider Initum. This partnership resulted in the development of an AI-based cataloguing solution which was created in just 10 days. Built on the Microsoft Power Platform, this low-code application is capable of gathering information from a book's cover, archiving it, and verifying the details. In addition, KBR developed the Allez app in-house to scan library records. Volunteers use the app by assisting in the verification process to ensure accuracy of the records data. The AI-based solution went live in October 2022, with strong support from top management of the library. Along the way, KBR encountered several challenges, including staff shortages, time constraints for integrating the system into daily operations, and various technical difficulties. Overall, the AI-based solution transforms the workflow of librarians at KBR. It has made cataloguing books more efficient, ultimately enhancing the quality of the library services.

Keywords Royal Library of Belgium · KBR · National Library · Artificial intelligence · AI · Retrocatalography · Microsoft Power Platform · Allez app · Low-code · Volunteers

A.-L. Schumann
Department of Politics and Public Administration, University of Konstanz, Konstanz, Germany
e-mail: anna-lea.schumann@uni-konstanz.de

I. Mergel (✉)
Department of Politics and Public Administration, University of Konstanz, Konstanz, Germany

Fraunhofer FOKUS, Fraunhofer Institute for Open Communication Systems, Berlin, Germany

School of Management, Public Management, University of Vaasa, Vaasa, Finland
e-mail: ines.mergel@uni-konstanz.de

I. Mergel, C. Schmidt (eds.), *AI Innovations in Public Services*,
https://doi.org/10.1007/978-3-032-01344-6_7

1 Introduction

The Royal Library of Belgium (KBR) is the National Library of Belgium with the mission to collect all Belgian publications, preserve Belgium's cultural and historical heritage, and provide society with information and cultural experiences [1]. It is the National Scientific Library and preserves a heritage collection of around eight million records [1]. It is a federal institution that reports to a minister and has financial control.

The KBR employs around 250 staff members. Among them, one employee is responsible for training the AI model. This individual possesses a background in librarianship but is not necessarily proficient in IT. Although training the AI model is a lot of work for one person, it also provides a lot of freedom to experiment. For future expansion of their AI projects, the KBR will require more personnel resources.

KBR developed a cataloguing AI solution within only 10 days in collaboration with a software company named Initum. The company is known for its innovative, user-friendly solutions that add value to its customers [2]. The project, called Retrocatalography, involved creating an application with the Microsoft Power Platform that can gather information from a book's cover, archive it, verify it, take a picture of it, and then analyse it using AI to check whether everything has been detected accurately [3]. The Power Platform allows for low-code application development using Microsoft's pre-developed components. There was no specific budget, but the expenses for the application, cell phones, etc., amount to around 20,000 Euros as of today. The AI application went live in October 2022.

In this chapter, we investigate the Retrocatalography project at the KBR. Our focus is on how the KBR implemented its AI solution, along with the needs and challenges linked to this implementation. We begin with a brief overview of the project, followed by an analysis of the needs that led to the adoption of AI and the skills and competencies necessary for the librarians involved. Furthermore, we identify the key actors in developing the AI solution and the challenges they encountered. Finally, we summarise the results of the AI project, the value it (co-)created, and the lessons learned throughout the process.

2 Description of the Project

Initially, the KBR had various proposals for digitising its records, such as scanning paper cards with the artefacts' records. However, this plan was turned down because some of the cards had already been scanned, while others were handwritten and in poor condition to be scanned. Eventually, the KBR resolved to begin the digitisation process from the original records instead of the library cards. The librarians searched their catalogue to determine which records were available in digital format and which were not. For those records that were not available, they searched through physical stacks and scanned the title page. A system was in place to detect the author, title, publisher, year of publication, and other relevant information from the scanned document. This process worked well for records with similar title page templates. However, many title pages were unique in design. As a result, the KBR began working with the company Initum using Microsoft's AI tool to create applications and automated processes to address this [3]. The so-called Power Platform includes an AI component and an AI builder, allowing librarians to train their models based on the title pages of records, such as books or maps.

To use the developed tool efficiently it is crucial to identify the necessary information beforehand to import records into the catalogue. The required information includes the title, subtitle, author, and other relevant details. The information needs to be located on the cover page, and the order of the title page elements needs to be identified. This involves, for example, identifying whether the title comes before the author or vice versa. Depending on the layout, different collections may be needed.

After tagging the information of the artefact, the AI model is trained with an initial corpus, and librarians scan the records, for example, the colophon of a contemporary book, a publisher's emblem, or imprint, usually located on the title page of a book. The colophon typically includes the ISBN of a book, which can be used to search for the book in library databases. If a library has already provided a detailed book description, the KBR extracts the metadata and includes it in its catalogue as open data from other National Libraries to expand its catalogue and avoid extra work. As one of the interviewees states, AI extensions will speed up the process with minimal human input: "*So, in the end, it should be a process that we're just scanning the book, and everything is collected, and there's small review, and then it's pushed to the KBR database. That should be the goal of the total project.*"

KBR has also developed an in-house app called Allez, which is separate from its library management system. Using the app, volunteers are presented with a scan of an image or metadata and asked to verify whether the AI information is correct or incorrect. To validate the data, the KBR has posted a job offer for volunteers who can work with the app. After the records were verified and validated in the Allez app, KBR exported them to their catalogue: "*We check it, we clean it a bit, and then we import it in our catalog.*" It is important to note that AI technology continues to improve with time, and less human work is necessary to correct data: "*Now actually [the AI] can read very well the difference between the authors, ... and the titles. Before, I need a lot of time to correct one. Now in the same time I can correct five. It means the artificial intelligence works better and better.*"

2.1 Need(s) Behind the AI Implementation

KBR still holds many books in its stacks that need to be listed in its online catalogue. Some books are still described only on paper cards, making it impossible for patrons to find these records in the library's online catalogue. Before the COVID-19 pandemic, this wasn't a significant issue, but during and after the pandemic, librarians asked patrons to reserve artefacts through an online reservation system. It became apparent during this transitory period that only around 50% of the records were available online, which creates challenges for patrons to reserve books they need and puts librarians in a time-intensive situation to aim to locate the physical records. As a result, this topic has come to the attention of library management, and they are working to find solutions to digitise the remaining records.

2.2 Skills and Competencies Required for Librarians

At the KBR, the interviewees have identified as one of the most critical competencies for excelling in the use of AI the motivation and a keen interest in the field: "*But I think the main thing you have, and this is something I have for the moment, you have to be interested in it and you have to be willing to take your time. Sometimes, when there's a YouTube video, you really have to look for thirty minutes to the same YouTube video to really understand what they want to do.*"

Learning the Power Platform process requires education to understand its steps, but it can be self-taught. However, fusion development, where the IT department works with the library staff involved in the AI project, is suggested to understand each other better.

Furthermore, library staff need the expertise to ensure that AI-generated results are correct, as one of the interviewees stated: "*... if AI has discovered a book or analysed a book, you do a review, check if everything is correct, and change where it's not correct. Again, it's less time because you already have everything written that is discovered and just do the corrections where needed. You gain a lot of time with that solution.*"

2.3 Actors Involved in the Development of AI Solution

KBR works closely with the company Initum to create applications using the Microsoft Power Platform. The collaboration between the library and the company is described as the following: "*We have a good collaboration, we had a good understanding what they want to have, what they want to see. My experience is positive, very positive.*" Furthermore, "*... [name of the responsible person in the KBR] knows the process, [name of the consultant] knows the technology and we need to bring that together*". These quotes show how the inclusion of an external partner helps the KBR staff to learn from the external service provider and how they pool their resources.

Along with hiring an external service provider, the KBR collaborates with seven to eight volunteers who scan and validate records in the Allez app, created by the library itself, to correct scans separately from the library management system. Most of these volunteers are retired and wish to contribute meaningfully and culturally to the work of the library as one of them highlights in the following quote: "*I go one time a week to the KBR to see my colleagues, the professional colleagues, a little bit chitchat, chitchat, and then to do the work and one coffee because I like that too.*"

An external company recently supported the volunteers by helping them scan more records.

The close collaboration between KBR, its external service provider, and the volunteers can be described as co-production. This term refers to the interaction of various actors aimed at co-creating public value [4]. Co-production consists of five phases: co-commissioning, co-design, co-implementation, co-delivery, and co-assessment [4].

Co-commissioning marks the initial phase where KBR began its partnership with the external service provider, Inetum-Realdolem. Together, they explored potential AI solutions tailored to the library's needs and ultimately chose to utilise Microsoft's Power Platform.

The co-design phase involved collaboratively designing and training the AI model based on the Power Platform. Furthermore, the external service provider assisted KBR with technical support by their in-house developed app, Allez.

During the co-implementation phase, KBR closely collaborated with both the external service provider and volunteers, who worked on scanning and verifying records to ensure the Allez app accurately read and represented the data.

Co-delivery involved marking records in the online catalogue according to whether the information of the record was created by a librarian or generated by AI. Notably, co-design, co-implementation, and co-delivery phases run concurrently, influencing one another [4].

Finally, co-assessment serves as a retrospective phase of co-production [4].

Table 1 summarises the roles of different actors in each phase of co-production, detailing how they support KBR in implementing AI and creating public value.

Table 1 Co-production phases of the AI project of the Royal Library of Belgium (KBR)

Co-production phase	Description of the phase	Application in the case
Co-commissioning	Prospective co-production phase	Collaboration with Inetum-Realdolem, where Inetum-Realdolem consulted KBR with a possible AI solution. They decided to go with Microsoft's Power Platform.
Co-design	Concurrent co-production phases	KBR and Initum trained an AI model based on the Power Platform, and Initum provided KBR with support using their in-house developed app, Allez.
Co-implementation		KBR collaborated closely with Initum and volunteers, who scanned and verified records to ensure that the Allez app was reading and reflecting the data correctly.
Co-delivery		A remark in the online catalogue indicates whether the record information was created by a human or an AI.
Co-assessment	Retrospective co-production phase	

2.4 Organisational Level

The KBR library leadership was receptive to AI and allowed the responsible employee to find an AI solution. Overall, their assessment was that "*It's not necessary to have one AI department because AI is too big to have one use. I think every department has to have an AI component in it to see where can we use AI....*" In addition, it is more critical to have library staff who is "*...open for it, ... [is] willing to look into it, to test it, to see can it work, can it not work*".

KBR sees it as essential to advocate and foster a culture in the library that is interested in AI and its use. In KBR, library management empowers employees with flexibility in AI projects.

2.5 External Actors

The KBR has decided to use the Power Platform, a Microsoft AI tool included in the Windows 365 package. The costs are relatively affordable, and since the library already has a license for the package, it only needs to pay per employee who utilise the AI application. The KBR collaborates with a company called Inetum-Realdolem, which supports them with the Power Platform. However, the KBR creates the in-house AI workflow, the Allez app. Despite this, the company assists the KBR with coding questions.

The KBR suggested that National Libraries should cooperate more to improve their category classification and subject indexing with the help of AI: "*So, I think every library is a bit searching for a way to give an answer to the same problems. I think there we can help each other.*" They propose that in the long run, each National Library should have its local dataset, which can then be combined to create a general dataset that AI can use for subject indexing. The KBR emphasised that these ideas are intended for the future. Additionally, collaborating in low-code, which allows for less coding and enables faster application development, could be an effective approach to utilising AI projects with other libraries in Belgium in the future.

2.6 Challenges

The KBR faces the challenge of including more staff members and simultaneously increasing the number of records that can be catalogued and at the same time serving as input for the training of the AI tool. This fact implies that the library leadership might have to increase the resources for the project and adopt it as part of its official mission. In addition, library staff struggle to integrate AI into their daily work due to time constraints, as one of the interviewees suggested: "*So, it's a bit difficult between finding the time to do and willing to do it.*" Training a model comes with several technical challenges. One such challenge is handling situations where the model is not functioning optimally and needs to be retrained automatically. However, there has been a recent development where models can automatically retrain themselves based on the data collected. Another challenge is deploying the model in different environments, such as development, test, and production environments. Microsoft is investing a lot of money in the Power Platform to address this challenge and is making significant progress in introducing new functionalities and possibilities. Finally, the budget for AI projects at the KBR is challenging: "... *we don't have a lot of money, so we have to think about every euro we spend*."

3 Results

3.1 *Organisational Level*

AI in the KBR has added to the transformation of how librarians work daily: "*So, it helps people to be faster in their work. That's why AI is really important in the future, I think, it's to make work being faster, efficient, and make, I think, also boring work more advanced because reading a book back plane and try to categorise it, it's a really boring work*." However, not all employees in the library have been able to identify the value of low coding and the Power Platform.

3.2 *Value Created and Co-created*

The value gained from implementing AI focuses on the increase in output: KBR now has a more detailed overview of its collection, making it more user-friendly for patrons with specific requests: "*The value is that we want for ourselves we want to have a better view what do we have*." This means that patrons can now find more records in the online catalogue to fulfil their requests. Additionally, patrons can quickly identify if a record in the catalogue was generated by AI, as this information is transparently displayed in the following remarks: "*When I search the title, ... now I get a record, and then it says also for a remark, it's AI-generated. So,* the reader knows *that it's AI generated*." In addition, the library staff now needs less time to collect information, making it possible to catalogue more books efficiently and effortlessly. Finally, the data quality within the library will improve by the end.

3.3 *Lesson Learned*

The key competencies for excelling in AI development include motivation and a strong interest in the field, as well as the necessary education to understand the concepts. Furthermore, creating an AI solution is an ongoing process, as one interviewee noted: "*But little bit by little bit, the way we are working now was one year of work, trial, and error ... You cannot say from the beginning, 'That's very good.' No, you have the idea, you have the tools, and then you have the planning, and then all together we came to the way where we are now today here.*"

4 Conclusion

In this chapter, we investigated the Retrocatalography project at the KBR, focusing on implementing its AI solution and the associated needs and challenges. In 2022, KBR collaborated with external provider Initum to develop a cataloguing AI solution using the Microsoft Power Platform, completing the project in 10 days.

These needs arose during the COVID-19 pandemic, addressing the urgent need for online access to library books. However, many titles are still only catalogued on paper cards, hindering patrons and librarians from locating these records quickly in the library's online system. The top management of the library has supported exploring an AI solution from the beginning of the project.

Through close collaboration among KBR, the external service provider, and volunteers, the application can capture information from a book's cover, archive it, verify data, take a photograph, and then analyse the information using AI to ensure accurate detection of all relevant details. The Power Platform facilitates low-code application development by leveraging Microsoft's pre-developed components.

However, the KBR faced challenges such as staff shortages and a continuously rising number of records. Furthermore, due to time constraints, it is challenging to integrate experimenting and working with AI in daily work. There are also some technical challenges, including situations where the AI model is not functioning optimally and needs to be retrained automatically. Lastly, the budget for AI projects at KBR is a challenge.

Experimenting with the newly developed AI-based solution is transforming how librarians work at the KBR. This technology enhances internal processes, allowing librarians to concentrate more on intellectual tasks. With the AI solution, cataloguing books becomes more efficient and effortless, ultimately leading to improved quality within the library. The KBR now has a more precise overview of its collections, making it more user-friendly for patrons with specific requests. Additionally, patrons can quickly see whether a catalogue record was generated by AI, as this information is transparently displayed in the remarks section.

However, not all library staff recognise the value brought by this advancement. To excel in AI development, librarians need key competencies, including motivation, a strong interest in the field, and adequate education to grasp the underlying concepts. Table 2 summarises the Retrocatalography project at the KBR and gives an overview of the main results.

Acknowledgements The work for this chapter was supported by the European Union's Horizon Europe Research and Innovation Programme under Grant Agreement ID 101061516.

Appendix

Table 2 Summative overview—Royal Library of Belgium (KBR)

<table>
<tr><td colspan="4">Case and project name</td></tr>
<tr><td colspan="4">Retrocatalography at the Royal Library of Belgium (KBR)</td></tr>
<tr><th>Country</th><th>Number of employees</th><th>Type of AI solution</th><th>Year and maturity level</th></tr>
<tr><td>Belgium</td><td>Approx. 250 employees at KBR</td><td>Cataloguing AI solution with the Microsoft Power Platform</td><td>Application Go-live: October 2022
Legal Deposit Updates (Development): Spring 2024</td></tr>
<tr><td colspan="4">Project description</td></tr>
<tr><td colspan="4">KBR developed a cataloguing AI solution in 10 days with a company named Initum in 2022 and then started to feed the tool with data until 2024. The project, called Retrocatalography, involved developing an application with the Microsoft Power Platform that can gather information from a book's cover, archive it, verify it, take a picture of it, and then analyse it using AI to check whether everything has been detected accurately. The Power Platform allows for low-code application development using Microsoft's pre-developed components.</td></tr>
<tr><th>Need(s) behind implementation</th><th>Actors involved</th><th colspan="2">Challenges</th></tr>
<tr><td>Some books are still only described on paper cards, making it impossible for patrons to find these records in the library's online catalogue. The COVID-19 pandemic has highlighted the need to digitise these records
There was a need to promote collaboration between departments within KBR to explore AI and develop an AI solution.</td><td>Close collaboration with the software company Initum. Collaboration with seven to eight volunteers who scan and validate records. In addition, an external company recently supported the volunteers. The library management supports exploring an AI-based solution.</td><td colspan="2">The main challenges are a staff shortage and a rising number of records. The library staff is finding it difficult to integrate AI into their daily work due to time constraints. Technical challenges include, for example, situations where the AI model is not functioning optimally and needs to be retrained automatically. Lastly, the budget for AI projects at KBR is a challenge.</td></tr>
</table>

(continued)

Table 2 (continued)

Case and project name		
Retrocatalography at the Royal Library of Belgium (KBR)		
Results		
Organisational level	**Value created and co-created**	**Lesson learned**
AI within the KBR revolutionises how librarians work, making processes more efficient and allowing librarians to focus on intellectual work. However, not everyone in the library currently recognises the value that AI brings.	The KBR now has a clearer overview of its collection, making it more user-friendly for patrons with specific requests. In addition, patrons can easily identify if a record in the catalogue was generated by AI, as this information is transparently displayed in the remarks section. Moreover, the AI solution makes it possible to catalogue more books efficiently and effortlessly, and the quality within the library will improve by the end.	The key competencies for excelling in AI development include motivation and a strong interest in the field, as well as the necessary education to understand the concepts.

References

1. About KBR (n.d.), https://www.kbr.be/en/about-kbr/. Accessed 13 Feb 2025
2. Inetum in Belgium (n.d.), https://www.inetum.com/en/belgium. Accessed 13 Feb 2025
3. KBR: artificial intelligence helps the Royal Library of Belgium quickly catalogue books (n.d.), https://www.inetum.com/en/story/kbr. Accessed 13 Feb 2025
4. I. Mergel, N. Edelmann, N. Haug, Co-production phases in the development and implementation of digital public services. Perspect. Public Manag. Govern. **8**(2), 1–13 (2025)

Anna-Lea Schumann is currently pursuing a master's degree in Politics and Public Administration at the University of Konstanz. Her research interests focus on applying modern working practices within public administration and their implications for public value creation. In her bachelor's thesis, she explored the use and implementation of design thinking in libraries. She has gained initial practical experience through various internships in public administration, providing her with valuable insights into the operational methods and processes of the public sector.

Ines Mergel is a University Professor of Public Administration in the Department of Politics and Public Administration at the University of Konstanz and a Fellow of the National Academy of Public Administration (Class of 2018). After holding positions at the Harvard Kennedy School of Government as a Doctoral Fellow and Postdoctoral Fellow (2002–2008), Professor Mergel was awarded tenure at the Maxwell School of Citizenship and Public Affairs (Syracuse University, NY) in 2014 (2008–2014) and then served as Associate Professor with tenure (2014–2016). Professor Mergel is a member of the supervisory board of the e-Governance Academy (Estonia). Other board memberships can be found here. Professor Mergel is a founding member of the international initiative Teaching Public Service in the Digital Age, which aims to integrate digital skills into the teaching and training of public managers. As part of this initiative, Professor Mergel was appointed a Schmidt Futures Innovation Fellow in 2022.

AI for Access: Strategic Innovation at the Dutch National Library

Barbara van der Vaart and Carsten Schmidt

Abstract Digitisation and access to information became increasingly important during the last two decades. At the same time, the challenges for all kinds of public services and organisations, also National Libraries, to hire new qualified staff members became even more challenging. To cover the needs and overcome the hurdles at the same time, the National Library of the Netherlands decided to introduce AI solutions and incorporate them into the traditional workflows like cataloguing. In 2023, the "Retrotool-Project" was initiated. The goal is to develop an automated metadata tool to accelerate and streamline cataloguing while ensuring data security, transparency, and ethical AI use. This tool will enable human-AI interaction to support cataloguers by automating repetitive tasks, allowing human experts to focus on complex metadata refinement. The "Retrotool-Project" can be seen as an example to introduce AI into a National Library to improve efficiency, quality, and accessibility of metadata while maintaining human oversight.

Keywords The Netherlands · National Library · Koninklijke Bibliotheek · Artificial intelligence · AI · Automated Indexing · Large language models · Bibliographic data · Retrotool · AI-assisted metadata extraction · AI in cultural heritage

B. van der Vaart
LIBER Europe, The Hague, The Netherlands
e-mail: barbara.vandervaart@libereurope.org

C. Schmidt (✉)
Department of Politics and Public Administration, University of Konstanz, Konstanz, Germany
e-mail: carsten.schmidt@uni-konstanz.de

I. Mergel, C. Schmidt (eds.), *AI Innovations in Public Services*,
https://doi.org/10.1007/978-3-032-01344-6_8

1 Introduction

1.1 The National Library of the Netherlands (KB)

The Koninklijke Bibliotheek (KB), the national library of the Netherlands, is headquartered in The Hague. Established in 1798 and officially designated as the Royal Library in 1806, the KB has functioned as an independent administrative entity since 1993, receiving its primary funding from the Ministry of Education, Culture, and Science. Its mission is to collect, preserve, and provide access to all publications related to the Netherlands, ranging from medieval manuscripts to modern digital resources.

Currently, the KB employs around 500 staff members and houses approximately seven million publications, including books, magazines, and newspapers. In addition to its physical collection, the KB offers digital services such as the national Online Library (providing e-books and audiobooks) and Delpher, a platform granting access to millions of digitised pages. Since 2015, the KB has a coordinating role for the Dutch public library network.

1.2 Metadata Generation at the KB

Koninklijke Bibliotheek explains the importance of metadata in library management on its Web site: "Good metadata are important for bringing people and information together. They give meaning to the collection, making it easier for users to search through it. Good metadata ensure that the KB's collection will remain visible, preservable and usable in the future" [1].

The work on AI tools in KB started several years ago. One interviewee explained: "We started about eight years ago in the field of AI, and for four reasons: first, to improve our internal processes; second, to enhance our services; third, to contribute to the public debate on AI implementation; and fourth, to provide high-quality data for AI development." To help cataloguers with their metadata work, the KB looked for solutions to automate the process of generating metadata. In 2020, the KB began to develop a tool called Demosaurus, an earlier project aimed at assigning authors and keywords to books in the cataloguing system that was previously used. This tool supported the completion of two complex data fields: it assisted in assigning keywords to titles, making it easier for users to find the information they are looking for, and it facilitated the linking of authors to the author thesaurus, a process known as thesaurisation [2]. In its initial phase, the tool specifically focused on children's books. However, due to lack of funding, the project was discontinued and is no longer in use.

In 2023, the KB started the development and implementation of an automatic metadata generation tool called Retrotool. The project was introduced in 2023 and has since achieved significant operational milestones. This current Retrotool is a new and improved version that covers a wider range of materials and applies automatic metadata generation to physical books. It uses Optical Character Recognition (OCR) and AI technologies, such as Large Language Models (LLMs), to extract bibliographic data directly from books and create basic catalogue records. This process offers greater efficiency and accuracy than its predecessor.

2 Description of the Project

2.1 Automatic Metadata Generation: Retrotool

The KB's extensive collection comprises millions of books, newspapers, and magazines, both in physical and digital formats. The Collection Data department, staffed by approximately 30 cataloguers, processes metadata for about 50,000 physical items annually. Metadata, such as title, author, genre, and publication year, play a crucial role in ensuring the accessibility and discoverability of the library's collection. It facilitates efficient searching, retrieval, and exchange of bibliographic records at national and international levels. The catalogue also records each book's location within the KB. Without this information, the book becomes untraceable and effectively lost [3].

Over time, a substantial backlog of uncatalogued materials has developed due to factors such as restricted access during the COVID-19 pandemic and the transition to a new library system with different metadata standards. To address this backlog, the KB introduced Retrotool, an AI-powered solution for cataloguing older publications lacking metadata. Using OCR, Retrotool captures key bibliographic details from the title page and colophon, processes them through an LLM (currently Microsoft's ChatGPT), and assigns them to appropriate cataloguing fields. The tool then cross-references the KB catalogue to determine if the item already exists. If not, a basic bibliographic record is generated for cataloguers to refine before the final entry into the system.

2.2 Development and Implementation

The development of Retrotool was inspired by similar projects at the National Libraries of Finland and Belgium. After an initial proof of concept was completed in October 2023, the first basic functionalities were tested. Collaboration with a technical partner, although new to library systems, allowed for an iterative development process where feedback from cataloguers was rapidly integrated.

By April 2024, a fully functional prototype was tested, leading to refinements such as the ability to generate XML files compatible with the KB's cataloguing system. By September 2024, Retrotool was considered ready for production use.

However, certain administrative processes, such as finalising long-term support contracts, remain in progress.

Currently, Retrotool operates as a *Software as a Service (SaaS)*, hosted externally by the technical development partner. In the future, the KB plans to migrate the system physically in-house to maintain full control and ownership.

2.2.1 Initiation of the Retrotool

The KB has long recognised the necessity of investing in automated cataloguing processes to enhance efficiency and address the existing challenges in bibliographic management. Recent government funding, allocated as part of broader initiatives to improve public communication following the Dutch healthcare benefits scandal, the so-called *toeslagenaffaire*, has made this possible. This political scandal involved false allegations of welfare fraud by the Tax and Customs Administration against thousands of families receiving childcare benefits. It drew widespread public outrage and media attention, and it had significant political consequences, ultimately leading to the resignation of the Rutte cabinet in 2021.

The government funding was subsequently used by the KB to improve automated processes aimed at addressing the significant cataloguing backlog. A key project is Retrotool, focusing on cataloguing older books, primarily from the 1800s onward, which lack existing data. Using text recognition, Retrotool extracts information directly from the books, reduces manual input errors, and helps identify duplicates. This allows the cataloguers to concentrate on refining more complex bibliographic details, speeding up the process of uploading accurate descriptions to the catalogue.

2.2.2 Operational Process of the Tool

New as well as old publications are continuously added to the collection. As one interviewee explained, it was only in 1974 that the KB officially adopted the goal of systematically collecting all publications published in or about the Netherlands that meet its inclusion criteria, inviting all publishers to provide copies. Before then, not all publications were added to the collection. Retrotool is used to address these gaps in the collection, which are often filled through donations of (private) book collections, totalling thousands of books per year.

The operational process of Retrotool is as follows: the tool scans the colophon and title page using OCR technology, after which it combines this information with data from the Internet and an LLM (currently Microsoft's ChatGPT) to generate a basic record. An interviewee said: "The main purpose of this tool is to remove the doubles from the retro collection, which is gigantic, and to create a basic description of each book. We only have to check it, make minor additions, and then it is ready to be uploaded to the catalogue." Another interviewee explained: "The tool reads the title page and colophon of a book, extracts key information, checks if the book is already catalogued, and if not, generates a basic description that a cataloguer can refine before finalising the entry." The extracted fields are then automatically checked with the library's catalogue on whether the book is already listed. If this is not the case, eight fields serve as a foundation for further cataloguing by a cataloguer, who completes the fields and then adds the record to the catalogue. Additionally, the tool enhances basic descriptions, providing a more detailed catalogue entry. An interviewee explained: "It takes away most of the repetitive tasks and allows cataloguers to focus on the more complex parts of bibliographic description."

2.2.3 Needs Behind the Implementation

Due to several factors such as the COVID-19 pandemic and the introduction of a new library system, the cataloguing department has accumulated a significant backlog. One interviewee said: "We have about 150,000 titles that we still have to describe in the catalogue. At our current rates, we would need about 15 years to catch up on that entire backlog if nothing else were to arrive at our library. So, we started to look at smarter solutions, and AI was one of the first things we considered removing repetitive tasks and allow us to focus on more complex issues." However, new items continue to arrive, so smarter solutions were explored, particularly in AI and automation, especially to streamline repetitive tasks. This would allow the cataloguers to focus more on complex cataloguing aspects and help to address the backlog more efficiently. However, human intervention remains essential in every stage, and the specific expertise of the cataloguers is what completes the process. Furthermore, an interviewee said: "One of the projects that is part of that larger whole is Retrotool, which I'm currently functioning as a project manager of. It consists mostly of books from 1800 onward that lack any existing metadata, requiring us to rely solely on text extraction from the book itself and external sources." Retrotool, therefore, is designed to assist, not replace, cataloguers—helping to make informed decisions faster and ultimately providing access to these works much sooner. An interviewee explained: "We are not replacing cataloguers with AI. Rather, we are giving them tools to make their work more efficient. AI handles repetitive tasks, but human expertise is still needed to ensure accuracy and contextual understanding."

2.2.4 Research and Development Approach to Innovation

The KB employs a *research and development-driven approach* to innovation, integrating AI and emerging technologies to enhance its services. This innovation process begins with exploratory research, guided by an internal strategic agenda that identifies impactful areas for investigation. To support this approach, the KB establishes cross-departmental research groups, bringing together expertise from various divisions. In the case of Retrotool, collaboration was established between cataloguers from the Collection Data Department and the Development team to explore and evaluate potential automated metadata generation solutions. An interviewee said about the development process: "We use a structured approach: first, exploratory research, then proof of concept, then a minimal viable product (MVP), and finally, a fully operational prototype before full implementation."

Furthermore, the KB employs a *funnel approach* to innovation, progressing through distinct phases: exploration, proof of concept, and the development of a minimum viable product (MVP). Each project undergoes iterative testing and refinement, resulting in robust prototypes. Recently, Retrotool reached the prototype phase, enabling the automated generation of metadata descriptions. Throughout its development, and in close collaboration with a commercial technical partner aligned with the KB's AI principles, feedback has been systematically gathered from the Department Head, team leaders, and cataloguers within the Collection Data Department to refine the tool's functionality.

To ensure efficient technological implementation, the KB follows a *selective outsourcing strategy*, partnering with external providers for specialised expertise while retaining in-house development for core functionalities. This hybrid model allows the KB to incorporate cutting-edge technology while maintaining institutional control over critical processes. By early next year, Retrotool is expected to be fully integrated into the KB's standard cataloguing workflows. An interviewee said about future plans: "Retrotool currently operates as Software as a Service (SaaS), hosted by our partner company, but eventually, we plan to bring it in-house to ensure full ownership and control."

2.3 Actors Involved

The Retrotool project is based on the need to invest in automated cataloguing processes to enhance efficiency and address the existing challenges in bibliographic management. It is part of a broader initiative to improve public communication following the Dutch healthcare benefits scandal, the so-called toeslagenaffaire, described above. Table 1 provides greater detail on who the internal actors are in the Retrotool project and the activities that they developed in the project. The description follows the approach according to Mergel et al. (2025); co-production consists of five phases: co-commissioning, co-design, co-implementation, co-delivery, and co-assessment [4].

Table 1 Co-production activities in the Retrotool project at the Dutch National Library

Phase	Co-production type	Description
Co-initiation	Prospective co-production phase	The National Library of the Netherlands identified the need for AI-driven cataloguing due to a backlog of 150,000 uncatalogued books. The initiative was internally proposed by KB leadership, cataloguing staff, and AI researchers. The project was inspired by similar initiatives from other EU MS, e.g. FI and BE, with funding support from the Dutch government
Co-design	Concurrent co-production phases	Development of a prototype, integrating OCR and LLM (Microsoft ChatGPT, later moving to open-source LLMs) for metadata extraction. The co-design process involved cataloguers, AI specialists, and external developers, ensuring that the AI-assisted cataloguing process aligned with librarian expertise. Feedback loops were introduced to refine metadata accuracy
Co-implementation	Concurrent co-production phases	The prototype was tested by cataloguers and metadata specialists in early 2024, leading to adjustments in metadata field selection, XML export compatibility, and system integration. The tool was iteratively improved through librarian feedback, ensuring that AI-assisted cataloguing met NL bibliographic standards. Collaboration with external AI developers helped refine the tool's machine learning capabilities
Co-use/production moment	Concurrent co-production phases	Retrotool was officially deployed in September 2024, supporting cataloguers in processing new and historical materials. The system allows cataloguers to validate AI-generated metadata before the final entry. External research collaborations continue, with KB exploring further enhancements, such as automated thesaurisation and extended metadata fields
Co-evaluation	Retrospective co-production phase	KB conducts ongoing evaluations based on cataloguer feedback, metadata accuracy, and processing efficiency. External research institutions and AI experts are involved in assessing the tool's effectiveness, ethical considerations, and long-term sustainability. The transition to open-source AI models is a priority for future improvements

2.4 Challenges

While Retrotool is a significant step forward, several challenges remain:

1. **Use of Generative AI**: The KB currently employs Microsoft's ChatGPT to classify bibliographic data. However, due to concerns about data sourcing, transparency, and intellectual property rights, the goal is to transition to an open-source

large language model (LLM). The use of GPT-NL is being considered once this LLM is further developed.

2. **Employee Concerns**: Some cataloguers express apprehension about AI replacing human roles. However, Retrotool is designed to *assist rather than replace* human expertise, automating repetitive tasks to allow cataloguers to focus on more complex bibliographic descriptions. The expertise of cataloguers remains indispensable, as their input and guidance are crucial for the AI tool's effectiveness. Human oversight is essential when integrating information from an LLM into the catalogue, ensuring that all data generated by both the LLM and OCR is carefully reviewed. Ultimately, it is the responsibility of human experts to determine what should and should not be included in the catalogue. An interviewee described it that way: "There is still a very significant part of human intervention. AI removes repetitive tasks from bibliographic descriptions, allowing cataloguers to focus on the more nuanced aspects."

   The key to the success of Retrotool lies in striking the right balance between automation and manual labour and to apply AI responsibly. It is essential to identify the operations that can (and should) be automated, those that require additional attention from the cataloguer, and the functionalities that offer the greatest benefit to the cataloguers themselves [5].

3. **Ethical and Legal Considerations**: Questions surrounding the permissibility of AI-driven metadata generation within a national library context remain under discussion. An interviewee said: "The KB has explicitly said that we do not want to support commercial AI models that are built on illegally acquired text and information. While we currently use Microsoft's ChatGPT, we aim to transition to an open-source model in later versions of Retrotool." Ensuring compliance with data ethics and privacy regulations is a priority. It was precised by an interviewee: "We want to ensure that we're using AI ethically and transparently and moving away from commercial AI is a step in that direction." (…). Another interviewee commented: "In our case, we use a Microsoft version of ChatGPT, but we do not want it to share our data; instead, the data stay with us. We pose the questions, but these are not shared with the LLM for learning purposes; there is a checkbox for this that we can tick. We do not want our questions to be used to improve the LLM." Another interviewee explained: "We are developing an AI roadmap inspired by the French National Library's approach. This will help us systematically track our AI projects and ensure they align with our ethical principles."

   Regarding the legitimacy and unique role of national libraries in the future, an interviewee remarked: "I believe it is important for National Libraries and the library sector to establish clear standards for ethical values concerning AI applications and not leave this entirely to the commercial sector."

3 Results

3.1 Impact and Value Creation of the Retrotool at the KB

The introduction of Retrotool has influenced the workflow and development of metadata management inside the KB and caused significant positive results: Retrotool has demonstrated to provide important benefits for both the KB and its users, contributing to improved efficiency, accuracy in bibliographic data and by improved access to the collections. One interviewee said: "By making metadata generation more efficient, we are improving public access to books. If books are in our repository without metadata, they might as well not exist for the public."

3.1.1 Efficiency Gains

One of the most notable advantages of Retrotool is its ability to accelerate the cataloguing process, thereby significantly reducing backlog processing time. By taking over tasks in metadata generation, the tool enables cataloguers to work more efficiently, allowing for a higher volume of materials to be processed in a shorter timeframe. An interviewee said: "The tool allows us to describe and catalogue books at a much faster rate, making previously inaccessible books available to the public sooner." This is particularly important given KB's extensive collection, which includes both newly acquired and historical publications, and the significant backlog that has accumulated over the years.

3.1.2 Enhanced Accessibility

The timely inclusion of records in the KB catalogue ensures greater public access to historical materials. Previously uncatalogued or inaccessible items can now be integrated into the library's digital cataloguing systems, allowing researchers, scholars, and the public to discover and utilise a more comprehensive range of resources. This aligns with the KB's mission to preserve and provide access to Dutch cultural heritage.

3.1.3 Value Creation for the KB

Retrotool has created substantial value in two primary areas: internal cataloguing processes and data and collection management. By efficiently handling basic bibliographic descriptions, the tool optimises workflow efficiency without replacing human cataloguers. As it takes away repetitive tasks from cataloguers, it allows them to apply their valuable expertise where it truly matters: to focus on more complex aspects of bibliographic description, such as subject classification, metadata refinement, and curatorial decision-making. This targeted use of automation ensures that human expertise remains central to the cataloguing process while alleviating repetitive, time-consuming tasks.

3.1.4 Broader Societal Impact

Beyond its institutional benefits, Retrotool enhances public access to the KB's collections, ensuring that previously unprocessed materials are available for academic and public use. By improving the discoverability of historical documents and rare books, the tool plays a crucial role in supporting research, education, and cultural preservation.

In conclusion, Retrotool marks a significant advancement in metadata management at the KB, successfully integrating automation with human expertise. By enhancing cataloguing efficiency and improving public accessibility, the tool serves as an important new asset to the modernisation of the KB's cataloguing system. However, while automation streamlines the processes, the expertise of the KB's skilled cataloguers remains indispensable, in order to ensure the accuracy, contextualisation, and intellectual integrity of bibliographic records. An interviewee said: "We still rely on cataloguers' expertise, but we now have a way to process and integrate descriptions more efficiently, helping to clear the backlog."

3.2 Lessons Learned

Retrotool was developed in an iterative project style, which started with a transition phase and piloting and led to full implementation. During the different steps of implementation, several key lessons are identified:

1. *Iterative development is crucial*: Close collaboration between cataloguers and technical developers by rapidly integrating feedback from cataloguers into the tool led to a system tailored to the library-specific needs.
2. *AI awareness and training are essential*: Addressing staff concerns through training and transparency is necessary for successful adoption of the AI tool by staff.

3. *User involvement may further improve outcomes in future AI projects*: Cataloguers have been actively and successfully engaged in the development process. Involving library patrons in future innovation projects could further enhance KB's service offerings.

   Even if Retrotool is already fully implemented, development and lessons learned are not finished. Looking forward, continued refinements, including new AI functionalities (such as text recognition of handwritten manuscripts) and expanded metadata fields, will further optimise Retrotool's impact in national bibliographic management.

4 Conclusion

The implementation of Retrotool at the KB demonstrates the potential of AI as a valuable support tool in cataloguing, by streamlining repetitive metadata tasks while ensuring that human expertise remains central to complex decision-making. Rather than replacing professional cataloguers, the tool enhances their efficiency, allowing them to focus on higher-order intellectual tasks. By accelerating the cataloguing process, Retrotool has played a crucial role in reducing the backlog of 150,000 books, significantly cutting down the time required for metadata generation.

Despite these efficiency gains, human oversight remains essential. AI-generated metadata must be carefully reviewed and refined to maintain the accuracy and quality of catalogue records. The KB recognises the ethical implications of AI adoption and is committed to transparency. As part of this effort, the institution aims to transition from proprietary AI solutions, such as Microsoft's ChatGPT, to an open-source language model, to safeguard greater alignment with ethical standards and institutional values.

Looking ahead, Retrotool's scalable architecture provides a basis for further refinements, including expanding metadata capabilities and enhancing automation while preserving human professional oversight. Collaboration with the Royal Library of Belgium and other institutions highlights the potential for shared learning in AI-driven cataloguing innovations. By bringing Retrotool in-house in the near future, the KB aims to ensure long-term control, enhance customisation, and sustain the tool within its metadata workflows.

Acknowledgements The work for this chapter was supported by the European Union's Horizon Europe Research and Innovation Programme under Grant Agreement ID 101061516.

Appendix

See Table 2.

Table 2 Overview of the Retrotool project at the National Library of the Netherlands

<table>
<tr><td colspan="4">Case and project name</td></tr>
<tr><td colspan="4">Automatic metadating project: Retrotool</td></tr>
<tr><td>Country</td><td>Number of employees</td><td>Type of AI solution</td><td>Year and maturity level</td></tr>
<tr><td>The Netherlands</td><td>500</td><td>Creation of an AI tool for the automatic metadating of book publications from 1800</td><td>The project was initiated in mid-2023. Retrotool was developed and tested, and in September 2024 it was officially implemented</td></tr>
<tr><td colspan="4">Project description</td></tr>
<tr><td colspan="4">Retrotool was developed to address cataloguing backlogs by processing the retro collection—old books that were acquired but not yet catalogued. Using a document camera (OCR), the tool captures information from the title page and colophon, and artificial intelligence organises it into cataloguing fields. The tool then checks if the book is already in the catalogue. If not, it adds the book with a basic description, which a KB staff member can further refine</td></tr>
<tr><td>Need(s) behind implementation</td><td>Actors involved</td><td colspan="2">Challenges</td></tr>
<tr><td>Diminishing the backlog in the cataloguing of books, with the additional benefit that repetitive tasks are taken over, allowing the cataloguers to focus more on complex cataloguing aspects</td><td>KB Management: Deputy director (interviewed) and the head of research (interviewed)
Development team
Collection Data Department: Head of Department, Innovation Coordinator (interviewed), and Interim Innovation Coordinator (interviewed)
Four cataloguers who tested and currently work with the tool
Technical company that developed the tool</td><td colspan="2">Ethical challenges (use of LLM created by Microsoft is opaque) and apprehension by employees that AI would make their work obsolete</td></tr>
<tr><td colspan="4">Results</td></tr>
<tr><td>Organisational level</td><td>Value created and co-created</td><td colspan="2">Lesson learned</td></tr>
<tr><td>Department of Collection Data</td><td>This initiative expands public access to a broader collection of KB publications while enabling cataloguers to focus on the more critical aspects of bibliographical descriptions. By automating repetitive and tedious tasks, it allows them to apply their valuable expertise where it truly matters</td><td colspan="2">The focus of the innovation process remains on expanding and improving the tool, with iterative feedback from cataloguers and other staff incorporated at various stages
AI awareness and training is essential; addressing concerns by staff through training and transparency is necessary for successful adoption of the AI tool by staff</td></tr>
</table>

References

1. Koninklijke Bibliotheek, *Working with Metadata* (KB, National Library of the Netherlands, n.d.), https://www.kb.nl/en/over-ons/expertises/metadata. Accessed 10 Feb 2025
2. D. Haagsma, Uitzoekassistentie van de Demosaurus. Vakblad voor Informatieprofessionals **08** (2021) https://zenodo.org/records/5705945
3. W. Van Wezenbeek, *Wilma Ontdekt: 50.000 Boeken, Kranten en Tijdschriften per Jaar* (KB, de Nationale Bibliotheek, 2024), https://www.kb.nl/blogs/wilma-ontdekt-50000-boeken-kranten-en-tijdschriften-jaar
4. I. Mergel, N. Edelmann, N. Haug, Co-production phases in the development and implementation of digital public services. Perspect. Public Manag. Govern. **8**(2), 1–13 (2025)
5. M. Buesink, AI gedreven ondersteuning voor en door catalogiseerders. Vakblad voor Informatieprofessionals **05** (2024) https://informatieprofessional.maglr.com/kb-onderzoekskroniek12

Barbara van der Vaart has many years of experience in international project management and has worked as a project coordinator and policy officer in academic research projects and governmental and international organisations. Before joining LIBER, she worked on two ERC Grant projects at Delft University and Leiden University. She obtained an MSc degree in Cultural Anthropology at Utrecht University, where she also studied Child and Adolescent Psychology.

Carsten Schmidt focuses on concepts and methodologies for e-government in the European Union and the associated countries, as well as the related aspects of digital infrastructure. Particular attention is paid to the areas of the once-only principle, European large-scale pilot projects, and sustainability. Before, he was involved in different positions (Project Director, Work Package Manager, etc.) in European large-scale projects like mGov4EU, TOOP, e-SENS, and e-CODEX. He worked for the Ministry of Justice NRW, Germany, the Technical University of Tallinn (TalTech), and the University of Tartu, Estonia.

How to Make Millions of Documents Accessible Through AI and a Digital Library? The Case of Gallica, French National Library

Antoine Henry

Abstract The chapter introduces Gallica, a project hosted by the Bibliothèque nationale de France (BnF). Since its inception in the fourteenth century, the library has been developing new missions and striving to make collections more accessible. One key tool for the BnF is Gallica, an online digital library that concentrates much of the R&D conducted by the library to ensure accessibility. Since 1997, the project has been experimenting with new features, including HTR, OCR, image, and data mining, to facilitate research within its vast collection of ten million documents. The library employs an incremental approach to scaling up proof-of-concepts into industrialised innovations that can be used by its 60,000 daily users. Meanwhile, the development of artificial intelligence contributes to cultural changes within the library. Through its central role, the national library also shares its achievements with other libraries in France and at the European level.

Keywords Handwritten Text Recognition · Optical Text Recognition · Digital Library · Data mining · Image mining · Deep learning · Bibliothèque nationale de France (BnF) · Gallica · Artificial intelligence

1 Introduction

The French National Library, known as Bibliothèque nationale de France (BnF), has its roots in the royal library established by Charles V in 1368. Today, it operates as a public institution under the supervision of the Ministry of Culture. The library is divided into two main locations in Paris: Richelieu, which serves as the historical site, and François-Mitterrand.

A. Henry (✉)
University of Lille, ULR 4073—GERiiCO—Groupe d'Études et de Recherche Interdisciplinaire en Information et Communication, Lille, France
e-mail: antoine.henry@univ-lille.fr

I. Mergel, C. Schmidt (eds.), *AI Innovations in Public Services*,
https://doi.org/10.1007/978-3-032-01344-6_9

As the legal deposit institution since 1537, the BnF is responsible for preserving and archiving all printed materials published in France. This mission includes now Web legal deposit, with over 2 petabytes of data stored online. The library is one of the largest in the world and plays a significant role in its community.

In 2023, the BnF had 2262 employees, an annual budget of €253 million and the library welcomed over 1.4 million visitors.

2 Description of the Project

The project that is studied is Gallica [1]. Gallica is an online digital library created by the Bibliothèque nationale de France (National Library of France), offering a vast collection of French and international cultural heritage [2]. This comprehensive resource provides access to a wide range of materials, including books, journals, newspapers, manuscripts, maps, photographs, and other multimedia content. Approximately 100 people contribute to Gallica, with 19 employees solely devoted to the project. These staff members are spread across various departments, such as the IT Department, Collection Department, and the Cooperation Department, which serves as the central hub for Gallica. The Cooperation Department plays a crucial role in guiding the initiative, with ten of its members hailing from the IT Department and nine from the collaboration section.

Gallica mostly uses OCR (optical character recognition) and HTR (handwritten text recognition). According to an AI expert from the library: "The first experiments took place in 2010. At the time, the BNF was already involved in a number of research projects, particularly at the European level, with major research projects in the 2010s, 2007s and 2015s focusing on the digitisation of cultural heritage on a European scale. The stakes were mass digitisation, mass OCR and handwriting recognition." Those technologies are important to ensure the accessibility of documents that have been digitised, although the concept of artificial intelligence (AI) had not been mentioned at the time. In addition, the project also uses natural language processing (NLP), data mining, and image mining. This allows users to do textual research on images or digitised documents. With the rise of deep learning (2014), for them it's also an opportunity to have a "hybridisation of approaches, types of collection and types of documents." This way, they could make a massive digitisation and pursue the processing using the same technological pipeline.

Figure 1 is a schema of how AI has been implemented in the library [3]. We are here able to see which projects were contributing to which fields.

Figure 1 illustrates the evolution of the AI-related projects in the library. We can identify the various technologies involved in Gallica according to the needs (analysis, language processing, text/image recognition). The BnF articulates an internal process for projects at the national or European level. Indeed, as pointed out through interviews, the library is very active at the European level (i.e. the working group dedicated to AI at the Conference of European National Librarians—CENL—is led by a French expert from the BnF), even if she still has capacities to do internal development.

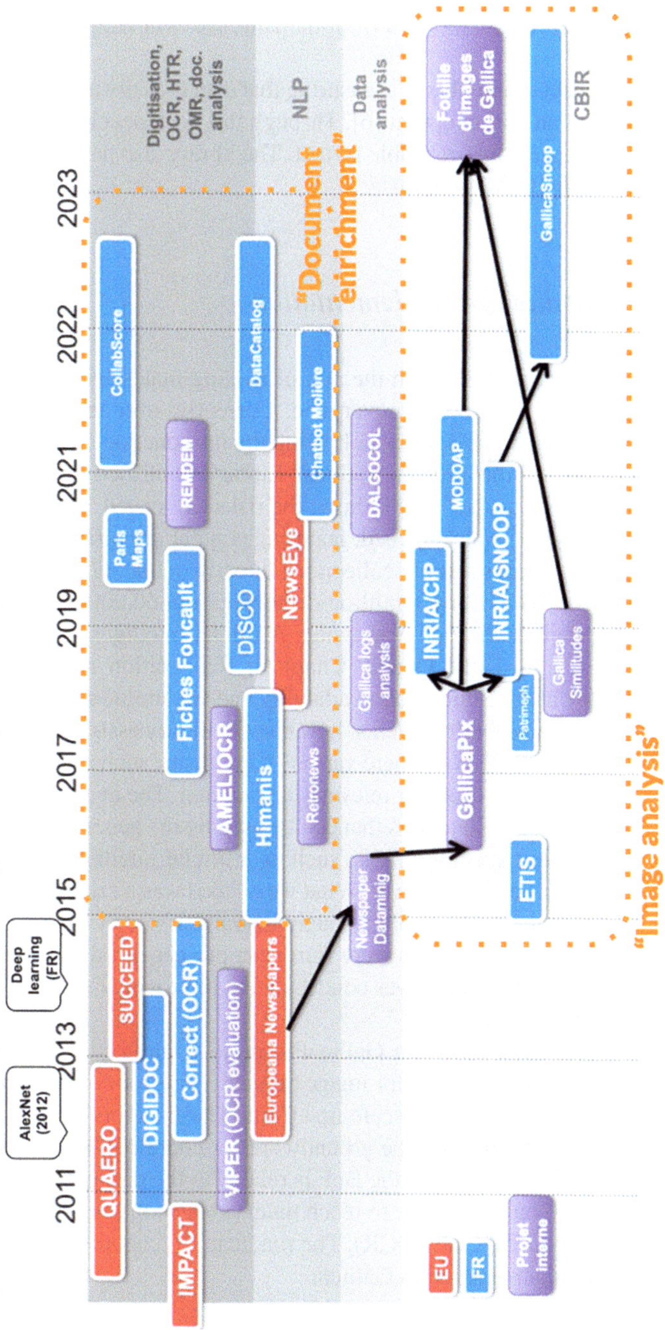

Fig. 1 Timeline of the development of AI in the national library. (Source: Jean-Philippe Moreux [4])

All these projects contribute in the end to Gallica (https://gallica.bnf.fr/) or to the global catalogue of the library https://catalogue.bnf.fr/index.do. Related to the ecosystem of Gallica, additional services from the BnF, like Mandragore [5], are also available online.

An important aspect of the library is ensuring that data is easily accessible. That's why the BnF created an API endpoint [6]. Through this API, developers can access data from Gallica in a machine-readable format. The library also has a data endpoint to request raw data: https://data.bnf.fr/

2.1 Need(s) Behind the Implementation

Gallica was established in 1997 with the aim of making materials free from intellectual property rights accessible to everyone. Currently, over ten million documents are available online via Gallica. Following the introduction of Google Books in 2005, the director of the French National Library published an article titled "Quand Google défie l'Europe," highlighting the risks associated with this project. As a result, Europeana [7] was launched, featuring content primarily from Gallica.

To enable people to access BnF's collections directly online, Gallica is engaged in digitisation efforts. With over ten million documents and 60,000 daily users, it is among the largest digital libraries worldwide. Artificial intelligence has been utilised through technologies like Optical Character Recognition and Handwritten Text Recognition to enhance document readability and streamline search processes. With such a vast collection of documents, how can the library assist users in finding what they are looking for? This is where various AI projects, such as image mining, come into play to help users discover relevant information. The head of Gallica was emphasising that: "We need functions that can be used by the general public, everywhere. These aren't very specific things, such as artificial intelligence capable of reading stock market codes or whatever. What we needed was a relatively 4×4 technology, so to speak, that could be used throughout Gallica."

Among the significant milestones were European projects for digitising press in 2008, 2012, and 2015. These initiatives contributed to improving OCR and the digitalisation of BnF's collections.

Another notable milestone is the GallicaPix project, initiated in 2016, which employed a deep-learning approach for image mining. This proof of concept proved successful, prompting the launch of scale-up efforts. These factors contribute to the reflection of AI in libraries and lay the groundwork for coordinating efforts.

The AI roadmap (2021) [8] from the BnF is related to the purpose of the library, and it's contributing to building tools to reach them (image mining, AI cataloguing, content personalisation, HTR, and OCR). The roadmap [9] encompasses four main projects that are interconnected with Gallica:

- **Image mining in Gallica** (querying images in Gallica based on similarity and generated keywords)
- **Handwritten text recognition (HTR) to be integrated into Gallica** (such a technology applies to handwritten texts but also to ancient printed works and texts written in less spoken languages)
- **Cataloguing** (daily cataloguing support, automatic mechanism expansion and improvement, implementation of LRM model, etc.)
- **Personalised content recommendation with an ethical perspective** (that is to say, respectful of diversity and data privacy, etc.)

2.2 *Actors Involved*

Gallica was started by the Bibliothèque nationale de France. As mentioned, the project is managed by the Cooperation Department with the support of departments like IT or the Collection Department.

Initially, the library conducted research and development. Later, they began collaborating with research teams, such as INRIA or ETIS Lab, on specific projects. The BnF also partners with European projects like Quaero [10], Europeana Newspapers [11], and NewsEye [12].

Two of their partners are the National University Library of Strasbourg (BNUS) and the National Library of History of Arts (INHA). Through Gallica, the BnF has federated a group of 276 partner organisations that use the platform. The idea of this partnership is the following: the BnF gives access to Gallica's backend in order to be used by the other library, and in exchange, the partner library gives access to its documents that could complete BnF's collections. These partners meet one or twice a year to discuss their needs, but the prioritisation and decision-making are ultimately made by the BnF: "Based on these needs, which may be those of partners or users, our own or those of partners, through surveys, feedback from the field, the emails we receive, requests, we draw up a roadmap which we consider to be a priority, which again, the choices are made on the basis of pragmatic factors, i.e. budgets, the ability to implement these new services or the improvement of existing services."

Table 1 describes the co-production phases of the project "Gallica", launched by the Bibliothèque nationale de France (BnF). The co-production types indicate the level of collaboration and involvement from various stakeholders in each phase based on the phases described by Mergel et al. [13]. Co-initiation was driven solely by BnF's willingness to start the project. In contrast, co-design involves concurrent phases with libraries collecting feedback and needs, while co-implementation features simultaneous collaboration with technical/research partners. The co-use/production moment brings together a group of libraries using Gallica as a white-label product, leveraging it in exchange for shared documents among 276 partners. Lastly,

Table 1 Synthesising the work that the national library is doing to collaborate

Phase	Co-production type	Description
Co-initiation		None, it was the willingness of the BnF to launch the project
Co-design	Concurrent co-production phase	The library is collecting feedback/needs and then chooses what to implement and how
Co-implementation	Concurrent co-production phase	With libraries like the BNUS or INHA and technical/research partners like INRIA or Mistral
Co-use/production moment	Concurrent co-production phase	With a group of libraries that are using Gallica as White-label product (30 cases). They can use Gallica in exchange for their documents. They have 276 partners that are using Gallica
Co-evaluation	Retrospective co-production phase	The evaluation is done by the BnF itself

the co-evaluation phase is retrospective, meaning that the evaluation was conducted by BnF itself.

2.2.1 Organisational Level

The project is led by the cooperation department and is under the supervision of the direction of services and networks. Figure 2 shows where the cooperation department (in charge of Gallica) is located in the organigram of the library.

There is specific support at the organisational level, as Gallica is explicitly identified in the AI roadmap. The project has a specific political sponsor, Tiphaine Vacqué, who is in direct relation with Kevin Riffault, the managing director.

2.2.2 External Actors

For the purpose of the project, they are working with partners that are mostly research teams (e.g. INRIA, a research centre in France) or technical partners (e.g. IT companies). Those actors are contributing to the implementation of a specific technology or contribute to answering a specific need. This point is difficult to handle as they are looking for actors who are able to work on technologies that are evolving at the same time. Besides, the library needs to have competencies to manage and maintain up and run the system. Those difficulties put a lot of pressure on the internal team.

We can note that for now, individual patrons and their representatives and associations are not involved in the discussion or the development of those functionalities. Even if a Gallica community did exist on Twitter (we were speaking about Gallicanautes), feedback from direct users is more informal or through investigations made by the audience studies department.

Fig. 2 Organigram of the BnF (June 2024)

2.3 Challenges

Gallica, a significant project, comes with numerous challenges. In an institution like the BnF, where AI is transforming the way people work, internal culture is shifting towards greater technological adoption. An internal expert expresses that "We have defined 4 main priorities, which are not exclusive, but there are 4 priorities. There's the image mining project, which aims to create an iconographic repository based on Gallica that will identify all the illustrations. There's handwriting recognition to do OCR on everything, not just printed matter. Help with indexing and cataloguing is very wide-ranging. It can help with current cataloguing. Every year, 70,000 or 80,000 books are published. It can also enrich existing cataloguing, the retrospective of the general catalogue. Indexing can also mean, for example, better indexing of the web archive collection, and ensuring that it's not just 5 pet-aoctet of massive data sets. That was the third. The fourth is conservation aid. These are more optimisation and decision-making technologies. How to optimise storage and shop organisation? A new site is going to be built in Amiens to house the press collections. How do we take all these collections here and optimise their migration to Amiens depending on the physical space available and the demand for consultation here? This is clearly a problem of optimisation. For us, it's a bit of a novelty."

Yet, we need to acknowledge that, even if it's a priority for the library, some employees remain hesitant to digitise everything, fearing it may deter visitors from visiting the library.

The biggest challenge currently is scaling up experimentation to industrial product levels. Although experiments have shown promising results, implementing them at a production level requires substantial investment and remains difficult. Indeed, one IT expert stresses that "What already exists, 20 years–30 years of production, it's harder to make information systems that are running at full speed evolve than it is to create. It's paradoxical, but it's easier to create something from scratch. The very destructive side of deep learning, which evolves very quickly, and which has an iterative life cycle, is both an advantage and a disadvantage, because you create models from data and you can spend your time improving the models, so it's a fairly new approach for a central IT department." In the meantime, the library must ensure high-quality services, necessitating verifying that new functionalities work well and integrating them smoothly into its current IT environment.

Another pressing issue is evaluation. AI projects are costly, but assessing their impacts is currently challenging. Scaling up experimentation also raises questions about evaluation. With limited funding, the library must decide which features to develop for various user groups (citizens, companies, other libraries) and tailor its approach to meet their specific needs and practices.

3 Results

3.1 Organisational Level

With 27 years of experience thanks to Gallica, the BnF has gained significant expertise in handling projects related to artificial intelligence (AI). Initially, these projects were not labelled as AI-related, but with the emergence of deep learning and breakthroughs, the BnF established an AI team to support this evolution. Today, this phenomenon is also part of the library's roadmap, supported by a dedicated sponsorship at the political level.

The AI team coordinates initiatives on the field and shares them to maximise their impact.

3.2 *Value Created and Co-created*

Gallica is a showcase for the BnF and its expertise in the AI field. By implementing this kind of technology, the library is creating public value at various levels:

- To other libraries by sharing with them the outcomes of the project (like in the context of the CENL or through associations like Liber or IFLA). Also, directly when libraries (like the BNUS) [14] are using Gallica for their own collection.
- To patrons through the implementation of this technology in their services. This could help users of Gallica or the general catalogue to access more precisely what they were looking for. This could also be a way to ease this process of finding, as their systems require important information literacy (e.g. to know how to do some research).
- To the private sector, for those who are using resources from the BnF for their activities and currently tech companies that are looking for qualitative structured data to improve their models.

AI presents various opportunities for creating value at different levels within the BnF:

- Service level: AI can contribute to achieving the library's mission by facilitating users' access to documents. For instance, OCR and HTR technologies enable digitisation of materials, image mining enhances search capabilities, and AI cataloguing tools streamline document indexation.
- Internal level: Librarians can benefit from AI tools that assist with various internal tasks, such as identifying documents requiring restoration and improving content classification.
- Process level: AI applications can also improve library processes, both internally and externally. By optimising workflows, staff can focus on higher-value tasks, ultimately leading to better services for users.

3.3 *Lesson Learned*

At present, there are few feedback/lessons learned as the projects are still in their experimental stages with little evaluation of performance metrics. The library has not yet established methods to assess the efficacy of its prototypes. Interviewees highlighted the importance of gathering people from various services to be part of AI projects to make sure they will contribute to it and that they understand how AI can be useful for them (and not a threat). To achieve that, they suggest working on the improvement of AI literacy within the library.

However, AI presents various opportunities for creating value at different levels within the BnF:

- Service level: AI can contribute to achieving the library's mission by facilitating users' access to documents. For instance, OCR and HTR technologies enable digitisation of materials, image mining enhances search capabilities, and AI cataloguing tools streamline document indexation.
- Internal level: Librarians can benefit from AI tools that assist with various internal tasks, such as identifying documents requiring restoration and improving content classification.
- Process level: AI applications can also improve library processes, both internally and externally. By optimising workflows, staff can focus on higher-value tasks, ultimately leading to better services for users.

4 Conclusion

To conclude this case about Gallica, we could enlighten that Gallica "plays a part in this because everything in Gallica is in one big well of saved data for eternity. That's what we're trying to do. Once we've archived and preserved all that, it's distributed. That's where Gallica comes into its own, providing access to the collections for as many people as possible." This citation of one interviewee makes the correlation between the fundamental missions of the BnF and Gallica. As they aim to grow to 20 million documents by 4–5 years, otherwise as the head of Gallica states: "If you don't, this content won't be visible and will ultimately be useless." In this perspective, the need for technical support to ensure accessibility of collections is more prominent than ever.

As they are going deeper on their AI-driven digital transformation journey, they will face both challenges and opportunities. On the one hand, the adoption of AI requires significant investments in infrastructure, training, and personnel, which may be a barrier for some libraries, particularly those with limited resources. Additionally, there are concerns about data privacy, bias, and job displacement that must be carefully addressed. However, on the other hand, the potential benefits of AI far outweigh these challenges. By leveraging AI, National Libraries can unlock new levels of efficiency, innovation, and user engagement, ultimately enhancing their role in supporting lifelong learning, cultural development, and social progress.

Acknowledgements The work for this chapter was supported by the European Union's Horizon Europe Research and Innovation Programme under Grant Agreement ID 101061516.

Appendix

See Table 2.

Table 2 Overview of the Gallica project at the French National Library

Case and project name			
Gallica—French National Library			
Country	**Number of employees**	**Type of AI solution**	**Year and maturity level**
France	2128	OCR, HTR and image/data mining	1997, well underway/major milestones accomplished
Project description			
Gallica is the digital library of the BNF. This digital library gives access to more than ten million free documents			
Need(s) behind implementation	**Actors involved**	**Challenges**	
Information retrieval, cataloguing, ease the research inside the collections	Mostly internal (IT, Collection, and Cooperation departments), external partners like BNUS, INHA, INRIA, or technical partners (i.e. Mistral)	Moving from prototyping to implement and launch live	
Results			
Organisational level	**Value created and co-created**	**Lesson learned**	
A specific department is in charge of Gallica; this is the coordination department. The project has a sponsor at the political level and is an important project for the BnF related to AI	New services for users, new services for librarians and for partners (like other libraries), and change at the process level to ensure a smoother experience as well for users and for employees	A specific department is in charge of Gallica; this is the coordination department. The project has a sponsor at the political level and is an important project for the BnF related to AI	

References

1. https://gallica.bnf.fr/accueil/fr/content/accueil-fr?mode=desktop
2. Additional publications are being shared by the library in open access: https://bnf.hal.science/BNF_DSG/
3. To follow the activity of the BnF, you could also follow the work of AI4LAM a working group about the use of AI in Library, Archive and Museum: https://sites.google.com/view/ai4lam/working-groups-and-chapters
4. To go deeper inside the work done at the BnF, Jean-Philippe Moreux, an AI expert at the library, is publishing papers about experiments that have been done: https://www.researchgate.net/profile/Jean-Philippe-Moreux/research
5. Mandragore is a digital platform developed by the Bibliothèque nationale de France. The database is giving access to 200,000 illuminations, drawings, seals and bookbinding decorations already described, with structured information and features like image mining
6. An endpoint is a connection where data sources send their data in a structure way in order to be process: https://api.bnf.fr/
7. https://www.europeana.eu/fr
8. https://www.bnf.fr/sites/default/files/2022-01/Poster_AI%20Roadmap_BnF_202112.pdf
9. https://www.bnf.fr/en/artificial-intelligence-bnf
10. The project could be found here: https://actions-recherche.bnf.fr/BnF/anirw3.nsf/IX01/A2013000354_quaero
11. The project could be found here: https://www.europeana.eu/en/collections/topic/18-newspaper
12. The project could be found here: https://cordis.europa.eu/project/id/770299
13. I. Mergel, N. Edelmann, N. Haug, Co-production phases in the development and implementation of digital public services. Perspect. Public Manag. Govern. **8**(2), 1–13 (2025)
14. https://www.bnu.fr/fr/numistral

Antoine Henry is an assistant professor in information and communication sciences and a member of GERIICO's Axis 4, whose theme is the circulation of information and the organisation of knowledge. His research work focuses mainly on digital issues (AI, digital commons, ethics of algorithms), the transformation of organisations, and collective intelligence.

He is also a member of the board of directors of the French chapter of the scholarly association ISKO and a member of the research group of the Centre Internet et Société (UPR 2000 of the CNRS) in which he co-manages the working group AI, art, and creativity.

From Metadata to Meaning: Applying AI in the National Library of Estonia

Carsten Schmidt

Abstract The National Library of Estonia (NLE) plays, defined by its legal framework, a dual role on the one side as a National and on the other side as a Parliamentary Library, uniquely integrating these functions to preserve Estonia's cultural and digital heritage. NLE was founded in 1918 and supports the development of all Estonian libraries. Furthermore, it leads research in the humanities and social sciences and is a hub for library and information science innovation. With 250 staff members and a budget of EUR 33.39 million, the NLE advances nationwide e-services and professional training for librarians. In 2019, the NLE launched two AI-driven projects, "Automatic Indexing" and "Ask Us". As automated and AI-driven services becoming more and more important, the idea was to address challenges in manual processes and improve user services. The Automatic Indexing project develops machine learning and AI to streamline publication tagging, enhancing accuracy, consistency, and efficiency while reducing costs. Ask Us, part of Estonia's "Bürokratt" initiative, integrates generic building blocks and chatbot technology to improve accessibility to library services. Both projects concluded in 2023, delivering prototypes and reusable technical components. During the project phase, NLE faced several challenges, including staff scepticism towards AI and adapting IT governance. Staff engagement through regular updates, workshops, and collaborative testing built the basis for acceptance and trust. All initiatives emphasise the commitment to implementing technology for library modernisation and, at the same time, preserving Estonia's linguistic and cultural identity.

Keywords Estonia · National Library · Artificial Intelligence · AI · Chatbot · Automated Indexing · Eesti Rahvusraamatukogu · Digital Transformation · e-Government · Sustainability

---

C. Schmidt (✉)
Department of Politics and Public Administration, University of Konstanz, Konstanz, Germany
e-mail: carsten.schmidt@uni-konstanz.de

I. Mergel, C. Schmidt (eds.), *AI Innovations in Public Services*,
https://doi.org/10.1007/978-3-032-01344-6_10

1 Introduction

The Estonian National Library (Estonian: Eesti Rahvusraamatukogu) is a national public institution in Estonia that operates according to the National Library of Estonia Act. The National Library of Estonia (NLE) was initially established on December 21, 1918, as the Parliamentary Library of Estonia. The NLE employs about 250 staff members and operates with a total budget of € 33.39 million, which includes allocations for its e-library (€ 232,000), e-rental solutions (€ 115,000), and ICT costs (€ 1.01 million) [1].

Today, it continues serving as a parliamentary library and national cultural hub. The NLE plays a vital role in preserving the nation's digital heritage, overseeing the Estonian Web Archive to collect and store Web pages significant to Estonia's society and cultural history.

As a centre of excellence, it supports the development of libraries nationwide by offering centralised e-services, collecting library statistics, coordinating field-specific terminology, and providing professional training for librarians. Its research focus lies in the humanities and social sciences, and it leads library and information science development through standardisation and terminology efforts. One of the interviewees said: "*I think libraries are in a really good position for AI because we have been working for many years with structured, high-quality data. But cataloguing is extremely labour-intensive. AI can help by automating metadata tagging for books, newspapers, and other publications.*"

In 2019, NLE initiated two artificial intelligence-driven projects: Automatic Indexing and the Chatbot service *Ask Us*. Both projects resulted 2023 in prototypes and provided reusable (technical) components. The Automatic Indexing system has achieved significant milestones, with plans to implement the service soon. Meanwhile, the Ask Us service will be enhanced with a chat function and a virtual assistant to streamline user interactions. Within the two projects, a prototype and reusable technical components were developed. The maturity levels are major milestones accomplished (*Automatic Indexing*). In the coming months, the complete version is planned to be implemented. The full version will consist of a chat function and a robot for the NLE (*Ask Us*).

2 Description of the Project

The Estonian government has developed a predominant strategy for using AI as a service or solution for the different departments. The so-called AI "Kratt" strategy, adopted by the government in July 2019, seeks to boost the take-up of AI in both the private and public sectors [1]. The implementation of AI and the initiation of the project are integral parts of the government's general approach. It is foreseen, if possible, to use AI for all aspects of public services. One interviewee said: "*I think a big driver is actually the like Estonian government; General, kind of progressive thinking in this area.*"

The NLE became part of the national AI initiative, which was also caused by the substantial amount of data that is building a sound basis for the development and training of AI. An interviewee explained: "*I think libraries are in a really good position for AI because we have been working for many years with structured, high-quality data. But cataloguing is extremely labour-intensive. AI can help by automating metadata tagging for books, newspapers, and other publications.*"

The NLE uses two parts of the project: the Chatbot and the automated indexing project.

The "Ask Us" Chatbot Project

The "Ask Us" project is part of the Estonian government's overarching "Bürokratt" project [2]. The central approach is to create a solution that will serve as a central Chatbot model for all government institutions. Bürokratt is an interoperable network of Chatbots on the Web sites of public authorities that allows people to obtain automated information from these authorities through a chat window [3]. This approach aims to prevent redundant developments and allows easy customisation to meet the various needs of the different departments and agencies, e.g. the NLE. To enhance the value, Bürokratt provides a single point of access to information for individuals and officials. The extensibility and future expansion of the Bürokratt network to other organisations is paramount. An interviewee explained: "The Chatbot is part of a broader national AI strategy. It can handle general inquiries and even redirect users to different government agencies. This ensures users get accurate information 24/7 without needing human intervention."

Bürokratt is a horizontal project that does not focus on only one organisation; it uses a distributed design, where the different Chatbots used by the agencies are independently developed but interconnected, based on generic technical building blocks provided to various government organisations. An interviewee said: "We are developing a network of Chatbots across public institutions in Estonia. The idea is that a user can ask one Chatbot a question, and if it is not library-related, it will redirect to another relevant Chatbot within the system." The information provided by the Chatbot is generated via the Automatic Indexing project and staff members of the NLE. The case illustration will focus mainly on the Automatic Indexing project.

Automatic Indexing Project

One of the main tasks of the National Library is the collection, long-term preservation, and accessibility of all publications published in Estonia and their registration in the database of the Estonian National Bibliography (ERB). The database ERB registers data about national publications. National publications include all publications published in Estonia in all languages and publications published abroad in Estonia, including works by Estonian authors and their translations, regardless of their physical format (paper, electronic). The principles for compiling ERB are defined in the document "Principles of National Bibliography Compilation".

The publications in the NLE collections are described and tagged manually. To achieve this, experts inside NLE review each publication and allocate tags to the content. The allocation is based on the beliefs of the staff members and what they think accurately reflects its content. This process does not utilise artificial intelligence or algorithms. Consequently, there are several concerns:

1. Tags created by the employees may not always be the most suitable or logical from the user's perspective.
2. This methodology may not consistently produce the most objective and accurate results.
3. Tagging in this manner is highly resource-intensive for the library (i.e. the state).
4. Ensuring consistent tagging for all publications on the same topic is challenging.

2.1 Need(s) Behind the Implementation

Tagging items is a labour-intensive and time-consuming task that demands significant personnel resources not only in the National Library of Estonia (NLE). The whole process heavily depends on the knowledge and judgments of the individual librarians or information specialists responsible for selecting tags, which can result in inconsistencies in the tags assigned to other editions of the same publication. Because tagging has so far been a predominantly manual job, the potential for human error and subjective interpretation is high, leading to variability in the quality and accuracy of the tags. The lack of standardisation can create challenges for users of NLE who rely on tags created by the librarians to find information, as inconsistent tagging can make it difficult to retrieve specific information.

Besides that, the manual nature of the tagging process can be time-consuming and costly. Organisations like NLE must invest in training personnel to continuously ensure they have the expertise to tag items accurately. Even with training, the subjective nature of tagging means that discrepancies are almost inevitable. To address these challenges, NLE decided to explore automated tagging systems that utilise AI and machine learning. The NLE has a solid starting point for AI projects. It preserves a considerable amount of data. An interviewee explained: "*The National Library has a legal deposit obligation, meaning we collect all published books and documents in Estonia. This makes us a natural hub for AI-driven language processing and indexing.*" The different components that are under construction can analyse the content of regular books or handwritten text. They can generate text based on the analysed content. This is leading to greater consistency and increased efficiency. However, even if the results of the automated indexing reach, in general, a higher quality, human experts' supervision is necessary to ensure consistency and, at all times, the same level of quality.

The project aimed to develop a prototype that applies machine learning and AI to automate publication content analysis and tagging. During the project, it was recognised that it is relevant if the subject to be tagged is a book or, e.g. a newspaper article. An interviewee explained: "*We developed two AI prototypes: one for automated subject indexing of books and another for newspaper articles. Books worked well because they contain rich content, but short articles were more challenging due to the different methodologies used by librarians versus AI.*"

NLE has developed a multi-modal AI that includes components of subject indexing with meta-tagging and content indexing, plus OCR and meta-tagging. Essential aspects of the project were the support of the Estonian language by reusable technologies independent from large tech companies, the reduction of costs, the enhancement of processes, and ensuring the consistency of metatags. One expert stated, "*This is not one specific solution, but it's composed of about a dozen different modules. We want to make these components publicly accessible as open-source software.*"

Furthermore, by implementing machine learning and AI, the prototype will be able to analyse publications' content automatically [4] and generate relevant tags simultaneously. This will significantly reduce the required (manual) effort, lowering the tagging process's expenses. Besides that, the automation of processes will expedite the tagging, allowing faster management and increased availability of tagged publications. One interviewee said: "*The AI tool analyses books and other publications, extracts metadata, and suggests subject tags. Librarians then validate and refine them. This hybrid approach ensures accuracy while reducing workload.*"

One interviewee emphasised that automated systems can apply standardised criteria uniformly, reducing the variability and subjectivity inherent in manual tagging. This consistency will ensure that all publications on similar topics are tagged coherently and allow for better searchability and organisation.

Furthermore, the project had the additional goal to contribute to developing technologies supporting the Estonian language. By creating sophisticated AI tools customised explicitly to the Estonian language, another task was to promote the growth and refinement of linguistic resources and technologies specific to Estonia. This will benefit the library and support broader applications in other fields requiring advanced language processing capabilities.

The project aims to conduct a comprehensive analysis and develop a prototype and solution capable of analysing and automatically tagging the content of a publication when the full text is available.

The project is separated into two main phases:

1. **Detailed Analysis Report**: The first phase starts with an in-depth analysis of the methods and tools used to analyse the content and tagging. The assessment will highlight the strengths and limitations of the existing system, on the one hand, and, on the other hand, it is foreseen to identify the requirements and the prerequisites for augmentation. Furthermore, the technical specifications for the prototype will be outlined. The report also includes an evaluation of the potential impact of automated meta-tagging on the different workflows, efficiency, resource allocation, and accuracy. Additionally, it will explore the integration of Estonian language technologies to ensure the prototype is tailored to the linguistic nuances of Estonian publications.
2. **Prototype Development**: This second phase will be built on the results of the first phase and the detailed analysis, and it will focus on creating a functional prototype. The prototype will include machine learning systems and AI algorithms for an automated analysis and meta-tagging. It handles various publication types and ensures tags are accurate and consistent. The development process

included iterative testing and refinement to address any challenges identified during initial trials. The ultimate goal is to produce a robust and scalable solution seamlessly integrated into the library's digital infrastructure.

2.2 *Actors Involved*

Numerous individuals are involved in the AI projects at the National Library NLE. These include the head of development at the NLE, who also oversees other public libraries in Estonia, and internal and external project managers for the two AI projects. Additionally, internal and external experts with experience in artificial intelligence, data management personnel, development team members, and the individuals currently performing the tasks that are slated for automation all play crucial roles in these projects. The following description of co-creation types indicates the level of collaboration and involvement from various stakeholders in each phase based on the phases described by Mergel et al. [5] (Table 1).

2.2.1 Organisational Level

The National Government sets the general AI strategy and provides funding and policy direction for AI adoption in public institutions, including libraries. Within the National Library of Estonia (NLE), the Head of Library Services Development is responsible for implementing AI-related components within the institution. It also has the task to oversee the AI-related developments and ensure the reusability in other public libraries in Estonia, and the alignment with national strategies. The Data Science and Digital Humanities Team, led by the library's sole data scientist, plays a key role in the technical implementation of AI. These people are responsible for the machine learning models, data structuring, and metadata extraction, collaborating with external IT developers to refine AI tools. Librarians and cataloguers are actively involved in training, validating, and improving AI-generated metadata. Their involvement shall ensure that the AI-based indexing will be aligned with traditional cataloguing methodologies and provide real-world feedback to developers. The IT and Infrastructure Team supports AI integration into the library's digital infrastructure, ensuring data security, storage, and system scalability. Finally, Library Leadership and Policy Makers must see beyond the borders and ensure the long-term AI strategy, securing funding, managing ethical concerns, and ensuring AI aligns with the library's mission of preserving and providing access to Estonian cultural heritage.

2.2.2 External Actors

In the different AI projects, two private companies, TEXTA OÜ and Net Group OÜ, are involved as external vendors. These companies are responsible for developing AI prototypes and reusable technical components to automate subject indexing,

Table 1 Co-production process in the Automatic Indexing project at the NLE

Phase	Co-production type	Description
Co-initiation	Prospective co-production phase	The National Library of Estonia identified the need for AI in cataloguing and subject indexing. The initiative was internally proposed by the library's leadership, data scientists, and librarians, and supported by the Estonian government and funding bodies. External IT firms and universities were approached to explore AI feasibility
Co-design	Concurrent co-production phase	A prototype was developed, integrating machine learning models for subject indexing. Collaboration included library staff, data scientists, IT companies, and academic researchers. External AI developers provided expertise in OCR, NLP, and metadata extraction, while librarians trained AI models with existing catalogue data
Co-implementation	Concurrent co-production phase	The AI system was deployed in a pilot phase, tested by librarians and IT teams. External AI developers worked on fine-tuning models, while cataloguers validated the AI-generated metadata. Continuous testing occurred with feedback loops between users, developers, and researchers to improve accuracy
Co-use/production moment	Concurrent co-production phase	AI tools are now used for metadata extraction, subject indexing, and cataloguing. Librarians oversee AI results, correct errors, and refine models. The system is accessible to multiple Estonian libraries, enabling broader adoption. Open-source modules support external researchers
Co-evaluation	Retrospective co-production phase	AI tools are evaluated based on librarian feedback, user acceptance, and indexing accuracy. Formal assessments involve research institutions, government agencies, and external experts. Continuous improvements focus on reducing biases, increasing training data, and enhancing AI-human collaboration

metadata extraction, and cataloguing. Aside from these IT vendors, the National Library of Estonia (NLE) collaborates with academic institutions, such as the University of Tartu and Tallinn University. These institutions contribute linguistic expertise and research in natural language processing (NLP) to enhance AI's ability to process Estonian-language texts. Other Estonian public and academic libraries, including the University of Tartu Library and the Estonian Literary Museum, participate in testing and implementing AI solutions. They help refine models to ensure AI-driven cataloguing works effectively across different institutions. At the European level, NLE engages with Nordic national libraries, particularly Finland and Norway, to exchange best practices, open-source AI tools (e.g., Annif), and research on AI-driven library solutions. Finally, the Estonian government and funding bodies support AI projects by providing financial resources and ensuring alignment with the national AI strategy. They promote the adoption of AI in public institutions while addressing ethical, legal, and data security concerns.

2.3 Challenges

IT regulation was a significant challenge in AI implementation, especially in 2019. Since 2018, the National Library of Estonia (NLE) has outsourced IT services and project development to the Information Technology Centre for the Ministry of Finance. However, after assessing service needs, it was decided that the library should regain control over IT development while the IT Centre continued workplace maintenance. This led to the re-establishment of NLE's IT Department to provide greater flexibility, also in the AI projects.

Besides that, librarians of NLE are described as people who often worry that implementing new technologies will render their jobs obsolete. There's a concern about what their future roles will be. One interviewee said: "*Many librarians are set in their ways and not very open-minded about change.*" It takes time to bring in new, younger, and more flexible people who understand the value of these innovations. Initially, it can be challenging to create a shared understanding of what AI is doing in the library and what the librarian's role will be, especially with things like automatic cataloguing or coding examples. This also has an impact on the development of AI solutions, as AI cannot self-learn new subject terms and needs continuous librarian input.

However, the users and patrons of the NLE are described as very open-minded. They are eager to use the new technologies. For example, university students and other customers are thrilled to have API access to NLE data or scientific books. They are very supportive and provide valuable feedback about improving and moving forward with projects. Therefore, the support of staff members is essential. An interviewee explained: "*AI can index already known words using existing ontologies. But it cannot recognise or add completely new subject terms, that still requires human input.*"

Further challenges are data quality issues and AI accuracy caused by limited Estonian-language datasets. They hinder OCR and metadata extraction and require constant human validation. Additionally, ethical and legal concerns limit AI's scope, which is mainly based on data privacy and copyright restrictions.

In general, AI development requires high investment and specialised personnel, which NLE fights to attract. Because of the lack of internal IT specialists, AI tools depend on external developers, which creates a risk to long-term sustainability.

Addressing these challenges requires investment, collaboration, and training to ensure AI supports, rather than replaces, human expertise.

3 Results

The implementation and prototyping of the solution have created different kinds of impact. The results influence various levels inside the NLE. It also widens the role of the NLE from an organisation that stores information and provides data. One interviewee explained: "*Libraries are transitioning from just being book repositories to becoming data providers. AI helps us systematise and structure this data for wider reuse.*"

3.1 Organisational Level

The National Library of Estonia (NLE) aims to increase efficiency and accuracy through AI-driven metadata extraction, subject indexing, and cataloguing [6]. AI automates labour-intensive tasks, reducing the cataloguing time from manual efforts to near-instant processing. As a result, this will not only lower the costs, it will also expand accessibility by enabling the cataloguing of previously unprocessed materials such as Web archives, PDFs, and news articles. By leveraging machine learning models and OCR, AI improves metadata consistency, though human oversight remains essential to correct errors and refine outputs. Additionally, AI makes large-scale data processing feasible and will support researchers by providing structured linguistic and cultural analysis datasets.

To stay updated on AI advancements and best practices, NLE relies on internal knowledge sharing and participation in conferences and collaborations. Employees attend AI and library technology conferences, after which insights are disseminated through internal newsletters, workshops, and briefings. Digital humanists and data scientists share findings in short presentations or written reports in the library's internal weekly updates. The collaboration with especially the Nordic but also the European libraries provides valuable knowledge on AI tools and methodologies, e.g. Finland's Annif [7] for automated subject indexing. This ensures that NLE remains aligned with global AI trends in library science while fostering internal capacity-building.

To overcome scepticism, it is vital to keep the people who are not working on a day-to-day basis in the project informed and involved. In the NLE case, the project's responsible people ensure regular communication and updates. NLE publishes an in-house newsletter highlighting the week's news and developments every Friday. This helps keep all staff members informed about what's happening in the IT field.

3.2 Value Created and Co-created

The implementation of the AI solution created different kinds of values and results. First, it has reduced the time to catalogue per item from 30 to 45 min to a nearly instantaneous metadata generation. In parallel, it has changed and enriched the work of the staff members. They became responsible for reviewing the outcomes of the AI work and ensuring quality while enabling scalability. An interviewee explained, "*We're not trying to fully automate cataloguing. The goal is to widen the bottleneck—librarians use AI-generated suggestions and then validate or correct them.*" Furthermore, the automation of tagging improves discoverability and standardisation across publications. It also created the necessary resources for processing materials like Web archives, PDFs, and historical newspapers that were previously unindexed due to resource constraints. One interviewee said, "*AI improves accessibility by making previously unindexed documents searchable. This helps both researchers and the general public find relevant materials more efficiently.*"

The development and piloting process was accompanied by various internal and external stakeholders, e.g. librarians, IT vendors, researchers, and users. They collaborate across the different phases, from prototype to implementation. University students and researchers' feedback helps to refine the results.

3.3 Lesson Learned

It was reported that the employees of the NLE have a low level of trust in AI solutions. Therefore, keeping them informed about ongoing developments is crucial to build confidence and transparency. NLE also conducts workshops, and whenever someone attends a conference, whether in-house or external, they share their insights with the team upon their return. This might be through a brief 15-min talk or by writing a short article for the NLE newsletter. One interviewee explained: "*In our case, if we are doing something, then we have every Friday going out, it's like in-house newspaper when we are saying out what is this week's news. We are communicating to all librarians what's happening in this field. Of course, we have this, as I already mentioned, we have three digital humanists working in library. They are sharing their knowledge, making some workshops here. Also, when some conference will be enhanced in-house or outside, they are coming back and then they are sharing their knowledge. If somebody wants to know something about it, they are making very, very quick let's say ten or fifteen minutes speak [of] what they heard and sometimes even small article to our everyday newspaper.*" This way, NLE keeps everyone updated, involved, and informed about the latest developments and advancements. The development of AI solutions should be carried out meticulously to ensure success and trust.

First, the process should start with a thorough analysis of the state of play of the methods and tools used for the services and by the staff in the library. This analysis will help to identify different areas for improvement and help to create a solid foundation for AI implementation.

Second, the focus should shift to the prototype. A functional prototype will serve as a proof of concept. It demonstrates the potential benefits and allows addressing possible employee concerns. The case of the NLE has highlighted the importance of involving the staff during this phase. The gathering of feedback is the basis for necessary adjustments and the alignment of the solution with needs and expectations. Another aspect is the preservation of the Estonian language. One interviewee explained: "*If we don't have AI tools that understand Estonian, we risk our language becoming less relevant in the digital world. The National Library plays a key role in preserving digital Estonian heritage.*"

Once the prototype has been refined and thoroughly tested, the final step is to move it into production. This phase should only proceed when the AI solution works reliably and effectively. Continuous monitoring and support will be necessary to ensure smooth integration and address any issues that may arise.

4 Conclusions

The National Library of Estonia (NLE) has demonstrated a forward-thinking approach by integrating modern AI technologies into its operations, focusing on enhancing efficiency and supporting digital transformation.

Projects such as "Ask Us" and especially "Automatic Indexing" are on the one hand contributing to the commitment to modernising the services of the NLE while addressing challenges in manual processes, resource allocation, and technological adoption. On the other hand, these initiatives allow to streamline the library's internal workflows and also deliver the opportunity to position NLE as one of the leading National Libraries in leveraging AI within the public sector. Moreover, by contributing to developing Estonian language technologies, NLE is pivotal in advancing linguistic resources and tools for broader applications and ensuring independence from global software companies, especially for minor languages.

Implementing these projects underscores the importance of balancing innovation with stakeholder engagement, e.g. via co-creation activities. In parallel to the implementation, challenges, e.g. the need to involve further (technical) experts and the scepticism of the employee on the integration of AI into traditional workflows, have emerged. NLE's focus on transparent communication and continuous training has fostered trust and collaboration among its staff. The employment of additional staff, the involvement of external experts, and the cooperation with companies have on the one side strengthened the library's technical capabilities and on the other side ensuring the development of robust, scalable, and re-usable solutions.

Looking ahead, the successful implementation of these AI-driven projects has the potential to provide a sound foundation for NLE to expand its technological ambitions. The full deployment and integration of the AI-based solutions in the services of the NLE will increase user accessibility, reduce operational costs, and improve service quality. Additionally, these advancements pave the way for NLE to explore further AI applications, such as personalised recommendations and advanced data analytics, to meet evolving user expectations and establish the National Library as a data provider.

Digital transformation is continuously reshaping the role of libraries globally, and NLE is well-positioned to lead by example. To summarise, prioritising innovation, fostering collaboration, and addressing the human aspect of technological change in a National Library can ensure the relevance of the library as a cultural and technological cornerstone in the national digital infrastructure.

Acknowledgements The work for this chapter was supported by the European Union's Horizon Europe Research and Innovation Programme under Grant Agreement ID 101061516.

Appendix

See Table 2.

Table 2 Overview of the AI projects at the NLE

<table>
<tr><td colspan="4">Case and project name</td></tr>
<tr><td colspan="4">Automatic Indexing and enquiry answering service Ask Us</td></tr>
<tr><th>Country</th><th>Number of employees</th><th>Type of AI solution</th><th>Year and maturity level</th></tr>
<tr><td>Estonia</td><td>250</td><td>Multi-modal AI including components of subject indexing with meta-tagging and content indexing + OCR and meta-tagging</td><td>2023/ Prototype and major milestones accomplished</td></tr>
<tr><th colspan="4">Project description</th></tr>
<tr><td colspan="4">The goal is to develop a prototype utilising machine learning and AI to automate publication content analysis and tagging</td></tr>
<tr><th>Need(s) behind implementation</th><th>Actors involved</th><th colspan="2">Challenges</th></tr>
<tr><td>Tagging items is a labour-intensive task that demands significant resources. This process relies heavily on the knowledge and judgments of individual taggers. Additionally, the manual nature of tagging can be time-consuming and costly</td><td>Head of development at the NLE, internal and external project managers, experts with experience in AI, data management personnel, development team members, customers, and vendors</td><td colspan="2">It is vital to keep the people who are not working on a day-to-day basis in the project informed and involved</td></tr>
<tr><th colspan="4">Results</th></tr>
<tr><th>Organisational level</th><th>Value created and co-created</th><th colspan="2">Lesson learned</th></tr>
<tr><td>The project is coordinated by the Head of Library Services Center and his team. It is supported by the Estonian government and part of the overarching AI strategy</td><td>• The users and patrons are described as very open-minded. They are eager to use the new technologies. They are very supportive and provide valuable feedback on improving and moving forward
• It can be challenging to grasp what AI is doing in the library and what the librarian's role will be, especially with things like automatic cataloguing or coding examples</td><td colspan="2">It was reported that the employees of the NLE have a low level of trust in AI solutions. Therefore, keeping them informed about ongoing developments is crucial to build confidence and transparency in the process. Furthermore, it is important to do it step by step:
• Detailed analysis
• Prototyping
• Production (this phase should only proceed when the AI solution works reliably and effectively)</td></tr>
</table>

References

1. New e-Estonia factsheet: National AI "Kratt" Strategy—e-Estonia | Knowledge sharing platform, https://iskm.issa.int/node/13601. Accessed 8 June 2025
2. European Commission, White Paper on Artificial Intelligence—a European approach to excellence and trust (2020), https://ec.europa.eu/info/publications/white-paper-artificial-intelligence-european-approach-excellence-and-trust_en. Accessed 8 June 2025
3. AI Chatbot to replace and improve governmental e-services—e-Estonia, https://e-estonia.com/ai-Chatbot-to-replace-and-improve-governmental-e-services/. Accessed 8 June 2025
4. D. Ivanovic, B. Milosavljevic, Artificial intelligence applications in digital libraries. Library Hi Tech **40**(2), 365–384 (2022)
5. I. Mergel, N. Edelmann, N. Haug, Co-production phases in the development and implementation of digital public services. Perspect. Public Manag. Govern. **8**(1), 1–13 (2025)
6. L. Dempsey, Library metadata and linked data—the transition to a more interconnected future. Insight **34**(1), 1–12 (2021)
7. O. Suominen, P. Király, Annif: DIY automated subject indexing using multiple algorithms. LIBER Q. **30**(1), 1–25 (2020)

Carsten Schmidt focuses on concepts and methodologies for e-government in the European Union and the associated countries, as well as the related aspects of digital infrastructure. Particular attention is paid to the areas of the once-only principle, European large-scale pilot projects, and sustainability. Before, he was involved in different positions (Project Director, Work Package Manager, etc.) in European large-scale projects like mGov4EU, TOOP, e-SENS, and e-CODEX. He worked for the Ministry of Justice NRW, Germany, the Technical University of Tallinn (TalTech), and the University of Tartu, Estonia.

Implementing AI in the National Library of Spain: The ETSO Project and Stylometric Analysis of Golden Age Theatre

Alberto Peralta

Abstract The Biblioteca Nacional de España (BNE), founded in 1711, serves as Spain's national library, safeguarding one of the most significant collections of Spanish Golden Age theatre manuscripts. With a staff of 364 and an annual budget of €35.86 million, it is a cornerstone of Spain's cultural preservation efforts. In 2017, the ETSO project ("Stylometry Applied to the Theater of the Golden Age") was launched to address the lack of transcribed texts from this period. Using AI tools like Transkribus, ETSO has automated the transcription and modernisation of over 1800 theatrical works, achieving up to 97% accuracy for printed texts and 91% for manuscripts. The project is ongoing and continues to refine its methodologies while contributing to the CETSO corpus and the TEXORO search engine. The project faced challenges such as adapting AI to historical typefaces, modernising archaic spellings, and overcoming transcription errors in handwritten manuscripts. These were mitigated through extensive model training and interdisciplinary collaboration. ETSO demonstrates how AI can unlock cultural heritage, making historical texts accessible for research and public engagement and serving as a model for integrating technology into humanities projects.

Keywords Biblioteca Nacional de España (BNE) · ETSO project · Stylometry and AI transcription · Spanish Golden Age theatre manuscripts · Cultural heritage and digital humanities

---

A. Peralta (✉)
Department of Business and Economics, Faculty of Economics, Business and Tourism, Universidad de Alcalá, Madrid, Spain

College of Business, Abu Dhabi University, Abu Dhabi, United Arab Emirates
e-mail: alberto.peralta@adu.ac.ae

I. Mergel, C. Schmidt (eds.), *AI Innovations in Public Services*,
https://doi.org/10.1007/978-3-032-01344-6_11

1 Introduction

The preservation and study of cultural heritage are central to understanding historical and societal evolution. The Biblioteca Nacional de España (BNE), established in 1711, plays a pivotal role in this endeavour by safeguarding an extensive collection of Spanish Golden Age theatrical manuscripts and printed works. These texts, dating from 1492 to 1659, offer invaluable insights into the artistic, cultural, and societal dimensions of one of Spain's most prolific literary eras. Despite their significance, a large proportion of these works remain inaccessible due to the lack of digital transcription and modernised spelling [1].

The ETSO project ("Stylometry Applied to the Theater of the Golden Age") addresses this gap by leveraging artificial intelligence to transcribe and analyse these historical texts [1–3]. Specifically, the project employs tools like Transkribus [4] and Stylo [5] to overcome challenges posed by historical typefaces, archaic orthography, and handwritten manuscripts [6–9]. The central question of this research revolves around how AI can be applied effectively to automate the transcription of complex historical texts and facilitate their analysis for authorship attribution, literary studies, and broader academic engagement.

Previous research has demonstrated the potential of AI in similar fields, such as Optical Character Recognition (OCR) for modern texts and Handwritten Text Recognition (HTR) for historical manuscripts. However, these methods have shown limited effectiveness when applied to the intricate typefaces and diverse handwriting styles of Golden Age manuscripts. The ETSO project builds upon these advancements by developing AI models tailored specifically for Spanish Golden Age texts, achieving remarkable transcription accuracy of 97% for printed texts and 91% for manuscripts.

The rationale for this project stems from the urgent need to democratise access to cultural heritage and unlock the analytical potential of previously neglected historical texts. By transcribing and modernising over 1800 works, the ETSO project enriches the CETSO corpus and the TEXORO search engine, creating a robust foundation for further philological and literary research. This endeavour aligns with the BNE's mission to promote cultural preservation and public engagement with Spain's literary legacy.

The project employs a combination of machine learning techniques and interdisciplinary collaboration. AI models were trained on a large dataset of Golden Age texts, while scholars from various fields refined the outputs through iterative processes. Key findings include the successful attribution of previously anonymous works, such as *La francesa Laura*, to renowned playwrights like Lope de Vega. These findings demonstrate the transformative potential of AI in historical research and cultural preservation.

In conclusion, the ETSO project not only addresses the technical and methodological challenges of transcribing and analysing historical texts but also underscores the broader implications of integrating AI into the humanities. By bridging the gap between technology and cultural heritage, this initiative sets a precedent for future projects aiming to preserve and disseminate humanity's literary and historical treasures.

2 Description of the Project

Thanks to the AI-powered tool Transkribus (READ-COOP, 2024) and its Handwritten Text Recognition (HTR) techniques, Dr. Cuéllar and the ETSO team have trained three models, which are being used and refined by the research community, capable of automatically transcribing and modernising these documents with a high degree of accuracy: approximately 97% accuracy for printed texts and 91% for manuscripts. Through these models, ETSO has processed around 1800+ theatrical works contained in prints and manuscripts from numerous libraries, archives, and other digitised sources. The resulting transcriptions are now part of the CETSO Corpus and the TEXORO search engine, both part of the ETSO project. Moreover, they possess sufficient quality to undergo stylometric analysis, which reveals interesting authorship attributions.

2.1 Need Behind the Implementation of the ETSO Project

2.1.1 Problem

- An elevated percentage of printed and handwritten theatrical texts from the Spanish Golden Age period have never been transcribed into analogue or, of course, digital formats. Consequently, it is impossible to use these documents for searches of interest or for valuable computer analyses (such as stylometry, topic modelling, sentiment detection, etc.) that have been developing in recent years.
- Until ETSO, there were no automatic spelling modernisers for Spanish that could work over computer readable (i.e. transcribed) and non-readable (i.e. non-transcribed) copies of manuscripts.

2.1.2 Need

To automatically transcribe the Spanish Golden Age documents for stylometric analyses able to establish trusted authorship attributions.

2.1.3 Drivers

- A large number of documents (1200+) from the Spanish Golden Age were initially available to the IPs, collected from numerous open sources, such as AHCT, Artelope, Aula Biblioteca Mira de Amescua, BVMC, Moretianos, Teatro de Autores Portugueses do Séc. XVII, and others, as well as from other research groups, such as GRISO, ISTAE, Prolope, and others, and individuals and researchers [2].
- The discovery of the Transkribus tool [4] in the beginning of 2020 by the ETSO team (Dr. Cuéllar). The tool aims to be a solution for transcribing ancient manuscripts with a high degree of accuracy using machine learning. Developed by the READ-COOP group [7, 8], this tool features a powerful AI system for training in text recognition and, ultimately, for automatic transcriptions. It is also user-friendly and easy to learn, making it useful even for manual transcription of texts. Importantly, this tool is not limited to any specific language or alphabet; it is designed to recognise text regardless of the language or script used. The basic process involves accurately transcribing a sufficient number of words so that, later on, through an AI system with neural networks, the machine learns to link each part of the text to its corresponding transcription. By requiring tens or even hundreds of thousands of correctly transcribed words, the machine becomes capable of accurately transcribing the lines of new documents entered into it.
- The intervention of Dr. Germán Vega García-Luengos (Universidad de Valladolid) as the Coordinator of the Golden Age Theater Portal at the BNE, and the motivation of the senior management of the BNE, to incentivise the digitalisation and analysis of the Spanish Golden Age theatrical works [1, 2].

2.2 Actors Involved in the ETSO Project

The ETSO project was initiated by Dr. Álvaro Cuéllar (Universitat Autònoma de Barcelona) and Dr. Germán Vega García-Luengos (University of Valladolid), who played central roles in its co-design and implementation. Their teams collaborated with the research group on Lope de Vega PROLOPE [10] and over 200 researchers, students, experts, and collectors from various institutions. Patrons, including scholars and philologists, were actively involved in refining and utilising the tools, serving as evaluators and contributors to the development of models like CETSO and TEXORO. External collaborators, such as the READ-COOP developers, provided critical support for AI model training and deployment, enhancing the project's usability and effectiveness for a broad range of academic and cultural stakeholders.

Table 1 provides greater detail on who the internal actors are in the ETSO project and the activities that they developed in the project.

In addition, the ETSO project has been developed through the collaboration of a diverse and extensive group of researchers from various organisations external to

Table 1 The internal actors in the ETSO project

Value co-creation-related activity	Actors
Co-initiation	Dr. Álvaro Cuéllar (Universitat Autònoma de Barcelona) and Dr. Germán Vega García-Luengos (University of Valladolid) and their respective teams
Co-design	Dr. Álvaro Cuéllar (Universitat Autònoma de Barcelona) and Dr. Germán Vega García-Luengos (University of Valladolid), their teams and the research group on Lope de Vega PROLOPE (Universidad Autónoma de Barcelona)
Co-implementation	Dr. Álvaro Cuéllar (Universitat Autònoma de Barcelona) and Dr. Germán Vega García-Luengos (University of Valladolid), their teams and the research group on Lope de Vega PROLOPE (Universidad Autónoma de Barcelona) and 200+ researchers, students, experts, and collectors
Co-use/production moment	Dr. Álvaro Cuéllar (Universitat Autònoma de Barcelona) and Dr. Germán Vega García-Luengos (University of Valladolid), their teams and the research group on Lope de Vega PROLOPE (Universidad Autónoma de Barcelona), and 50+ researchers from across the world
Co-evaluation	Dr. Álvaro Cuéllar (Universitat Autònoma de Barcelona) and Dr. Germán Vega García-Luengos (University of Valladolid), their teams and the research group on Lope de Vega PROLOPE (Universidad Autónoma de Barcelona)

the Biblioteca Nacional de España (BNE). These organisations, representing a wide range of academic and cultural institutions, are listed alphabetically in Table 2. This collective effort highlights the interdisciplinary and international scope of the project, underscoring its significance in advancing the study of Spanish Golden Age theatre.

Moreover, the ETSO project has included 122 students from the Universidad de Valladolid collaborating with the team in the development and deployment of its tools.

The collaboration of the individuals from these external institutions is threefold:

1. Individuals and institutions have provided a large number of manuscripts and other documents (1200+) from the Spanish Golden Age needed to train the AI to accurately transcribe them.
2. Developers from READ-COOP group and researchers linked to this open-source platform helped train the first recognition models in Transkribus.
3. Researchers and interested individuals keep refining the CETSO and TEXORO tools [2, 3], populating the Corpus of documents and improving the search and recognition engines. In this process, researchers receive the value of the existing tools for the philological investigations conducive to PhD dissertations and evaluations of their research questions.

Table 2 The external actors in the ETSO project

Affiliation	Affiliation (continued)
Universidad Autónoma de Madrid	Università degli Studi di Milan
Universidad Complutense de Madrid	Universitá degli studi di Salerno
Universidad de Alcalá	Università degli Studi di Torino
Universidad de Burgos	Università degli Studi di Trento
Universidad de Castilla-La Mancha	Università degli studi Roma Tre
Universidad de Córdoba	Università del Piemonte Orientale
Universidad de Guadalajara	Università del Salento
Universidad de Jaén	Università di Bologna
Universidad de La Habana	Università di Firenze
Universidad de La Rioja	Università di Pavia
Universidad de León	Universitat de Barcelona
Universidad de Navarra	Universitat de Girona
Universidad de Salamanca	Universitat de les Illes Balears
Universidad de Santiago de Compostela	Universitat de València
Universidad de Sevilla	Universität Wien and Universitat Autònoma de Barcelona
Universidad de Valladolid	Université de Genève
Universidad del País Vasco	Université de Montréal
Universidad Internacional de La Rioja	Université de Neuchâtel
Universidad Nacional de Educación a Distancia	University of California
Università Ca' Foscari Venezia	University of Kentucky
Università degli studi di Cassino e del Lazio Meridionale	Uniwersytet Wrocławski
Università degli Studi di Firenze	West Virginia University

3 Challenges Faced by the ETSO Project

3.1 First Challenge: Limitations of OCR for Transcribing Ancient Spanish Manuscripts

To attempt the automatic transcription of ancient documents, there is a common process known as Optical Character Recognition (OCR). OCR is used for digitally converting modern texts with high efficiency, but it did not serve ETSO's specific purposes. The typefaces used in printing do not correspond to the typography employed today, and OCR processes, trained to recognise modern fonts, do not achieve the desired accuracy when the manuscripts are handwritten in the Spanish orthography of the fifteenth to sixteenth centuries. Moreover, in the case of ancient manuscripts, traditional OCR methods struggle to transcribe even a single word accurately (similar references can be found, for example, in [11]). Working with these automatic transcriptions would ultimately require more effort than transcribing directly from scratch, manually [12].

3.2 *Second Challenge: Modernising Archaic Spellings for Corpus Compatibility*

Additionally, the ETSO team needed to consider the challenging issue of spelling. To meet the ETSO's specific interests, the spelling of the works needed to be modernised, that is, updated to modern Spanish orthography. Only then can they be compared with the rest of the corpus, or body of literature already modernised by human teams, where the spelling adheres to current norms. Even if the automatic transcription process via OCR were flawless and managed to transcribe letters and words precisely, the resulting text would not serve ETSO's specific purposes because of the mismatch between current and old meanings. In other words, the transcription would be technically valid, but the words transcribed would remain in a state where they cannot be compared to other words in works currently in the corpus.

3.3 *Third Challenge: Inaccessibility of Digitised Golden Age Theatre Texts for Stylometric Analysis*

The vast quantity of printed and manuscript works—hundreds or even thousands—of Golden Age theatre, although digitised and housed in valuable portals such as the BNE or the Virtual Library Miguel de Cervantes, could not be used for analysis because they were not transcribed. In other words, the text could not be read or understood by the computer, making it impossible to utilise these works for stylometric analyses. Therefore, thousands of theatrical pieces that should have been included in ETSO were excluded from the project's reach.

Quoting Dr. Cuéllar while explaining the challenge ([13]: 102):

> ["In Figure 1, we can see an example of a typical page from a printed work of Golden Age theater, in this case from the play *Duelos de amor y lealtad* by playwright Calderón de la Barca. As evident, the typography, except for occasional peculiarities typical of such documents, is clear and legible for any modern reader, making transcription straightforward. However, standard computer processes are not equipped for handling this type of text."
>
> "We also observe an example in Figure 2 of typical pages from a manuscript, such as that of the anonymous work *La francesa Laura*. Immediately, the complexity of manuscripts becomes apparent—often with elevated reading difficulty or fragments impossible to transcribe even for trained historians or philologists."]

3.4 *Fourth Challenge: Inaccessibility of Digitised Golden Age Theatre Texts for Stylometric Analysis*

In 2020, Transkribus did not have any pre-existing models for recognising Spanish, so it was necessary to build one from scratch. The first step involved training the tool in print recognition, which led to the creation of the initial recognition model called Spanish Golden Age Prints 1.0. This model is now available for use by the research community. Additionally, a later, refined version of the model, incorporating modernised spelling to align with current Spanish, can also be freely utilised through the READ-COOP platform (see https://readcoop.eu/model/spanish-golden-age-prints-1-0/ and https://readcoop.eu/model/spanish-golden-age-theatre-prints-spelling-modernization-1-0/).

3.5 *Fifth Challenge: Developing Custom AI Models for Spanish Golden Age Texts*

Even with the proper tools to recognise print from old works, different errors in the resulting texts arise due to a range of reasons: especially cumbersome handwriting, the presence of crossed-out sections, document dirtiness, the translucency of the opposite side, and the luck (or lack thereof) of having the AI tools trained with documents of similar handwriting.

3.6 *Sixth Challenge: Increased Complexity and Error Rates in Manuscript Transcriptions*

Manuscripts are much more challenging than printed works and present additional complexities (see [11, 14]). Consequently, there is a significant increment in the number of errors in the automatic transcriptions of this type of text.

3.7 *Seventh Challenge: Ensuring Accuracy in Stylometric Analyses of Transcriptions*

In the case of printed works and manuscripts, automatic transcriptions can be used for stylometric analyses. However, the results must be handled cautiously due to the error percentage obtained by the recognition tool. In ETSO's example, the automatic transcription of some manuscripts revealed a very strong stylometric relationship with the repertoire of Lope de Vega—this playwright is the focus of the project up to now. He is, together with Miguel de Cervantes, the author of El Quijote, at the culprit of Spanish literature. They used the model-generated transcription as the base text for manual corrections and repeated the tests. These confirmed the initial result and associated the work with Lope's corpus across various analyses. Additionally, an intensive philological investigation led to the attribution of at least one anonymous work to this author.

4 Results of the ETSO Project

In synthesis, the ETSO project has advanced the preservation and study of Spain's Golden Age theatre through the innovative application of AI, bridging tradition and technology. In collaboration with the National Library of Spain (BNE), the project has successfully transcribed, modernised, and analysed a vast corpus of historical texts, uncovering hidden literary treasures such as the attribution of *La francesa Laura* and *Mujeres y criados* to Lope de Vega. By leveraging tools like Transkribus [4, 8] and Stylo [5], and fostering interdisciplinary collaboration among philologists, historians, and technologists, ETSO has overcome challenges in digitisation and transcription accuracy. Its efforts have not only enhanced access to these cultural assets for scholars and the public but have also set new standards for AI-driven research in the humanities.

Through this transformative work, ETSO exemplifies how technology can enrich cultural heritage and inspire deeper engagement with history [2, 3, 13, 14]. We now present these results in greater detail.

4.1 ETSO and the National Library of Spain: Bridging Heritage and Innovation

The Golden Age theatre represents a cornerstone of Spain's cultural history and universal dramaturgy, renowned for its artistic brilliance, a prolific array of authors and works, societal reach, and enduring global influence. Its legacy continues to thrive on contemporary stages, affirming its timeless appeal.

In this context, the BNE plays a pivotal role in preserving and studying this rich heritage. As the custodian of the world's most extensive collection of manuscripts and printed materials from the Golden Age theatre, the BNE provides unparalleled insights into this era's theatrical landscape. The ETSO project complements the BNE's efforts by uncovering critical aspects of the theatre's historical context, cementing its status as an invaluable cultural heritage. Furthermore, ETSO emphasises its relevance in modern performance, academic research, and the integration of cutting-edge technologies for preservation and dissemination.

ETSO aligns with the BNE's broader strategy to digitise and make its collections accessible for research. This mission peaked with the comprehensive digitisation of the Golden Age Theater Collection, which has been systematically made available online through the Biblioteca Digital Hispánica and Hemeroteca Digital portals since 2009. As former BNE director Ms. Ana Santos Aramburu aptly stated, "We are aware that the digitisation of culture serves to create wealth and has economic value in addition to its cultural significance" [15].

In collaboration with the research group on Lope de Vega PROLOPE [10], the BNE has undertaken long-term digitisation efforts, integrated within broader initiatives such as the Recognition and Enrichment of Archival Documents (READ) project [7, 8]. These initiatives have pioneered advancements in Handwritten Text Recognition (HTR), Key Word Spotting, Layout Analysis, and Automatic Writer Identification, setting new benchmarks for the preservation and exploration of historical texts [6, 9, 11–14]. Through these efforts, the ETSO project not only preserves the legacy of Spain's Golden Age theatre but also redefines how it is studied and appreciated in the digital age.

4.2 Unveiling Value Creation and Collaboration in the ETSO Project

The ETSO project exemplifies a transformative integration of technology and humanities, demonstrating how value creation and collaboration can uncover cultural heritage's hidden treasures. Leveraging advanced AI tools like Transkribus, the project has significantly enhanced the analysis of historical texts, enabling discoveries such as attributing La francesa Laura and Mujeres y criados to Lope de Vega. This achievement underscores the project's ability to unlock invaluable insights that traditional methods could not have accomplished alone.

Collaboration is at the heart of ETSO's success, involving diverse stakeholders, including scholars, students, collectors, and the BNE itself, under the leadership of Dr. Cuéllar. This co-creation effort has resulted in tools like CETSO, a corpus of transcribed works, and TEXORO, a search engine designed to facilitate text analysis, which together provide a robust foundation for future research.

The use of AI in the ETSO project has reduced researchers' workload by automating transcription and has also fostered a collaborative ecosystem where technology and human expertise converge. Researchers, technologists, and cultural institutions work together to refine AI models, ensuring accuracy while enabling rapid transcription of previously inaccessible texts. This co-creation process amplifies the value of AI tools, as they are continuously improved through interdisciplinary input and active engagement from a diverse network of stakeholders. By integrating technological innovation with collective human effort, ETSO exemplifies how collaboration can drive meaningful advancements in preserving and understanding cultural heritage, creating both public and academic value.

4.3 Unlocking Heritage Through AI: Lessons from the ETSO Project

The ETSO project has demonstrated that AI can facilitate large-scale projects, but its success heavily relies on initial human input. Tools like Transkribus and Stylo have significantly accelerated the transcription of historical texts, achieving high levels of accuracy—up to 97% for printed texts. However, human expertise remains essential for training these models, correcting errors, and ensuring continuous improvement.

Collaboration across disciplines has been another cornerstone of the ETSO project. By bringing together researchers, libraries, and digital service providers, AI tools created a shared platform where philologists, historians, and technologists could contribute their expertise. This collaboration highlights the potential of AI to act as a catalyst for interdisciplinary research and innovation.

The project also revealed critical challenges in handling historical data. Optical Character Recognition (OCR), typically used for modern texts, struggled with older typefaces and handwritten manuscripts. Additionally, modernising archaic spelling to align with current linguistic norms posed significant difficulties. These challenges underscore the need for AI tools to be tailored to the specific historical and linguistic contexts they aim to address.

AI has proven to be a powerful tool for discovery in the ETSO project, uncovering previously unattributed works, such as *La francesa Laura* and *Mujeres y criados*, which were attributed to Lope de Vega. This success highlights AI's potential to unlock new insights in historical and literary research, provided it is integrated with traditional analytical methods to validate findings.

The iterative nature of AI development has been another important lesson from ETSO. The team initially developed the Spanish Golden Age Prints 1.0 recognition model, which was later refined to include modernised spelling. This process illustrates the need for ongoing adaptation and refinement in AI-driven research projects to meet evolving goals and challenges.

Lastly, the ETSO project exemplifies the co-creation of public value through AI. By transcribing and modernising vast collections of manuscripts and printed works, the project has made these historical texts accessible not only to scholars but also to the public. This aligns with the BNE's mission to preserve and democratise access to cultural heritage, demonstrating the societal and educational potential of AI in fostering broader engagement with historical assets.

5 Conclusions

The ETSO project has emerged as a ground-breaking initiative that bridges the gap between technology and the humanities, positioning the National Library of Spain (BNE) as a leader in the digital preservation and analysis of cultural heritage. By addressing the pressing challenge of transcribing and modernising Spanish Golden Age theatrical texts, ETSO has significantly advanced our ability to uncover and analyse historical treasures. This project showcases how artificial intelligence can be a powerful enabler of large-scale cultural heritage projects, fostering interdisciplinary collaboration and democratising access to historical texts (a complete summary of the ETSO project can be found in Table 3).

Table 3 BNE: ETSO project—stylometry applied to Golden Age theatre

<table>
<tr><th>Country</th><th>Number of employees</th><th>Type of AI solution</th><th>Year and Maturity level</th></tr>
<tr><td>Spain</td><td>667 (as of the time of writing)</td><td>Transkribus, to automatically transcribe and modernise old prints and manuscripts with a high degree of accuracy
Stylo, to relate texts based on their lexical usage
Other stylometric techniques based on AI to process texts</td><td>2017
Implemented and ongoing</td></tr>
<tr><td colspan="4">Project description</td></tr>
<tr><td colspan="4">Thanks to the AI-powered tool Transkribus (READ-COOP, 2024) and its Handwritten Text Recognition (HTR) techniques, Dr. Cuéllar and the ETSO team have trained three models, which are being used and refined by the research community, capable of automatically transcribing and modernising these documents with a high degree of accuracy: approximately 97% accuracy for printed texts and 91% for manuscripts. Through these models, ETSO has processed around 1800+ theatrical works contained in prints and manuscripts from numerous libraries, archives, and other digitised sources. The resulting transcriptions are now part of the CETSO Corpus and the TEXORO search engine, both part of the ETSO project. Moreover, they possess sufficient quality to undergo stylometric analysis, which reveals interesting authorship attributions</td></tr>
<tr><td>Need(s) behind implementation</td><td>Actors involved</td><td colspan="2">Challenges</td></tr>
<tr><td>To automatically transcribe the Spanish Golden Age documents for stylometric analyses able to establish trusted authorship attributions</td><td>• Dr. Álvaro Cuéllar (Universitat Autònoma de Barcelona) and Dr. Germán Vega García-Luengos (University of Valladolid)
• Their teams
• The research group on Lope de Vega PROLOPE (Universidad Autónoma de Barcelona)
200+ researchers, students, experts, and collectors from 40+ institutions and private collections</td><td colspan="2">OCR limitations: Struggled with historical typefaces and handwritten manuscripts, often making manual transcription more efficient
Modernising spelling: Essential to align texts with modernised corpora for meaningful comparisons
Inaccessible works: Many Golden Age texts remained unavailable for analysis due to lack of transcription
AI model development: Spanish Golden Age Prints 1.0 enabled accurate transcription, later refined to include modernised spelling
Persistent errors: Issues like handwriting, crossed-out sections, and document quality caused inaccuracies
Manuscript complexity: Handwritten texts had higher error rates than printed works
Stylometry challenges: Required caution due to tool errors and potential biases in authorship attribution</td></tr>
</table>

Table 3 (continued)

Country	Number of employees	Type of AI solution	Year and Maturity level
Results			
Bridging Heritage and Innovation	**Unveiling value creation and collaboration**	**Unlocking Heritage Through AI**	
The Golden Age theatre, a cornerstone of Spain's cultural history, continues to thrive as a timeless artistic legacy. The BNE plays a vital role in preserving this heritage, housing the world's largest collection of Golden Age theatre manuscripts and printed works. Complementing these efforts, the ETSO project uses cutting-edge technologies to digitise, analyse, and modernise these texts, ensuring their accessibility for research and performance. In collaboration with the Lope de Vega PROLOPE group and initiatives like the READ project, ETSO has pioneered advancements in Handwritten Text Recognition and digital analysis, redefining the study and preservation of this invaluable cultural legacy	The ETSO project exemplifies the transformative potential of integrating technology and humanities, using AI tools like Transkribus to uncover cultural heritage treasures, such as attributing works to Lope de Vega. Its success is rooted in collaboration among scholars, students, and institutions, resulting in resources like the CETSO corpus and TEXORO search engine. By combining technological innovation with human expertise, ETSO reduces transcription workloads while fostering interdisciplinary co-creation, advancing the preservation and understanding of cultural heritage for public and academic benefit	The ETSO project demonstrates how AI can facilitate large-scale cultural heritage projects by accelerating transcription and analysis of historical texts, though human expertise remains essential for training models and ensuring accuracy. Collaboration across disciplines has been key, creating a shared platform for researchers and technologists to address challenges like handling historical typefaces and modernising archaic spelling. ETSO's AI tools have uncovered previously unattributed works and highlighted the importance of iterative development and refinement. By democratising access to cultural heritage, the project aligns with the BNE's mission, showcasing AI's potential to enhance both scholarly research and public engagement	

In answering the research question of how AI can be effectively leveraged to enhance the accessibility and understanding of Golden Age theatre, ETSO provides a clear and compelling response. Through innovative tools like Transkribus and the development of the CETSO corpus and TEXORO search engine, the project has transformed inaccessible manuscripts into digitised resources available for scholarly and public engagement. These efforts underscore the importance of integrating technological innovation with collaborative human expertise to address complex challenges in cultural heritage preservation.

The key lessons learned from ETSO emphasise the value of co-creation and collaboration across diverse stakeholders, including researchers, technologists, cultural institutions, and students. This synergy has not only facilitated the refinement of AI models but also demonstrated the potential for technology to unlock new avenues for literary and historical research. The project also highlights the iterative nature of AI development, where continuous improvement and stakeholder input are critical for success.

Despite its accomplishments, ETSO has faced challenges, such as adapting AI to handle historical typefaces, handwritten manuscripts, and archaic spellings. These challenges underscore the need for tailored solutions in historical research and signal opportunities for further development. Moving forward, the National Library of Spain can build on ETSO's success by expanding the scope of its digital humanities projects. Potential follow-up initiatives could include applying similar methodologies to other historical collections or enhancing public engagement through interactive digital platforms.

The outcomes of ETSO reinforce the BNE's mission to preserve and democratise access to cultural heritage. The digitisation and analysis of Golden Age theatre texts have not only preserved a critical aspect of Spain's cultural history but have also set a benchmark for integrating AI into the humanities. By creating tools and resources that serve both academic and public audiences, the project has demonstrated the transformative potential of combining technology with cultural stewardship. As the BNE looks to the future, its commitment to innovation and collaboration will be essential in continuing to unlock the value of Spain's cultural heritage for generations to come.

Acknowledgements The work for this chapter was supported by the European Union's Horizon Europe Research and Innovation Programme under Grant Agreement ID 101061516.

References

1. BNE, Bibliotecas, datos, inteligencia artificial: las nuevas rutas del conocimiento. Conference agenda (2023), https://www.bne.es/sites/default/files/repositorio-archivos/programa_jornada_ia_0.pdf and https://www.bne.es/es/agenda/bibliotecas-datos-inteligencia-artificial-nuevas-rutas-conocimiento
2. ETSO, Herramienta TRANSKRIBUS y la Estilometría aplicada al Teatro del Siglo de Oro. Presentation in Bibliotecas, datos, inteligencia artificial: las nuevas rutas del conocimiento (2023), https://www.youtube.com/watch?v=76uQN8jMenU.min12.41-40.31
3. ETSO (2024), https://etso.es/. Accessed 1 Apr 2024
4. G. Mueühlberger, L. Seaward, M. Terras, S. Ares Oliveira, V. Bosch, M. Bryan, S. Colutto, H. Déjean, M. Diem, S. Fiel, B. Gatos, T. Grüning, A. Greinoecker, G. Hackl, V. Haukkovaara, G. Heyer, L. Hirvonen, T. Hodel, M. Jokinen, P. Kahle, M. Kallio, F. Kaplan, K. Florian, R. Labahn, E.M. Lang, S. Laube, G. Leifert, G. Louloudis, R. McNicholl, J.-L. Meunier, J. Michael, E. Mühlbauer, N. Philipp, I. Pratikakis, J. Puigcerver Pérez, H. Putz, G. Retsinas, V. Romero, R. Sablatnig, J.A. Sánchez, P. Schofield, G. Sfikas, C. Sieber, N. Stamatopoulos, T. Strauß, T. Terbul, A.H. Toselli, B. Ulreich, M. Villegas, E. Vidal, J. Walcher, M. Weidemann, H. Wurster, K. Zagoris, Transforming scholarship in the archives through handwritten text recognition: Transkribus as a case study. J. Doc. **75**(5), 954–976 (2019). https://doi.org/10.1108/JD-07-2018-0114
5. M. Eder, J. Rybicki, M. Kestemont, Stylometry with R: a package for computational text. R J **8**(1), 107–121 (2016)
6. L. Padró, E. Stanilovsky, FreeLing 3.0: towards wider multilinguality, in *Proceedings of the Language Resources and Evaluation Conference (LREC 2012)*, (2012)
7. READ, The Recognition and Enrichment of Archival Documents (READ) project (n.d.), https://eadh.org/projects/read
8. READ-COOP (2024), https://readcoop.eu/. Accessed 1 Apr 2024
9. PRHLT (2024), HTR Website: https://www.prhlt.upv.es/handwritten-text-recognition/. Accessed 1 Apr 2024
10. UAB, *El Grupo Prolope, Colaborador de la Exposición Lope y el Teatro del Siglo de Oro* (UAB Sala de Prensa, 2018), https://www.uab.cat/web/sala-de-prensa/detalle-noticia/el-grupo-prolope-colaborador-de-la-exposicion-em-lope-y-el-teatro-del-siglo-de-oro-/em-1345667994339.html?noticiaid=1345778034284
11. P. Smith, *Handwritten Text Recognition of the Dunhuang Manuscripts: The Challenges of Machine Learning on Ancient Chinese Texts* (British Library, 2024), https://blogs.bl.uk/digital-scholarship/2024/03/handwritten-text-recognition-of-the-dunhuang-manuscripts.html
12. CoMUN-HaT, CoMUN-HaT: Contexto, multimodalidad y colaboración del usuario en procesado de texto manuscrito (2016), https://www.prhlt.upv.es/comun-hat-contexto-multimodalidad-y-colaboracion-del-usuario-en-procesado-de-texto-manuscrito/
13. A. Cuéllar, La Inteligencia Artificial al rescate del Siglo de Oro: transcripción y modernización automática de mil trescientos impresos y manuscritos teatrales. Hipogrifo (2023). https://doi.org/10.13035/H.2023.11.01.08
14. A. Cuéllar, *Cronología y Estilometría: Datación Automática de Comedias de Lope de Vega*, Texto, literatura, cultura, XXIX (Anuario Lope de Vega, 2022). https://doi.org/10.5565/rev/anuariolopedevega.483
15. A. Muñoz, Tecnología al rescate del Siglo de Oro. El Independiente (2018) https://www.elindependiente.com/tendencias/cultura/2018/11/27/tecnologia-al-rescate-siglo-de-oro/

Alberto Peralta is currently a researcher in the Department of Business and Economics, University of Alcala (Spain). He is also an assistant professor at Abu Dhabi University (UAE). Alberto does research in sustainable business model innovation, entrepreneurial economics, and value co-creation (innovation) in the public and private sectors. He also teaches strategic innovation, lean startup, and the creation of sustainable business models at several institutions.

Assessing Nineteenth-Century Library Collections with the "Living with Machines" Project at the British Library, United Kingdom

Justus Kühler and Ines Mergel

Abstract As part of its commitment to innovation and to improve the accessibility of the library's collection of resources from the long nineteenth century, the British Library ran the "Living with Machines" project between 2018 and 2023. The Library's project uses Artificial Intelligence (AI) technologies to improve access to historical collections. The library faced the challenge of making the extensive collections easier to interact and more accessible to users. The project was initiated to explore how AI and machine learning (ML) would impact historical research, with a particular focus on the impact of mechanisation in the nineteenth century. The project team was gathered from 2018 to July 2019. The project involved over 5500 volunteers and engaged the public through crowdsourcing tasks. The collaboration spanned various disciplines, including data scientists, historians and research software developers. The British Library also reached out to the public to ask for their help in commenting on the artefacts. Collaboration challenges arose when staff did not spend enough time understanding each other's disciplines. According to the interviewees, librarians will need a solid grounding in "information organisation" when it comes to working with AI solutions and outputs.

Keywords Digitisation of historical data · AI cataloguing · National Library · British Library · Artificial intelligence · AI · Living with Machines · Volunteers · User engagement

---

J. Kühler
Department of Politics and Public Administration, University of Konstanz, Konstanz, Germany
e-mail: justus.kuehler@uni-konstanz.de

I. Mergel (✉)
Department of Politics and Public Administration, University of Konstanz, Konstanz, Germany

Fraunhofer FOKUS, Fraunhofer Institute for Open Communication Systems, Berlin, Germany

School of Management, Public Management, University of Vaasa, Vaasa, Finland
e-mail: ines.mergel@uni-konstanz.de

I. Mergel, C. Schmidt (eds.), *AI Innovations in Public Services*,
https://doi.org/10.1007/978-3-032-01344-6_12

1 Introduction

The British Library, based in London, is the national library of the United Kingdom and one of the largest libraries in the world. It houses approximately 170–200 million items from various countries. It was founded on 1 July 1973 under the British Library Act 1972 and was formerly part of the British Museum. Today, the library employs around 1700 staff, and it had a budget of over 177.4 million euros in the financial year 2022/2023 [1].

As part of its programme for innovation and accessibility, the British Library launched the "Living with Machines" project running from 2018 to 2023. This initiative used machine learning (ML) to analyse and interpret extensive historical datasets [2]. Therefore, the project made use of solutions such as Computer Vision, a broad term for analysing and describing patterns in visual content [3]. Optical Character Recognition (OCR) and Natural Language Processing (NLP) were used to digitise newspaper materials: "*In Living with Machines, we did a lot of different experiments using things like computer vision and natural language processing that have specific uses for different kinds of research projects. We'll collaborate a lot with people where they're applying a particular method on a specific collection, and we help assemble the collection that they could use for that work, and then we can publish datasets that are derived from that project or machine learning models and other outputs on our research repository.*" By digitising archive material such as newspapers and maps, the project made these resources accessible for research purposes and at the same time tackled bias in historical data. During the project, the organisation developed and tested AI models for tasks such as named entity recognition and the digitisation of the library's extensive collections. The project strengthened interdisciplinary collaboration between specialists from different research fields such as historians, data scientists and linguists. In line with the British Library's mission, the project fostered collaboration between the Alan Turing Institute, partner universities and the British Library. User engagement was also at stake during the Living with Machines project. Users interacted with the library's existing datasets, helping to improve their accuracy and quality.

2 Description of the Project

The project in the British Library was initiated to address challenges in managing vast and diverse collections, driven by the need to enhance access, improve discoverability and understand the impact of digitisation on user engagement. It also was initiated to explore the impact of AI and ML on historical research, focusing on the effects of mechanisation in the mid-nineteenth century. It aimed to anticipate future transformations in research methodologies and access to historical data. It was launched through collaboration between the Alan Turing Institute, which is the British Institute for Data Science, including AI and the British Library. The project was funded by the Arts and Humanities Research Council (AHRC) [4].

Initiated in 2018, the team was assembled gradually, completing its composition by July of the following year. Involving over 5500 volunteers, the project engaged the public through crowdsourcing tasks. One interviewee described the involvement of diverse volunteers as follows: "*I think that the point was that people who volunteered on Zooniverse weren't necessarily self-consciously museum goers, unlike people who went to the exhibition. So, it was a really new group of audiences to the library and to the Turing who hadn't previously had any relationship with either of the institutions.*" Collaboration spanned disciplines, including data scientists, historians and research software engineers, with members joining gradually between 2018 and 2019 within the team of the British Library [5].

2.1 Need(s) Behind the Implementation

The British Library project uses AI to improve access to historical collections. The goal was to explore the impact of AI and ML on historical research. The interviewee states that there are two reasons which motivate the experimentation with AI that is to (1) improve the accessibility of collections and (2) to use these resources as data and create some sort of public value: "*There's two ways that I think about AI in the library; one is improving our ability to make our collections more findable, getting people to collection items that they can then use for their research, to find stories for creative uses, entrepreneurial uses, whatever. The other is people using our collections as datasets and studying them for their form rather than as individual items.*"

Therefore, it can be interpreted that it aims to make collections more accessible, provide contextual understanding and ensure inclusiveness in accessing historical materials. Also, for people not visiting the library that much: "*I think that the point was that people who volunteered on Zooniverse weren't necessarily self-consciously museum-goers, unlike people who went to the exhibition. So, it was a really new group of audiences to the library and to the Turing who hadn't previously had any relationship with either of the institutions.*"

2.2 Actors Involved

The project was made possible by the collaboration of the Alan Turing Institute, the British Library, the Arts and Humanities Research Council (AHRC) and several universities in the UK.

Involving over 5500 volunteers, the project engaged the public through crowdsourcing tasks. One project member explained: "*The main point of public interaction was the crowdsourcing work that we did where we designed crowdsourcing tasks where the annotations that people/members of the public made would contribute to the building of a research dataset that would either be used to train a machine learning model and expand up our queries or used as an output in its own. The trick there was understanding what kinds of results would be useful for different disciplines in the project.*"

From an organisational perspective, the project was financed by the UK Research and Innovation (UKRI) Strategic Priority Fund, which comprises a total of around 988 million euros. Around 1% of the entire fund was allocated to the "Living with Machines" project at the British Library, around 11 million euros (approx. 9.2 million Pounds) [6].

The project was conducted highly interdisciplinary, including data science, history and research engineering. This fostered collaboration between the Alan Turing Institute, partner universities and the British Library. Based on Mergel et al. (2025) [7], we identified the following co-production phases in the implementation of AI (Table 1):

2.2.1 Organisational Level

The project received backing from the Alan Turing Institute and AHRC, securing funding from the UK Research and Innovation (UKRI) Strategic Priority Fund. In addition, the British Library collaborated with other UK institutions from the GLAM (Galleries, Libraries, Archives and Museums) sector, such as the National Football Museum and the National Railway Museum, to collect items researched and collected by the British Library's interdisciplinary experts [8].

Roles such as the library's project managers, data scientists, librarians and historians contributed to the project's success with their expertise and resources. This interdisciplinary approach contributed also to the main challenges of the project, missing understanding of the colleagues' work which is more time-consuming and considered to be rather boring: "*I think there was quite a lot of difficulty in finding because it was such an interdisciplinary project or multi-disciplinary project, finding things that resonated for everyone. We probably didn't spend enough time*

Table 1 Co-production process in the development and implementation of AI at the British Library

Co-initiation	Funding is provided by the UK Research and Innovation (UKRI) Strategic Priority Fund. This fund is an investment of 830 million pounds (approx. 988 million euros), which has been used to support 34 multidisciplinary and interdisciplinary research programmes in two investment waves. 9.2 million pounds (approx. 11 million euros) was made available for the "Living with Machines" project
Co-design	The project was conceived by the Alan Turing Institute, the British Library, the Arts and Humanities Research Council (AHRC) and several universities across the UK
Co-implementation	Experts from various fields such as computational linguists, historians, data scientists and librarians worked on the "Living with Machines" project and developed several data sets for further use and AI training
Co-use/production moment	The datasets were used both by the interdisciplinary library experts and by anonymous users who had free access to the datasets and used them for their own research purposes
Co-evaluation	–

sharing and really understanding what was inspiring for each other's disciplines and what the gaps were in each other's disciplines (...). So, it's not a technical issue, except for the scale of the collections, making anything a bit harder and slower. It's more of a collaboration issue where the time that it takes to coordinate and discuss takes away from time doing things, but it's also part of the work. I think we hadn't really anticipated—I think from the library, we knew, but I think for the researchers, they hadn't quite understood some of those compromises that would be necessary."

2.2.2 External Actors

The project engaged external vendors such as the Alan Turing Institute, an organisation working independently from the British Library but integrated in the same building. It was founded in 2015 as the National Institute for Data Science [8]. The close, also physical, relation between the Library and the Alan Turing Institute allowed for even closer collaboration facilitating the launch of the Living with Machines Project: "*the Alan Turing Institute is based physically in The British Library, so we knew we had an opportunity to work with all the data scientists and the cool people who were coming in to work with Turing.*"

The partners of the project were also other universities such as Cambridge, East Anglia, Exeter, Queen Mary University of London, the King's College, and the University of Edinburgh. Users and patrons, including researchers and historians, likely played a role by providing feedback, participating in crowdsourcing activities and utilising project tools for research to enrich the analytical scope and data quality. One interviewee describes this: "*They got to take part in that, and also the questions that they asked during the process really shaped how we thought about something of the work. Particularly, in the first crowdsourcing task that I designed, we asked does this accident involve the machine. Defining a machine actually turned out to be quite tricky because the 19th century definitions of the machine were different than what we would generally think of now. Even things like a potato peeler could be a machine, and we wouldn't think of a potato peeler as being a machine now.*"

2.3 *Challenges*

Despite the success of the project, it was also characterised by challenges. Challenges included interdisciplinary collaboration, technical expertise, staff rotation, copyright and access issues, and project management, but also the challenge of coordinating and agreeing on the core purpose of the project, as one of the interviewees from the library explained: "*Everyone had a different idea of what a research question is because everyone came from a different discipline.*"

The large list of internal and external collaborators was challenging. The interviewees noticed that the collaborators did not spend enough time understanding each other's disciplines and the resulting differences in methods and theoretical background: *"It's more of a collaboration issue where the time that it takes to coordinate and discuss takes away from time doing things, but it's also part of the work. I think we hadn't really anticipated—I think from the library, we knew, but I think for the researchers, they hadn't quite understood some of those compromises that would be necessary."*

Essential but perceived "boring" tasks like cleaning datasets and matching metadata were often overlooked due to the pressure on researchers to publish papers and yielding for results quickly: *"So, it was not always easy to get as much attention on those boring bits when people were felt pressure because they were on this high-profile project to also be publishing papers all the time. In some ways, it was less productive for people who were looking at how many papers they could get to add to their CV because everything is slower when you're working across disciplines and when you're doing that negotiation around what's important to you."*

2.4 New Skills for Librarians

Librarians involved in the AI projects of the British Library require a diverse skill set focusing on information literacy. Additionally, proficiency in digital tools and platforms is essential, enabling them to effectively navigate digital collections and utilise AI technologies like "machine learning" and "computer vision" tools for tasks such as "digitisation" and "metadata tagging": *"Then there's work around discovery; tagging images or tagging texts with entities/things detected by computer vision in images from books or things detected in text, people's names, places, concepts, whatever, as well as things that are more aimed at a metadata level for the whole item and not just looking at the text as a corpus. So, we bounce between different levels of where we apply these technologies and what they mean."*

However, the interviewee also emphasised that collaboration does not change just because it is collaboration with AI, but that this type of technology also requires patterns of communication and collaboration that are already in use: *"(...) there's a continuity between AI and other methods. A lot of what we did ended up being AI, but it wasn't called AI when we started doing it, partly because AI is more of a marketing term than a technical term. Providing access to sources at scale, thinking about the logistics of ingesting things, running processes at scale, queries at scale, that doesn't really change with AI."*

3 Results

3.1 Organisational Level

Overall, the project improved the accessibility and inclusivity of the library's collections, enhanced public engagement through exhibitions, workshops and crowdsourcing initiatives. But it has not fundamentally changed the organisation, as can be seen from the statement above. The research results were oriented towards the feasibility within the complex project context and the many stakeholders. Although it was an AI project, many analytical tasks and methods remained unchanged and did not change fundamentally. The interdisciplinary collaboration and communication led to an adaptation of the methods used, but also did not change fundamentally: "*There's lots of different things that have happened, but they aren't necessarily as evident from the core. The way that you interact with the library hasn't necessarily changed that much as a result of these AI pieces of work.*"

3.2 Value Created and Co-created

The focus of the Public Value creation within the British Library had its focus on increasing the accessibility of vast and extensive collections coming from the nineteenth century. Furthermore, there was also the creation of stronger interdisciplinary collaboration among humanities and data science. The synergies of both disciplines were put together in the library itself as one interviewee explained: "*One of the outcomes in the project, actually we did a few public workshops or workshops at conferences, but also we trial things with wherever we could in the digital scholarship training program so that people in the library were learning as the project learned different methods. But also so that hopefully it meant that if you did a workshop or a tutorial in public, it had a trial run with people who would give you useful feedback.*"

The already mentioned data-crowdsourcing task can be mentioned as one major outcome of the living with machines project: "*The main point of public interaction was the crowdsourcing work that we did where we designed crowdsourcing tasks where the annotations that people/members of the public made would contribute to the building of a research dataset that would either be used to train a machine learning model and expand up our queries or used as an output in its own. The results of these crowdsourcing tasks align with definition of Public Value Creation which is the result of a public sector organisation collaborating with its environment and also strengthens the individual and normative basics on which the activities of a public sector organisation rely such as accountability, accessibility and ethical behavior of employees*" [10].

3.3 Lesson Learned

The main lesson that was learnt is to promote project members' understanding of their tasks. This is critical when it comes to the production of research results and the phases that involve solving tasks that are perceived as rather "boring". In connection with this realisation, the interviewee also states that the time pressure in the research process promotes this development of a lack of understanding: "*I think there was quite a lot of difficulty in finding because it was such an interdisciplinary project or multi-disciplinary project, finding things that resonated for everyone. We probably didn't spend enough time sharing and really understanding what was inspiring for each other's disciplines and what the gaps were in each other's disciplines, because things that are really established in one field might be new in another. But also, a lot of the practical work, because everyone was a researcher, even the software engineers were publishing papers based on their work. Some of the really boring stuff isn't necessarily something that you can publish a paper on.*"

4 Conclusion

The Living with Machines Project started in 2018 with the collaboration of the British Library, the Alan Turing Institute and the Arts and Humanities Research Council (AHRC) with the goal of enhancing interdisciplinary collaboration by using new technologies such as AI. The narrower focus of the project was to explore resources and extensive collections from the British Library, coming from the "long nineteenth century", making resources such as maps and newspapers available for the broader research community.

Beginning in 2018/2019, the initiative utilised Computer Vision, natural language processing (NLP) and optical character recognition (OCR) technologies to achieve its goals. It brought together interdisciplinary teams, including the Digital Research Team, data scientists, historians and research software engineers, as well as over 5500 public volunteers engaged through crowdsourcing tasks. While the collaborative effort was key to the project's success, it also presented challenges. These included difficulties in achieving mutual understanding between disciplines, delays caused by coordination and negotiation efforts, and overlooked technical tasks, such as cleaning datasets and matching metadata, due to the pressure on researchers to publish. Additional challenges stemmed from staff rotation, copyright restrictions and balancing preparation with the delivery of project milestones.

Despite these obstacles, the project created substantial value. It increased the public engagement with historical data resources, strengthened interdisciplinary collaboration with external and internal actors and made the library's collection more accessible for patrons.

Several key lessons emerged from the initiative: Effective interdisciplinary collaboration required early resource allocation. Balancing the need for timely delivery with adequate preparation can mitigate delays and improve outcomes. Overall, the project underscores the potential of AI to transform historical research while maintaining a focus on inclusion and innovation in the digital age.

Acknowledgements The work for this chapter was supported by the European Union's Horizon Europe Research and Innovation Programme under Grant Agreement ID 101061516.

Appendix

See Table 2.

Table 2 Overview of the AI project at the British Library

Case and project name			
British Library			
Country	**Number of employees**	**Type of AI solution**	**Year and maturity level**
United Kingdom	1700 (2011)	Natural Language Processing/OCR	Starting year 2018/2019
Project description			
The project at the British Library was initiated to address challenges in managing vast and diverse collections, driven by the need to enhance access, improve discoverability and understand the impact of digitisation on user engagement. Aligned with the library's mission, it aims to make collections more accessible, provide contextual understanding and ensure inclusivity in accessing historical materials			
Need(s) behind implementation	**Actors involved**	**Challenges**	
The project was initiated to address the challenges of managing large and diverse collections driven by the need to improve access, increase discoverability and understand the impact of digitisation on user engagement	It involved collaboration between the Alan Turing Institute, partner universities and the British Library Involving over 5500 volunteers, the project engaged the public through crowdsourcing tasks. Collaboration spanned disciplines, including data scientists, historians and research software engineers	Team members sometimes did not spend enough time understanding each other's disciplines and their gaps Mundane tasks like cleaning datasets and matching metadata were often overlooked due to the pressure on researchers to publish papers. Collaboration slowed progress due to the time needed for coordination and negotiation	
Results			
Organisational level	**Value created and co-created**	**Lesson learned**	
Overall, the collaboration required adapting to these methods but didn't fundamentally change due to AI Although many tasks involved AI, it wasn't initially labelled as such. The core methods and technical data management remained consistent, whether AI or other computational techniques were used	Encompasses access and inclusion, education and awareness, community engagement and fostering innovation It strengthened initiatives such as exhibitions, crowdsourcing, workshops and innovation These values are in accordance with the institution's strategic mission	Lessons learned include fostering interdisciplinary collaboration, early resource allocation, balancing speed with preparation, ensuring long-term technical support, raising staff awareness and promoting knowledge sharing	

References

1. British Library, *Corporate Report British Library Annual Report and Accounts 2022–23* (British Library, 2023)
2. R. Ahnert, The living with machines report (2023)
3. V. Wiley, T. Lucas, Computer vision and image processing: a paper review. Int. J. Artif. Intell. Res. **2**, 22 (2018)
4. T.A.T Institute, Living with machines (2025), https://www.turing.ac.uk/research/research-projects/living-machines. Accessed 19 Feb 2025
5. L.w. Machines, Understanding history with new eyes (2025), https://livingwithmachines.ac.uk/about/. Accessed 19 Feb 2025
6. U.R.a. Innovation, Living with machines (2025), https://gtr.ukri.org/projects?ref=AH%2FS01179X%2F1. Accessed 19 Feb 2025
7. I. Mergel, N. Edelmann, N. Haug, Co-production phases in the development and implementation of digital public services. Perspect. Public Manag. Govern. **8**(2), 93–105 (2025)
8. Living with Machines exhibition (2025), https://livingwithmachines.ac.uk/living-with-machines-exhibition/. Accessed 19 Feb 2025
9. Alan Turing Institute, About us (2025), https://www.turing.ac.uk/about-us#:~:text=The%20Alan%20Turing%20Institute%2C%20headquartered,artificial%20intelligence%20to%20our%20remit. Accessed 19 Feb 2025
10. N. Haug, I. Mergel, Public value co-creation in living labs—results from three case studies. Admin. Sci. **11**(3), 74 (2021)

Justus Kühler is studying for a bachelor's degree in political science and public administration at the University of Konstanz. He is particularly interested in the latest developments in public administration that reflect the trend towards democratisation. He is particularly interested in the application of new forms of participation at the local level. He has already gained initial experience with municipal administration through his involvement in local politics.

Ines Mergel is a University Professor of Public Administration in the Department of Politics and Public Administration at the University of Konstanz and a Fellow of the National Academy of Public Administration (Class of 2018). After holding positions at the Harvard Kennedy School of Government as a Doctoral Fellow and Postdoctoral Fellow (2002–2008), Professor Mergel was awarded tenure at the Maxwell School of Citizenship and Public Affairs (Syracuse University, NY) in 2014 (2008–2014) and then served as Associate Professor with tenure (2014–2016). Professor Mergel is a member of the supervisory board of the e-Governance Academy (Estonia). Other board memberships can be found here. Professor Mergel is a founding member of the international initiative Teaching Public Service in the Digital Age, which aims to integrate digital skills into the teaching and training of public managers. As part of this initiative, Professor Mergel was appointed a Schmidt Futures Innovation Fellow in 2022.

Exploring Computational Descriptions for Metadata Creation for E-Books at the Library of Congress, United States of America

Anna-Lea Schumann, Justus Kühler, and Ines Mergel

Abstract The Library of Congress' (LoC) project "Exploring Computational Description" (ECD) is investigating the use of machine learning (ML) to create metadata for e-books that have not yet been catalogued. In-house the LC Labs carried out this initiative with the U.S. Programs, Law, and Literature Division and an external vendor. An initial budget of $250,000 from the National Digital Trust Fund was allocated for this experimental AI endeavour, prompted by a massive backlog of e-books. During the first project phase, five ML models were evaluated, and in the second project phase, human-in-the-loop prototypes that offer machine-generated terms to librarians were introduced. The integration of AI at the LoC has the potential to enhance cataloguing efficiency by automating repetitive tasks, thereby allowing librarians to focus more on intellectual tasks. At the same time, the project faced several challenges, including ensuring the reliability of AI-generated records, copyright concerns, and managing potentially harmful language in older texts used for training the models. Improving the accuracy of these models remains essential and depends on access to extensive digital data. However, human expertise remains crucial for ensuring high quality, and librarians need to develop a foundational understanding of ML to leverage these technologies effectively. The aim of the project is to develop innovative approaches that contribute to improving library practices.

A.-L. Schumann · J. Kühler
Department of Politics and Public Administration, University of Konstanz, Konstanz, Germany
e-mail: anna-lea.schumann@uni-konstanz.de; Justus.kuehler@uni-konstanz.de

I. Mergel (✉)
Department of Politics and Public Administration, University of Konstanz, Konstanz, Germany

Fraunhofer FOKUS, Fraunhofer Institute for Open Communication Systems, Berlin, Germany

School of Management, Public Management, University of Vaasa, Vaasa, Finland
e-mail: ines.mergel@uni-konstanz.de

I. Mergel, C. Schmidt (eds.), *AI Innovations in Public Services*,
https://doi.org/10.1007/978-3-032-01344-6_13

Keywords Library of Congress · Machine Learning · Metadata Creation · Cataloguing Automation · Human-in-the-loop · Digital Transformation · AI Ethics · Co-Production

1 Introduction

The Library of Congress (LoC), established in 1800 in Washington, D.C., is the de facto National Library of the United States. Initially housing a collection of legal texts in the Capitol Building, the LoC faced devastation during the War of 1812 when the British set the building ablaze, destroying its holdings. Following this, Thomas Jefferson sold his extensive and diverse personal collection of books and maps to Congress, laying the foundation for the library's broader scope. The LoC expanded rapidly over the years, aided by milestones such as the 1870 US Copyright Deposit Act, which significantly broadened its acquisitions. To accommodate its growing collection, iconic buildings such as the Thomas Jefferson Building (1897), the John Adams Building (1938), and the James Madison Memorial Building (1981) were constructed [1]. Beyond its physical collections, the LoC encompasses specialised facilities like the National Audio-Visual Conservation Center and initiatives such as the National Library Services for Blind and Disabled, the US Copyright Office, and the Congressional Research Service [1]. The LoC has more than 3000 permanent employees [1].

In recent years, the LoC has emphasised digital transformation and innovation. The Digital Strategy Directorate spearheads efforts in leveraging emerging technologies, collaborating with internal and external partners, and fostering modernisation through its strategic plan, "A Library for All: The FY2024–2028 Strategic Plan for the Library of Congress" [2]. Central to these initiatives is the Digital Innovation Division (LC Labs), launched in 2016, which drives experimentation and research. Since 2018, LC Labs has been instrumental in developing and accessing artificial intelligence (AI) tools for data management, accessibility, and analysis, reflecting the LoC's commitment to embracing technological advancements and addressing their implications [3].

This chapter explores how the LoC utilises machine learning (ML) for cataloguing. We focus especially on the "Exploring Computational Description" (ECD) project and examine how the library managed the project's first two phases, ECD1 and ECD2. First, we outline the necessity for an AI-based cataloguing solution and provide an overview of various AI-driven projects at the LoC. Next, we delve into the "Exploring Computational Description" project. We highlight the different actors involved in the project and the skills and competencies required for librarians. Additionally, we discuss the challenges and the value that has been (co-)created through the project execution. Finally, we conclude by sharing the lessons learned.

1.1 Need Behind the Implementation

Libraries are essential and trustable institutions for citizens and the public: "*The Library of Congress and libraries in general for the most part are still seen as trustworthy.*" Therefore, as one interviewee stated, it is important to "*just get our stuff into people's lives more easily, get ourselves out of the way, and make things more exciting. But then also this alternative model of attention to care for information integrity or truth.*"

To achieve LoC's vision of connecting all Americans to the library, LoC must explore new approaches that could significantly change its practices [2, 4]. The LC Labs are responsible for trying new methods, approaches, and technologies with external partners like universities and research initiatives [4]. In the past several years, the LC labs have also started experimenting with ML and AI. Moreover, one interviewee stated: "*We've already had the idea of automation for a very long time. Machine learning is the next level of that. If you have all these routine tasks or you have this very predictive work and you have all this data to help you identify patterns, why not take advantage of it?*"

For example, the LoC has a backlog of e-books that it receives, which has come to the attention of higher library management. As a result, the Principal Deputy of the Librarian of Congress, Mark Sweeney, has earmarked $250,000 from the National Digital Trust Fund, which is separate from the money given by Congress. This fund is used to contract out experimental AI work to a vendor.

1.2 AI Solutions in the LoC

The LoC is actively exploring the potential of ML and AI through various use cases and experimental projects. Key use cases for AI include creating machine-readable text from digitised documents using optical character recognition (OCR), developing standardised catalogue records from e-books and other digital materials, extracting historical copyright data, parsing legislative data, and experimenting with ML in the National Library Service for the Blind and Print Disabled [3].

The library has conducted several experiments to date, showcasing innovative applications of AI and ML. These include the *Speech-to-Text Viewer*, collaborative explorations with the Project Aida team, and initiatives under *Experimental Access* and *Humans-in-the-Loop* [3]. Other notable projects are the *Newspaper Navigator*, *Citizen DJ*, and *America's Public Bible*: *Machine-Learning Detection of Biblical Quotations Across LoC Collections via Cloud Computing* [3]. Additionally, efforts have focused on enhancing access and discovery of documentary images and using neural networks to broaden the reach of metadata in the project *Situating Ourselves in Cultural Heritage* [3]. These initiatives demonstrate the library's commitment to leveraging AI and ML technologies to expand access to cultural heritage and improve data usability. However, this illustration focuses on the project called *Exploring Computational Description (ECD).*

2 Description of the Project

In *Exploring Computational Description (ECD)*, the LC Labs and the U.S. Programs, Law, and Literature Division in Acquisitions and Bibliographic Access Directorate are currently working on a project to determine the feasibility of using AI and ML to create descriptive metadata for e-books that have not yet been catalogued. The project consists of three project phases: ECD1, ECD2, and ECD3 [5]. It was initiated in December 2021 and sponsored by the Principal Deputy of the Librarian of Congress and co-led by the U.S. Programs, Law, and Literature Division Chief and the Sr. Innovation Specialist in LC Labs [6]. It began in the Summer 2022 and involves collaboration with an external vendor, Digirati. The overall research question in the first project phase (ECD1) was: "*What are examples, benefits, risks, costs, and quality benchmarks of automated methods for creating workflows to generate cataloguing metadata for large sets of Library of Congress digital materials? And, what technologies and workflow models are most promising to support metadata creation and assist with cataloguing workflows? What similar activities are being employed by other organizations?*" [6].

Digirati tested five different models for ML and used two workflows for assisted cataloguing, creating a subject assistant suggestion prototype. In September 2023, the project team concluded the first part of the project, called "Toward Piloting Computational Description," and the team has moved on to the second part, ECD2 (2023–2024), which focuses on diverse human-in-the-loop prototypes that suggest machine-generated terms to librarians who then review them. Finally, in the last phase of the project, ECD3, the team uses the BIBFRAME system instead of the MARC system to test the most effective human-in-the-loop models and prototypes identified during the first two phases [5]. Since the interviews were conducted at the beginning of 2024, this case study focuses on the ECD1 and ECD2 projects.

Each project phase follows a framework consisting of three stages: (1) understand, (2) experiment, and (3) implement. The understand stage was described by one interviewee as follows: "*... understand what are you doing, who are the people, what is the data, what are the models, really understand and understand your own appetite for risk, understand how important is quality or how close to perfection does this need to be.*" Moreover, "*There are use cases where it's okay if there's a lot of error, where we were never going to process the stuff anyway and maybe it doesn't matter. And then, there are use cases where we're providing the only authoritative source on this. The trustworthiness of our whole institution relies on us getting this right...*" The expermentation stage "*... is the right place to do an experiment, ... and that experiment is all about gathering data.*" One interviewee stated the benefits of experimentation as follows: "*... we absolutely get information about the models that's wonderful, but we also learn a lot through really looking at results what is* *good enough or questions that are much easier answered when you're actually looking at the machine-generated stuff than when you're imaging.*" Finally, the implementation stage "... *rests on policies, principles, a roadmap, understanding staff*". All three phases are designed to support the evaluation of the following elements of ML: (1) data, (2) models, and (3) people. Data is crucial in ML, serving as input, output, and training material for models. The data includes collections, historic copyright, and legislative data, often in unique digital formats [7]. These real-world datasets can confuse AI models due to their messiness, imbalance, and historical content [7]. Models refer to the technologies and tools supporting ML algorithms' training, processing, and prediction. ML programs learn patterns from data without explicit instructions [7]. The effectiveness of a model depends on training, data processing, and delivery methods. In ML, people are essential to creating and using data and models. They design and program AI tools, and their expertise shapes potential ML use cases [7]. People are responsible for the quality of AI systems and must decide how to implement AI responsibly.

Additionally, a set of worksheets and questionnaires, freely available at GitHub (https://github.com/LibraryOfCongress/labs-ai-framework), have been created to help staff and stakeholders identify priorities for future AI enhancements and services [7].

In the project's initial phase, ECD1, the project team and the vendor undertook tests on five models and methods to detect or generate comprehensive bibliographic records from e-books. They used around 23,000 existing machine-readable cataloguing (MARC) records and e-books to train the models. Digirati was granted access to these 23,000 e-books, which were primarily in English, along with their corresponding MARCXML records sourced from various collections: open-access e-books, legal reports, e-deposit registration e-books, and cataloguing-in-publication e-books [8]. The primary objective was to generate token and text-classified records, a goal that was ultimately achieved [8]. Token classification is generally defined by identifying group tokens in records and assigning them to specific classes or categories [8]. In contrast, text classification involves identifying the sentiment, subject, or topic of the e-book [8]. However, the data provided was insufficient for the machine to accurately predict all the categories: "... *we gave them access to almost 23,000 e-books and the associated MARCXML to use as training data, which was not nearly enough training data.*" Nevertheless, for token classification methods, such as identifying title, the accuracy of the generated information ranged from 80% to 90% [8]. Regarding text classification, particularly for subject headings, the models encountered more challenges in predicting the correct information [8].

In the second project phase, ECD2, the project team concentrated on gaining a deeper understanding of cataloguers' needs and priorities of the LoC, with an emphasis on developing testable human-in-the-loop prototypes for catalogue assistance workflows [9]. This phase created three initial prototypes and one "clickable" prototype. Like ECD1, the team used e-books and MARCXML records from four collections: open-access e-books, legal reports, e-deposit registration e-books, and cataloguing-in-publication e-books [9]. In total, nearly 120,000 e-books were leveraged to train the models. The primary goal was to generate fully valid MARC records, replete with subfield information, and extract data from entire e-books [9]. Cataloguers reviewed the subject predictions produced by the models, indicating whether the suggestions were accurate or incorrect. The findings revealed that it is feasible to produce MARC records using ML methods, achieving an accuracy of 80% for the majority of fields and subfields [5]. However, accuracy dropped to approximately 50% when assessing subject fields [5].

2.1 Actors Involved

In the ECD, various internal and external actors come together in a process known as co-production. Co-production entails five interdependent phases: co-commissioning, co-design, co-implementation, co-delivery, and co-assessment [10]. Each phase engages various stakeholders, underscoring the collaborative essence of the initiative. In the following, we present the key actors in the ECD1 and ED2.

The ECD is led by the Senior Innovation Specialist in the LC Labs and the Chief of the U.S. Programs, Law, and Literature Division in the Acquisitions and Bibliographic Access Directorate.

The LC Labs were created to plan for the library's digital future and explore ways to utilise digitisation and digital collections to benefit the public. LC Labs act as an experimental space to test various projects and are included in the Digital Strategy Directorate. Since its inception, LC Labs has collaborated on many projects using AI and ML. The LC Labs consists of a small team of five full-time employees who recently welcomed their first programmer. One interviewee stated: "*There's no technical team in LC Labs, and none of the developers, designer, coders of the library work on our stuff. Everything LC Labs has done has been through partnerships in contracts, a lot of contracts. A lot of what the team has done over the years has led a program of exploration, experimentation—I think of it as broadening the horizons at the library or lowering barriers to innovation....*"

Part of the Acquisitions and Bibliographic Access Directorate is the U.S. Programs, Law, and Literature Division. This division, for example, catalogues copyright materials, supports ISSN infrastructure, or catalogues legal materials [11].

The U.S. Programs, Law, and Literature Division and the LC Labs collaborate. This relationship is described as follows: "*...collaboration has been great... it's been fantastic.*" About 12 cataloguers were also involved in testing, along with various other IT staff who helped move data and support the experiment.

In addition, both divisions work with the vendor Digirati in the ECD project. The vendor manages the development of the ML application. This collaboration is complemented by Digital Innovation Indefinite Delivery Indefinite Quantity (IDIQ), which is managed by LC Labs. This contract is valid for 5 years, during which vendors can submit task orders. Digirati was one of the vendors that successfully bid on a task order under this contract vehicle.

External vendors and digital service providers are contracted to contribute technical expertise and resources to the project. Research institutes and academic partners provide domain-specific knowledge and collaborate on various aspects. Users and patrons, such as cataloguers, participate through user testing and feedback sessions to ensure the project meets their needs.

Moreover, the LC Labs' planning framework helps connect staff with patrons and the library community: "*We're doing both, we are connecting with people, learning from them about what they care about and also, we are doing experiments with people, with our materials. We are exploring, we are not waiting until we get it because we don't know what it should be; how would we know? I think the fact that the framework is very vigorous and rigorous and it came out of actually engaging with people on these questions. It also came out of working with staff, it also came out of working with the library community and within the federal community.*"

Table 1 gives a brief overview of the co-production process based on Mergel et al. (2025) in the ECD 1 and ECD2 at the LoC:

2.2 *Skills and Competencies Required for Librarians*

Librarians need, besides cataloguing skills, necessary skills and competencies to effectively and responsibly utilise AI- and ML-based solutions. Therefore, it always requires a librarian with the necessary skills to comprehend and apply cataloguing principles effectively: "*You need to know how to catalogue and what to expect from*

Table 1 Co-production process in ECD1 and ECD2 at LoC

Co-commissioning	*Prospective co-production phase*	ECD was sponsored by the Principal Deputy of the Librarian of Congress and co-led by the U.S. Programs, Law, and Literature Division Chief and the Sr. Innovation Specialist in LC Labs.
Co-design	*Concurrent co-production phases*	Together with external vendor Digirati, the responsible project them tested different ML models (ECD1) and human-in-the-loop prototypes for cataloguing e-books (ECD2).
Co-implementation		These ML models were fed with data from e-books and checked for accuracy.
Co-delivery		The machine-generated records were reviewed and verified by professional cataloguers for their correctness.
Co-assessment	*Retrospective co-production phase*	Together with external vendors, the responsible project team noted that the initial set of 23,000 e-books (ECD1) was insufficient to create a dataset adequate for machine learning. They subsequently expanded the dataset by adding approximately 100,000 more e-books (ECD2).

what goes in a bibliographic record, for one thing, how to identify valid or invalid information, make decisions on name authorities, for instance, or subjects." This would involve identifying errors and generating new subject headings when required. This is not something that can be expected from a machine. Bias is another factor that needs to be taken into consideration. If cataloguers rely solely on machines to identify and apply subject-specific subjects to a particular resource, they may suggest biased options. Without someone with the necessary understanding and skills to identify and rectify this, the bias may perpetuate: "*There needs to be somebody going: 'Oh, wait. I don't think the machine did a good job here. I think we need to backtrack, start over.*'" In addition, librarians need at least a basic understanding of what ML and AI mean and how they work: "*I wish I had had a better understanding of what even machine learning meant, quite frankly, because it was sort of a duh moment when I said, 'What are you testing?'*" Furthermore, "*So understanding the basic concept was important, and I wish I understood that.*" Conversations with the vendors and workshops help to gain an understanding of the phenomena. In addition, it could be helpful if AI and ML are already part of the library science curriculum: "*So, having some sort of grounding basic and education in what that really is probably would be useful, to have a better understanding of what machine learning really means, how it can be used.*" Also, library staff should develop evaluation and assessment skills: "*So, it is going to always require careful curation, careful evaluation.*"

2.2.1 Organisational Level

The project has the support of the higher management of the LoC, as stated: "*In fact, this project was highlighted by the Librarian of Congress and the Chief Information Officer at a hearing before Congress... because Congress is, of course, interested in what are you doing with artificial intelligence, how do it's safe, how do we know that you can trust it, is it going to do horrible things, what about the ethical concerns...*" Furthermore, the tasks are: "*So, this current task order is going to be having librarians helping the machine make decisions, not expecting the machine to make decisions, but also using large language models to do some more of the work and see how that goes as opposed to say, natural language processing.*"

2.3 Challenges

During the project's first two phases, challenges were also encountered that should not be ignored. One challenge the LoC faced was deciding how transparent it should be with its patrons, mostly other libraries that use its catalogued records. Specifically, there is a question of whether patrons should be made aware if a record was created using ML and whether the record should include information about the confidence level of the ML-produced record: "*It's something we have to think about, what do we want to say, do we need to say something in our record that says 'this record was created with machine learning', do we need to say something about its confidence level?*"

A second challenge that needs to be addressed is the issue of copyright for the submitted e-books. One of the interviewees stated, "*If you're using rights-restricted material, where there's a copyright on content, can you use machine learning to feed the content into this black box of a machine and then what will it do with the content once the modelling is done? Will it delete it? Will it store it? Will it use it for some other purpose that you didn't realize?*"

Thirdly, the LoC is currently facing the challenge of determining the accuracy of ML-generated output. They are still figuring out what level of accuracy is considered acceptable: "*I think something we're still grappling with is accuracy and still trying to figure out what's good enough, what's close, what's relevant, is relevant the same as good enough or does it have to be a 100% one-to-one match.*" Moreover, "*... it's not close enough to acceptable levels to allow it to go on without human interventions and the human in the loop has been this mantra...*" To ensure the accuracy of the output, a cataloguer is required to identify possible mistakes and correctly input the information into the record.

Fourthly, identifying, for example, the title and author of an e-book through AI is a complex task due to the varying design of title pages. Each e-book has a unique typography, layout, and font size, making it difficult for ML to differentiate between, for example, the title and author. Moreover, predicting the content of an e-book requires the machine to scan more than just the initial 50 pages to identify the most frequently used terms in the book. However, identifying words and phrases that are not part of the controlled vocabulary remains challenging, and it is uncertain whether the machine can identify them successfully. In addition, the predicted words and terms generated by the machine are not always helpful nor provide any information about the e-book's content: "*Some of them are not useful, like 'it', 'one', 'she', 'this', not useful.*" As they are only machine-generated output, they cannot be corrected.

Fifthly, there are challenges when it comes to handling the content of books. One question that arises is how to deal with harmful and disrespectful language in these books, as well as how to handle cultural heritage. This can be particularly problematic with old books that contain such language and when these are used to train ML models. Therefore, it is important to consider how best to handle this issue because: "*If you give the machine, if you feed the machine harmful language, it will predict harmful language. Garbage in, garbage out. That is an ethical concern for sure.*"

In addition, training AI requires large volumes of data, including born-digital materials, which can be challenging: "*I think one of the most complicated things it is getting the training data right. So, definitely more is better.*"

Finally, there is a risk of ineffective solutions connected to the fear of investing resources into solutions that may not work or could worsen existing issues: "*The biggest risk is that we're going to pay for something that doesn't work, that we're going to implement something that makes things worse. ... and lose our credibility with the public and undermine people's faith in reality and truth.*"

3 Results

3.1 Organisational Level

The LC Labs promote the importance of experimenting with AI and ML at an organisational level. They are doing public affairs and presentations within the LoC: "*... we've done, as you can imagine, a lot of presentations internally.*" In addition, there are Congressional Hearings where the LoC must report their progress to Congress. For example, they provide updates on their experiments in the ECD project. One interviewee stated: "*So when we have these two Congressional hearings, a lot of what they wanted to hear about at the hearings were actually how are you using AI in copyright or Congressional Research Services. Members of Congress wanted to know are you doing to get our work done faster with AI.*" Furthermore, an AI working within the LoC provides input on policy and planning aspects of AI implementation.

However, LC Labs lacks the resources to educate more staff about the ML and AI technologies in the LoC: "*So, the idea of how do we tell more people that we can connect with them, we can't. So, we do the best we can. When we're invited to an internal meeting, we always go; we present.*"

In addition, an interviewee stated that AI is not changing the mission and the library's role: "*It's not like the machine is ever going to take over any concerns people have. Like, 'What are we going to need cataloguers for?' Using AI in a way is even more incumbent on expertise of cataloguers to be able to identify what's right, what's good enough.*"

3.2 Value Created and Co-created

Implementing and using ML and AI can create value for library staff and patrons within the LoC. The use of AI has the potential to enhance cataloguing output in numerous ways. For instance, AI can provide extractive or abstractive summaries, which can assist cataloguers in understanding the essence of a book without having to go through the entire book. Additionally, AI can take care of routine tasks, such as identifying information on the title page and freeing up librarians to focus on intellectual tasks. This can lead to more efficient use of time and resources. However, many library staff members are concerned that AI is replacing their jobs, but this is not necessarily the case. In the short term, AI creates more work because someone has to ensure it is functioning correctly, train and revise it, and continually monitor it. This leaves library staff more time to focus on intellectual tasks such as reviewing the model or correcting records: "*But I don't think that it's ever going to replace cataloguing or cataloguers or librarians. It'll augment, and for a while, it might even make it more work because it's more work to do some of these projects than it is to just catalogue the thing. But once you can make some headway with it, then maybe that project can go more smoothly and then you can focus attention on other things to study.*"

Successfully using AI-based technologies in the LoC also helps to create added value for other libraries in the country. After completing the records, the LoC sends them to the Online Computer Library Center (OCLC). Once there, the records are accessible not only in the LoC catalogue but also to everyone else. This means that other libraries can download the metadata and use it in their local library catalogue: "*Once they're complete, they go to OCLC, which means the world can access them. But they're also available in our catalogue that anyone could go to our catalogue and you put it into your record and your local catalogue.*" However, staff capacity and time thwart the project implementation: "*I'm not sure if we'll ever get to the point where we can use that metadata in any meaningful way or it's going to sit there, sort of this training data we had from our first task order and never actually use it. ... So, the cataloguing part won't even go live until probably spring of 2025.*"

Moreover, adopting AI in libraries is seen as a means of creating public value for society. However, one interviewee stated: "*The part about connecting with the public, for me, the degree to which our materials are—the materials that we steward are not meaningfully available to people in the ways that they would care to find them or have them is heart-breaking. We just don't have the resources to help make our materials part of people's lives because the paradigm that we're operating—every library is widely under resourced. We all are barely holding on to the processing that we can do with decreasing resources and increasing materials coming in and increasingly complex digital materials....*"

3.3 Lesson Learned

After the project's first two phases, some lessons were also learned. Especially after ECD1, the project team recognised that ML applications need more data to improve accuracy: "*... definitely would have given them as much of our content as possible*". In ECD2, they have increased the number of records to more than 120,000 e-books, hoping this will result in a more precise model. One interviewee stated: "*We only gave them 23,000 e-books. We could have given them 100,000. Now we're giving them 100,000, and hopefully, they'll have more success with the models they're using in this task order.*" This massive amount of digital content is necessary to describe the content of the e-books more accurately.

A second lesson learned is that there is a better understanding of what ML means necessary: "*I didn't understand and I don't think any of us really understood what a cataloguer-assisted workflow, what that meant, what does cataloguer-assisted workflow mean. It couldn't even—the concept didn't even make sense to me.*" However, upskilling helped to gain basic knowledge about the technology and process: "*And then we had a conversation, workshop conversation with different cataloguers, with people from the company, to try to talk about what would make your life easier or how do you find cataloguing e-books, what's difficult about that, what would make it easier.*"

4 Conclusion

In this chapter, we explored how the LoC utilised ML to catalogue e-books that have not yet been catalogued. We focused on the first two phases of the "Exploring Computational Description" (ECD) project. The project is run by the LC Labs and the U.S. Programs, Law, and Literature Division in cooperation with the external vendor Digirati. Notably, due to a backlog of e-books, the Principal Deputy of the Librarian of Congress has allocated $250,000 from the National Digital Trust Fund to contract experimental AI work.

In the first project phase, ECD1, five different models for ML were tested, and the vendor used two workflows for assisted cataloguing, creating a subject assistant suggestion prototype. The second project phase, ECD2, focused on diverse human-in-the-loop prototypes that suggest machine-generated terms to librarians. However, there were some challenges during the first two project phases, such as the trustable confidence level of AI-generated records, dealing with copyright content, or handling harmful or disrespectful language in older books, especially those used for training ML models. Moreover, the models' accuracy still needs improvement, and therefore, the ML models need large amounts of digital data.

Implementing and using AI in the LoC has the potential to enhance cataloguing output in numerous ways. Initial results show that AI can take over repetitive tasks, such as recording title information, which gives library staff more time for more intellectually demanding activities. Nevertheless, human expertise remains crucial for recognising errors and ensuring quality. However, introducing AI in libraries has also created new requirements: Library staff need to acquire basic understanding of ML to use and develop the technologies effectively.

Acknowledgements The work for this chapter was supported by the European Union's Horizon Europe Research and Innovation Programme under Grant Agreement ID 101061516.

Appendix

Overview of the ECD project at the Library of Congress

Case and project name			
Exploring Computational Description (ECD) at the Library of Congress (LoC)			
Country	**Number of employees**	**Type of AI solution**	**Year and maturity level**
USA	More than 3000 permanent employees	Using ML to create metadata for e-books that have not yet been catalogued	ECD 1: 2022–2023 ECD 2: 2023–2024 ECD 3: start 2024
Project description			
The LC Labs and the U.S. Programs, Law, and Literature Division are currently working on a project called Exploring Computational Description to determine the feasibility of using ML to create metadata for e-books that have not yet been catalogued. The project began in September 2022 (ECD1) and involves collaboration with an external vendor, Digirati. Digirati tested five different models for ML and used two workflows for assisted cataloguing, creating a subject assistant suggestion prototype. In September 2023, the first part of the project was concluded, and the team moved on to the second part (ECD2), which focused on diverse human-in-the-loop prototypes that suggest machine-generated terms to librarians			
Need(s) behind implementation	**Actors involved**	**Challenges**	
In order to fulfil LoC's goal of connecting all Americans to the library, LoC needs to investigate new approaches that could bring significant changes to its practices. LC Labs are tasked with experimenting with new methods, approaches, and technologies, and collaborating with external stakeholders such as universities and research initiatives. Additionally, there is support from the library management and funding from the National Digital Trust Fund to experiment with AI and ML	The LC Labs serve as an experimental space for testing different projects and are part of the Digital Strategy Directorate. The U.S. Programs, Law, and Literature Division primarily catalogues books and e-books and is part of the Acquisitions and Bibliographic Access Directorate. These two departments collaborate and work with external vendors such as Digirati or with research institutions and academic partners. Furthermore, the Planning Framework, developed by the LC Labs, helps to connect library staff with patrons and the library community	1. Should patrons, mostly other libraries, be informed if a record was generated using AI and whether the record should contain details about the confidence level of the AI-generated record? 2. Can we use machine learning and AI to process content that is copyrighted? What will the machine do with the content after the modelling is complete? 3. What level of accuracy is considered acceptable for an AI-generated output? To ensure accuracy, a cataloguer is still required to identify possible mistakes and input the information correctly into the record. This is closely related to creating quality standards and policies specifically for AI 4. AI struggles to identify the title and author of an e-book due to the varying design elements and typography. Additionally, predicting e-book content and identifying non-controlled vocabulary words remain challenging for AI. Additionally, the predicted words and terms may not always be useful or informative and cannot be corrected 5. How should we deal with harmful and disrespectful language in books and cultural heritage? This can be particularly problematic with old books that contain such language and when these are used to train ML models	

(continued)

Case and project name		
Exploring Computational Description (ECD) at the Library of Congress (LoC)		
Results		
Organisational level	**Value created and co-created**	**Lesson learned**
AI can provide extractive or abstractive summaries, which can assist cataloguers in understanding the essence of a book without having to go through the entire book. Additionally, AI can take care of routine tasks, such as identifying information on the title page and freeing up librarians to focus on intellectual tasks. This can lead to more efficient use of time and resources. Many library staff members are concerned that AI is replacing their jobs. However, this is not necessarily the case. In the short term, AI creates more work because someone has to ensure it is functioning correctly, train and revise it, and continually monitor it. This leaves library staff more time to focus on intellectual tasks such as reviewing the model or correcting records	LC Labs conducts public affairs has to report to Congress about its progress in experimenting with and implementing AI. However, LC Labs lacks the resources to educate more staff about ML and AI technologies in the LoC. The expertise of the cataloguers is even more valuable in identifying wrongly predicted content and errors. It always requires librarians with the necessary skills to comprehend and apply cataloguing principles effectively. Nevertheless, library staff need at least a basic understanding of what ML and AI mean and how they work	Create a guideline on how to deal with harmful and disrespectful language use Start with a large-enough dataset so that the AI tool can learn and provide more accurate results over time

References

1. *General Information* (n.d), https://www.loc.gov/about/general-information/. Accessed 9 Feb 2025
2. *A Library for All* (n.d.), https://www.loc.gov/strategic-plan/. Accessed 9 Feb 2025
3. *AI at LC* (n.d.), https://labs.loc.gov/work/experiments/machine-learning/. Accessed 9 Feb 2025
4. Library of Congress Blog, *Why Experiment: Machine Learning at the Library of Congress* (Library of Congress Blogs, 2023)
5. C. Saccucci, A. Potter, *Exploring Computational Description: Experiment Results*. (2024)
6. *Experiment: Exploring Computational Description* (n.d.), https://labs.loc.gov/static/labs/work/experiments/Documents/ECD1_Executive_Summary.pdf. Accessed 10 Feb 2025
7. Library of Congress Blog, *Introducing the LC Labs Artificial Intelligence Planning Framework* (Library of Congress Blog, 2023)
8. Library of Congress Labs, *Exploring Computational Description: Final Presentation* (Library of Congress Blog, 2023)
9. Library of Congress Labs, *Toward Piloting Computational Description: Final Presentation* (Library of Congress Blog, n.d.)
10. I. Mergel, N. Edelmann, N. Haug, Co-production phases in the development and implementation of digital public services. Perspect. Public Manag. Govern. **8**(1), 1–13 (2025)
11. *About the Organization* (n.d.), https://www.loc.gov/aba/about/. Accessed 9 Feb 2025

Anna-Lea Schumann is currently pursuing a master's degree in Politics and Public Administration at the University of Konstanz. Her research interests focus on applying modern working practices within public administration and their implications for public value creation. In her bachelor's thesis, she explored the use and implementation of design thinking in libraries. She has gained initial practical experience through various internships in public administration, providing her with valuable insights into the operational methods and processes of the public sector.

Justus Kühler is studying for a bachelor's degree in political science and public administration at the University of Konstanz. He is particularly interested in the latest developments in public administration that reflect the trend towards democratisation. He is particularly interested in the application of new forms of participation at the local level. He has already gained initial experience with municipal administration through his involvement in local politics.

Ines Mergel is a University Professor of Public Administration in the Department of Politics and Public Administration at the University of Konstanz and a Fellow of the National Academy of Public Administration (Class of 2018). After holding positions at the Harvard Kennedy School of Government as a Doctoral Fellow and Postdoctoral Fellow (2002–2008), Professor Mergel was awarded tenure at the Maxwell School of Citizenship and Public Affairs (Syracuse University, NY) in 2014 (2008–2014) and then served as Associate Professor with tenure (2014–2016). Professor Mergel is a member of the supervisory board of the e-Governance Academy (Estonia). Other board memberships can be found here. Professor Mergel is a founding member of the international initiative Teaching Public Service in the Digital Age, which aims to integrate digital skills into the teaching and training of public managers. As part of this initiative, Professor Mergel was appointed a Schmidt Futures Innovation Fellow in 2022.

Recommendations

Recommendations for the AI Implementation in Libraries

Ines Mergel, Justus Kühler, Anna-Lea Schumann, and Carsten Schmidt

Abstract AI implementation is part of the digital transformation efforts of National Libraries. To understand what the challenges are and derive recommendations for other libraries, we researched the AI implementation. Based on 90 interviews with library and AI experts, we identified ten European National Libraries and included the Library of Congress and the British National Library in our case analysis. Here, we derive the challenges that National Libraries face when implementing AI technologies. Based on these insights, we provide recommendations for libraries that plan to also implement AI solutions in their organisations. This chapter focuses on sustainable governance structures that ensure long-term strategic alignment of funding and implementation goals, the promotion of technical independence of international providers through internal competence and upskilling efforts, and the involvement of information specialists and users to ensure adoption and acceptance of AI tools. Furthermore, we highlight the importance of collaborative and interdisciplinary approaches as well as transparency, responsible data management, and ethical AI.

Keywords Policy · Strategy · Artificial Intelligence · Recommendations · AI · eGovernment · Libraries · Public Sector Innovation · Digital Transformation · Cultural Heritage · Metadata Quality

I. Mergel
Department of Politics and Public Administration, University of Konstanz, Konstanz, Germany

Fraunhofer FOKUS, Fraunhofer Institute for Open Communication Systems, Berlin, Germany

School of Management, Public Management, University of Vaasa, Vaasa, Finland
e-mail: ines.mergel@uni-konstanz.de

J. Kühler · A.-L. Schumann · C. Schmidt (✉)
Department of Politics and Public Administration, University of Konstanz, Konstanz, Germany
e-mail: Justus.kuehler@uni-konstanz.de; anna-lea.schumann@uni-konstanz.de; carsten.schmidt@uni-konstanz.de

I. Mergel, C. Schmidt (eds.), *AI Innovations in Public Services*,
https://doi.org/10.1007/978-3-032-01344-6_14

1 Introduction

National Libraries have been engaged in the implementation of AI technologies for several years [1]. Their efforts precede the time of the publicly available tools such as OpenAI or GenAI tools and focus predominantly on cataloguing solutions that are designed to support the data collection and artefact classification efforts that have become necessary with the emergence of new forms of writing and other types of literary outputs generated in the social media age [2].

As part of the EU LibrarIN research grant, we studied the implementation efforts of AI technologies as part of the digital transformation efforts of libraries. We started our inquiry by conducting 12 initial interviews with the executive directors of international library associations. We amended these interviews with additional interviews with 19 library experts who helped us understand how libraries are digitally transforming their services for their patrons and are aligning their internal digital processes using AI technologies. From these interviews, we identified National Libraries as pioneers in the implementation of AI. The interviewees pointed us to the most innovative National Libraries that they consider as role models for other libraries. Given that they were frequently mentioned as role models by many of our interviewees, we decided to focus on National Libraries instead of research libraries or other types of public libraries. As a result, we included ten National Libraries in the EU and added the Library of Congress (USA) and the British Library (UK). Using 59 interviews with National Library staff members in charge of implementing AI. To understand their challenges, we conducted a content analysis of the interviewees' statements and derived the challenges that National Libraries face during these technological transformation processes.

In the following, we highlight the type of challenges and derive recommendations on how other (National) Libraries might address them in their implementation processes. The findings are organised along the following recommendation dimensions: (1) ethical and legal considerations; (2) human resource issues, such as skills, human-in-the-loop, staff rotation, interdisciplinary collaboration; (3) technological expertise; (4) securing long-term, reliable funding.

2 Challenges for the Implementation of AI in National Libraries

2.1 Ethical and Legal Issues

The ethical and legal issues surrounding AI implementation that remain unresolved focus on the problems of data protection, copyright, and privacy, but also on the question of whether the AI use should be disclosed to patrons who are reusing the resulting data. Ethical considerations related to the use of AI, especially in relation to the context of language models, are pervasive. Several National Libraries emphasised the importance of considering ethical issues in developing and training AI models, particularly those using already materials related to sensitivity to ethical issues. This also includes the importance of ensuring that AI models are trained on appropriate data to mitigate bias and ethical concerns. Furthermore, the discourse highlights the dilemma institutions face regarding whether the decision to make their high-quality content available for training AI models, given the potential ethical implications and legal restrictions.

2.2 *Data Protection, Copyright, and Privacy*

The main challenges National Libraries are reporting focus on General Data Protection Regulation (GDPR) compliance and privacy issues.

In case archival artefacts are used for online displays or exhibitions that are based on private citizens' historical accounts, National Libraries need to resolve copyright issues as well as other technical integration and accessibility challenges with the rest of the library system. The copyright status of most records imposes limitations on the extent to which National Libraries can utilise them: "*Most of our collection, yes, is copyright protected, and there are legal, strict legal limits on what you can and cannot do with it.*" Similarly, submitted e-books (e.g., dissertations or publishers' e-books) face the challenge of the copyright law. One of the interviewees stated, "*If you're using rights-restricted material, where there's a copyright on content, can you use machine learning to feed the content into this black box of a machine, and then what will it do with the content once the modelling is done? Will it delete it? Will it store it? Will it use it for some other purpose that you didn't realise?*"

Especially in cases, where the AI-developed content will be placed on a public digital collection, copyright issues need to be resolved, as one of the interviewees highlights: "*There's a difference between just showing something works on one person's laptop, to we need to get developers in, we need to think about a public interface, we need to make sure that interface meets the accessibility standards that the library's website must have. That's a different phase of development work that necessarily also takes time. Another part of that, though, was the licensing issues to be able to show this material. Technically, they're copyrighted, the postcards, even though we're not always sure who produced them. It's not like a book where we know we have the author of this is X, Y, and Z.*"

2.3 *Resolving Data Bias Issues of International AI Products*

On the macro level, the development of AI by big commercial companies is a challenge and even a dangerous undertaking that conflicts with national security: "*[In] the current situation is quite dangerous because the development of the best AIs is basically being done by these big companies in California mostly or in China, and there's not that much transparency into what they are doing.*"

National Libraries see the need to develop their own unbiased AI tools not only to provide tools that can learn small languages but also to compensate for the bias of English language tools. One of the interviewees explained the role of National Libraries as follows: "*So, I see that the role of libraries as well as other public institutions could be to form a counterbalance against this, to try to use AI not to make money, but also for purposes that benefit society in general and also to counter bias, to try to come up with solutions to the ethical issues.*"

Therefore, libraries must constantly keep track of the AI development and direction to learn and apply AI in ways that benefit their local interests. In addition, there are challenges to using AI and handling copyright: "*We can do things in-house, usually, but giving out this material to researchers or even to companies, it's not clear if it's allowed. The laws around this are evolving, but it's a little bit of a grey area.*"

2.4 Disclosing AI Use to Patrons

One challenge that National Libraries face is deciding how transparent they should be with their patrons, mostly other libraries that use their catalogued records. Specifically, there is a question of whether patrons should be made aware if a record was created using AI and whether the record should include information about the confidence level of the AI-produced record: "*It's something we have to think about, what do we want to say, do we need to say something in our record that says 'this record was created with machine learning'" do we need to say something about its confidence level?*"

Some National Libraries have adopted a radical transparency approach. As an example, the German National Library data records are recognisable as having been created by machine or created intellectually by hand. Nevertheless, the question arises as to whether uniform labelling of AI-generated outputs is necessary and feasible over time: "*Perhaps even a kind of stamp, a watermark, indicating what kind of information was generated by AI.*"—an issue that is not yet resolved.

2.5 Keeping the Human Factor in the Loop

The human resource development and integration challenges focus on interdisciplinary collaboration, operational and task force development, organisational learning as part of the AI implementation process, and also on how librarians can overcome technological challenges.

2.6 Interdisciplinary Collaboration

AI implementation demands the expertise of many different stakeholders in National Libraries, and it can't be implemented top down as a strategic project initiated by top management and implemented by the IT department alone. The National Libraries we interviewed for this project identified the necessary interdisciplinary in-house collaboration as one of the significant challenges in the implementation process.

Given the broad inclusion of different departments within National Libraries, one of our interviewees mentioned that "*Everyone had a different idea of what a research question is because everyone came from a different discipline.*" The relatively large list of internal and external collaborators turns out to be a management challenge that needs time to overcome. Large-scale projects, such as AI projects, need to support the effort to understand each stakeholder's disciplines and the resulting differences in methods and theoretical background: "*It's more of a collaboration issue where the time that it takes to coordinate and discuss takes away from time doing things, but it's also part of the work. I think we hadn't really anticipated—I think from the library, we knew, but I think for the researchers, they hadn't quite understood some of those compromises that would be necessary.*"

At times, the project managers overlooked that each stakeholder had essential but mundane tasks to fulfil, such as cleaning datasets and matching metadata. These laborious tasks take a lot of time. The effort was often underestimated due to the pressure on the researchers to publish papers quickly: "*So, it was not always easy to get as much attention on those boring bits when people were felt pressure because they were on this high-profile project to also be publishing papers all the time. In some ways, it was less productive for people who were looking at how many papers they could get to add to their CV because everything is slower when you're working across disciplines and when you're doing that negotiation around what's important to you.*" The different notions of experiences, task-related burdens, and research needs require that AI implementation projects need to balance out the needs of the implementers, information specialists, and the researcher reusing the research-related data.

Fostering interdisciplinary collaboration, early resource allocation, balancing speed with preparation, ensuring long-term technical support, raising staff awareness, and promoting knowledge sharing emerged as essential measures to overcome collaboration challenges. As one of the interviewees stated, "*I think there was quite a lot of difficulty in finding because it was such an interdisciplinary project or multidisciplinary project, finding things that resonated for everyone. We probably didn't spend enough time sharing and really understanding what was inspiring for each other's disciplines and what the gaps were in each other's disciplines, because things that are really established in one field might be new in another. But also, a lot of the practical work, because everyone was a researcher, even the software engineers, were publishing papers based on their work. Some of the really boring stuff isn't necessarily something that you can publish a paper on.*"

AI tools enabled a shared platform where contributions from various scholars (philologists, historians, and technologists) could be pooled to enhance the transcription and analysis process. This also demonstrates that AI can be a catalyst for cross-disciplinary cooperation.

2.7 Operational and Workforce Development

Even though many National Libraries already have relatively large IT departments, implementing AI requires more developers and specialists for this emergent field of technology. In the first couple of years, the development of AI tools seemed to have emerged coincidentally. "*It wasn't planned, but it had a very positive effect on our development. The IT perspective offered new insights into methods and processes, enabling us to set a course that IT, which was too far removed from our specialist topics, could not achieve at the time.*" During the initial exploration phases of AI, National Libraries used the opportunity to gain experiences by building their own AI tools to gain the relevant experience. One interviewee stated: "*We needed this experience. We worked with an external company, learned a lot, and were able to redo everything. [...] You also need the mistakes to learn from them. And the good thing for us was that we had a managing director at the time who gave us this freedom, who invested money, who invested people, who gave us the freedom to tackle the issues.*"

The key competencies for excelling in AI development include motivation, a strong interest in the field, and the necessary education to understand the concepts. Furthermore, creating an AI solution is an ongoing process, as one interviewee noted: "*But little bit by little bit, the way we are working now was one year of work, trial, and error ... You cannot say from the beginning, 'That's very good.' No, you have the idea, you have the tools, and then you have the planning, and then all together we came to the way where we are now today here.*"

In the future, National Libraries will need high-level IT knowledge and skills to keep up with the current speed of development. This also includes the task of staying up to date on the newest developments, having access to training and education, and intentionally recruiting highly skilled specialists with expertise in technology were intentionally recruited.

Initially, National Libraries started to use fully automated AI processes strategically. Some of these decisions are currently being reviewed to determine whether a semi-automated process would be more advantageous, at least for specific applications. One interviewee commented: "*This is all justified, but experience shows that fully automated processes do not deliver the results that we would like. That's why these feedback processes with intellectual evaluation are more important.*"

Another interviewee highlighted that their next AI project will be staffed with people who will eventually use the tools: "*The technology is there to serve humans and bring humans along the way. It's always the way to go.*" Including librarians and information specialists from day one will help to develop internal AI expertise and competence, eventually improve AI literacy, and not rely only on external providers.

2.8 *Learning as Part of the AI Implementation Process*

The National Libraries in our sample also highlighted that it is crucial to approach machine learning and AI projects with a fresh and unbiased perspective, recognising the value in embracing mistakes as a part of the learning process. The fresh look perspective allows for an initial naivety and impartiality to make mistakes and learn from them. Consequently, top management must foster an environment that embraces experimentation, accepts missteps to allow mistakes, and encourages innovation. It is crucial to understand and recognise that such projects are iterative processes, necessitating the establishment of effective team dynamics as well.

As an example, in one of the National Libraries, the AI project team highlighted that only over time a better understanding of what machine learning means developed: "*I didn't understand and I don't think any of us really understood what a cataloguer-assisted workflow, what that meant, what does cataloguer-assisted workflow mean. It couldn't even—the concept didn't even make sense to me.*" However, upskilling helped to gain basic knowledge about the technology and process: "*And then we had a workshop conversation with different cataloguers, with people from the company, to try to talk about what would make your life easier or how do you find cataloguing e-books, what's difficult about that, what would make it easier.*"

Another National Library emphasised the need for iterative learning through prototyping: "The focus should shift to creating a functional prototype. The prototype will serve as a proof of concept, demonstrating the potential benefits and addressing any employee concerns. It is essential to involve the staff during this phase, gathering their feedback and making necessary adjustments to align the solution with their needs and expectations. Once the prototype has been refined and thoroughly tested, the final step is to move it into production. This phase should only proceed when the AI solution works reliably and effectively. Continuous monitoring and support will be necessary to ensure smooth integration and address any issues that may arise." Prototyping can then be tested with internal or external users as early as possible to gain insights into their needs and learn from their feedback.

Similarly, National Libraries should engage staff members who will use AI tools in the future to make sure the developed solution is trustworthy and efficient, that it meets the needs of its employees and enhances the library's operations. Engaging staff throughout the process will foster a collaborative environment and increase acceptance of the new technology. Therefore, keeping staff members informed about ongoing developments is crucial to build confidence and transparency in the process.

We also encountered several instances where library staff struggle to integrate AI into their daily work due to time constraints, as one of the interviewees suggested:

"So, it's a bit difficult between finding the time to do and willing to do it." Training a model comes with several technical challenges. One such challenge is handling situations where the model is not functioning optimally and needs to be retrained automatically. However, there has been a recent development where models can automatically retrain themselves based on the data collected. Another challenge is deploying the model in different environments, such as development, test, and production environments. Microsoft is investing a lot of money in the Power Platform to address this challenge and is making significant progress in introducing new functionalities and possibilities. Finally, the budget for AI projects at the [National Library] is challenging: "... we don't have a lot of money, so we have to think about every Euro we spend."

At the same time, librarians are concerned that the AI tools might replace human workers and lead to layoffs: "But what I'm worried about is that it's seen on the upper levels/management level as something that may help reduce staff ... That has, I think, been from the very beginning something that many people, in addition to myself, are afraid of, that it's been used—that it will be used in this way as an excuse to reduce staff." These fears are very real, given that information specialists are helping to train AI to conduct the jobs they have been doing for decades based on their education and experience. At the same time, some library staff have strong opinions about the low quality of the output of AI: "the quality is getting worse, and you're embarrassing yourself to the outside world. So that has been a factor because, of course, we also have a lot of mistakes in there, so the processes are not perfect, and especially in the library context, this perfectionism was and is very pronounced, which is also right and important."

However, in this phase of exploration and investment into AI development, we have not come across a case where National Libraries have replaced human workers.

2.9 Overcoming Technical Challenges

Integrating AI into the organisational structure is a multifaceted task. For many traditionally trained librarians or information specialists, it remains a challenge to adjust to AI's complexities, which extends to questions about methods and implementation. One interviewee summarises this: "*Looking back, I would say that it is very important that the institution is aware that this is not a sprint, but a marathon. It's not enough to select a method and implement it. That's a bit of a suggestion because the technology is developing so quickly. The methods are only a small part of the whole.*"

Furthermore, no technical applications should be implemented solely based on their current popularity, just because they are fashionable. Instead, only technical applications that provide demonstrable added value for National Libraries will also convince librarians that their implementation is favourable. One interviewee elaborated: "*We don't need to adopt technical applications that don't add value for us. We don't have to follow every trend. However, as a National Library, we need to be knowledgeable about this environment to have a say. What is effective, what can be effective, and what might be.*" Ultimately, a rethinking process towards ML and AI must take place at all levels in the library, which takes time: "*People expect quick results and are not prepared for the fact that it is so time-consuming and that the result will also look different to what they were used to before.*"

Implementing AI provides National Libraries with digital transformation opportunities: As an example, they might start a debate as to whether metadata in the familiar form is still needed at all. Over time, one of the National Libraries decided that metadata is still necessary but no longer needs to be created according to library rules. One interviewee described the discourse session: "*This also led to controversial positions because colleagues who are trained accordingly naturally have a completely different relationship to the library rules. And the discussion as to whether the results of the automated processes are good enough was also conducted from the point of view of whether the bibliographic rules are being adhered to. No, they are not adhered to, but the aim of the automated processes was exclusively to find and support.*" As a result, one National Library increased the number of eBooks they used to train their AI system from around 20,000 to 100,000 to increase the confidence in the accuracy of the output.

Another National Library expert suggests not starting with the most technological AI solution. For example, automated subject indexing requires skills and competencies in manual subject indexing and description. For this reason, they advise that beginners or non-professionals avoid using the tool. One interviewee recommended using the tool carefully and thoughtfully to improve metadata, but urged more cautious usage: "*I think that if it would be always used in a careful and well thought out manner, then it could actually make a difference or give us better metadata. But we have to, or we should maybe be, I think, a bit more cautious than we are now.*" Furthermore, they started embracing open access, data, and software. Progress has been slow, but there has been a gradual shift towards these principles.

Technological challenges also remain because of the quality of input and the status of sophistication of the AI tools: much of the needed input is not transcribed yet. While tools might recognise print from older books or texts, errors persist due to factors like challenging handwriting, crossed-out sections, document contamination or other soiling, or translucency.

2.10 Information Accuracy and AI Hallucination

As mentioned in the previous section, many National Libraries noticed that especially training large-language models requires vast volumes of data, including born-digital materials, which can be challenging: "*I think one of the most complicated things is getting the training data right. So, definitely more is better.*"

Another critical task is the evaluation of information librarians receive from AI applications, as AI tools are neither complete nor always neutral. At first glance, it becomes easier as everyone can now have access to knowledge. Still, the demands on librarians' information literacy requirements increase as the information needs to be evaluated by humans. Procedural questions focus on issues such as: Where does this information come from? How is this information labelled? Do I remember where the source was? What was the source? Is the source actually "clean"? One interviewee emphasised: "*I believe that libraries will face a debate about how we position ourselves as places where you can find reliable information and also information where it is clear how it came about.*"

Identifying, for example, the title and author of an e-book through AI is a complex task due to the varying design of title pages. Each e-book has a unique typography, layout, and font size, making it difficult for the AI to differentiate between, for example, the title and author. Moreover, predicting the content of an e-book requires the machine to scan more than just the initial 50 pages to identify the most frequently used terms in the book. However, identifying words and phrases that are not part of the controlled vocabulary remains challenging, and it is uncertain whether the machine can identify them successfully. In addition, the predicted words and terms generated by the machine are not always useful nor provide any information about the e-book's content: "*Some of them are not useful, like 'it', 'one', 'she', 'this', not useful.*" As they are only machine-generated output, they cannot be corrected yet.

As many libraries are aiming to determine the accuracy of AI-generated output, one of the open questions is what level of accuracy is considered acceptable: "*I think something we're still grappling with is accuracy and still trying to figure out what's good enough, what's close, what's relevant, is relevant the same as good enough or does it have to be a 100% one-to-one match.*" Moreover, "*... it's not close enough to acceptable levels to allow it to go on without human interventions and the human in the loop has been this mantra.*" To ensure the accuracy of the output, a cataloguer is required to identify possible mistakes and correctly input the information into the record. This is closely related to the necessity of creating quality standards and policies specifically for AI. It is therefore important—not just during the AI training phase—to keep human specialists' knowledge and expertise "in the loop" to continue to monitor the quality of the automatically generated output.

2.11 Resource and Funding Constraints

A remaining challenge—as is true for most publicly funded services—is the limited availability of financial resources. Some of our interviewees highlight that it remains a constant battle between personnel and material resources. Public tenders can have the potential to complicate project implementation, often resulting in significant delays in project implementation, with the growing demand for greater agility of administrative processes to facilitate better and faster, more efficient, and timely project execution.

Large language models, for example, require a substantial amount of energy and resources. One interviewee therefore suggested: "*And you should bear that in mind.*

Or are there simpler solutions that are also efficient but don't consume these resources?" At the same time, there is a risk of ineffective solutions connected to the fear of investing resources into solutions that may not work or could worsen existing issues: "*The biggest risk is that we're going to pay for something that doesn't work, that we're going to implement something that makes things worse. ... and lose our credibility with the public and undermine people's faith in reality and truth.*"

Other National Libraries have made the experience that while they might have received funds for early prototyping, they don't have enough resources to implement, launch, and maintain the resulting tools. It is therefore necessary to allocate more generous resources towards the AI projects that cover the whole development, implementation, and use cycle: "*...we should, or we should have put even more resources into it, yes. We should have invested, both in personnel and financially, as well as simply something like hardware, yes, and yes, I think that's what I would do differently.*"

3 AI Implementation Recommendations for Libraries

3.1 *Implementation Recommendation 1: Technical Independence of Large Vendors*

AI systems require structured, adaptable, and extensible (meta)data management. National Libraries must avoid reliance on external AI solutions that are heavily biased towards English language programming and outputs. Libraries should therefore ensure that in-house AI capabilities are available to limit external dependencies. The applied technical infrastructure should be scalable, interoperable, and reusable to allow for the learning and processing of a country's artefacts. This will be ensured by allowing for continuous testing and improvement of AI models, provision of sandboxes, and standardisation of AI-generated content and technical solutions. At the same time, technological developments are driven by large vendors, and we recommend that libraries find a balance between technical independence and continuing the conversations with big vendors to stay on top of the development.

3.2 *Implementation Recommendation 2: Keeping the Human in the Loop*

AI solutions are usually developed by the IT department or external vendors but need to be trusted by librarians and information specialists. Therefore, keeping them informed about the strategic and operational decisions is essential to allowing them to learn and adjust to the new circumstances. This is especially true given the many so-called AI hallucinations or, frankly, errors, that are resulting in correct-looking but erroneous outputs. Libraries should therefore keep humans in the loop to ensure that they consider the processes and outputs as trustworthy over time.

3.3 Implementation Recommendation 3: Collaborative Governance

To address cross-collaboration challenges in AI implementation projects, it is essential that library staff proactively address collaboration tasks across different departments. Moreover, training and guidance should be provided to develop, utilise, and share expertise. Knowledge acquisition should encompass technical knowledge as well as legal, conceptual, and ethical aspects. Interdisciplinary collaboration is crucial for the acceptance and adoption decisions of AI tools, and the governance structures should be aligned to allow for these digital transformation efforts. As part of the governance structures, it is necessary to create transparent decision-making processes, involve all team members early on, and share knowledge and training within and across the teams.

3.4 Implementation Recommendation 4: Sustainable Funding for Implementation and Maintenance

Sustainable funding models are necessary for long-term AI acceptance and adoption. Investment needs to be made in internal AI expertise and literacy, as well as workforce development. Collaboration with external experts, e.g., public-private partnerships, can accelerate AI creation and implementation, but should not be done at the expense of internal specialists who need to know how to use AI.

Energy-efficient AI models should be considered and prioritised (carbon footprint and sustainability), and cost-benefit analyses are useful to consider all available, cheaper options.

Both factors need to be part of the funding decision for AI.

3.5 Implementation Recommendation 5: Consider Implementation as a Digital Transformation Opportunity

Automation through AI tools must complement human expertise, not replace it, to avoid mistrust and rejection of AI solutions. We therefore recommend prototyping, sandboxing, incremental, and gradual implementation to reduce the risk of rejection by clients and information specialists. Especially, the involvement of users and internal experts is key to AI adoption. Their early engagement with end-users (librarians, researchers, public users). Rethinking the current requirements and processes together with users will allow libraries to transform their existing processes and help create public value digitally.

Ethical AI use must be embedded in operations, e.g., audits can ensure AI is biassing or providing misinformation.

AI governance frameworks should be continuously reflected, revised, and updated.

4 AI Policy Recommendations for Libraries

4.1 Policy Recommendation 1: Policy Should Be Guiding Rather than Stipulating

Most European countries in which we conducted our research have established AI policies that are complementing the EU's policies and provide country-level hints on how to deal with AI. Future policy amendments should however consider the fast-changing nature of the technology. In an environment that grows faster and innovates at higher rates than usual, it is difficult to keep up the policy framework that governs them. From our research, we recommend that national and supranational policy frameworks should support the implementation efforts by providing broad guidelines that allow for guarding heritage and national values, instead of stipulating the use and implementation approaches of AI.

4.2 Policy Recommendation 2: Invest in Digital Literacy of Librarians and Information Specialists

Many of the cases we showed in this edited volume highlight the work of highly specialised IT professionals who are experimenting with different types of AI tools. However, in order to be successful in the adoption and use of the tools, the countries need additional policies and funding to increase the digital literacy of library staff across the board—and not just for IT specialists. Similar to the growth of digital literacy among their patrons, libraries need the funds to invest in the digital literacy of their employees.

4.3 Policy Recommendation 3: Align European (Democratic) Values with AI Development and Policymaking

Libraries are the major guardians of national values and heritage. Policies supporting the AI implementation to preserve national heritage, therefore, need to be value-driven and aligned with human prosperity in the EU. Policies should therefore not follow a technology industry's values and logic—instead, they need to be aligned with human values deeply ingrained in the EU's public values. Many libraries will not have the resources and political influence to deal with large vendors to preserve their national values and small languages. We therefore recommend that any future national and EU policy amendments focus on value preservation.

5 Outlook and Possibilities for Future Research

We have shown here that Artificial intelligence has become increasingly important in recent years for the implementation of public services. This has also influenced and redefined the digital transformation of National Libraries.

On the one hand, by using AI, formerly complex procedures conducted by information specialists are automated and as a result can be faster, such as the generation of metadata, personalisation of user experiences, and enhanced discovery systems. On the other hand, the usage of AI raises ethical questions as well as challenges related to governance and operations. Based on the outcomes of the EU LibrarIN project and previous initiatives co-financed by the European Union and legislative acts as the so-called AI Act, we highlight here possibilities for future research.

5.1 Ideas for Future Research

Future areas of research should focus on, first, the possibilities of how libraries can work on the alignment of the adoption of AI solutions with existing ethical and legal frameworks. For example, the new AI Act of the European Union [3] or UNESCO's Recommendation on the Ethics of Artificial Intelligence. The documents pay special attention to the ethical implications of AI systems regarding culture, education, science, information, and communication. The document aims to guide policymakers and stakeholders on how to ensure that AI is developed and used ethically [4]. Researchers in the library sciences and in public management of libraries can, for example, identify the value of these policy frameworks. Furthermore, they can help explain bias mitigation and how humans can oversee AI-driven library services, for example, by the regulation foreseen bias detection and correction mechanisms (Art. 10 AI Act).

A second research gap that we have identified is the need to evaluate the possibilities and access to information across the different demographic groups. On the one hand, there is a strong theoretical discourse on how AI and algorithms bias and create digital divides. On the other hand, there is little empirical basis for how AI affects the different kinds of library user groups. This causes the risk that the libraries unintentionally become places of algorithmic exclusion rather than inclusion. Therefore, the research question could be whether AI can reduce or increase the existing digital divides in access to library systems.

Third, the options of human-centric approaches for the development of AI-based solutions were described. The next step could be to further elaborate on which approach of participatory AI design fits most for the public services and resource constraints of libraries and how the libraries can be served as testbeds. During the different phases, the possible research might identify which kind of participatory AI design may have an impact on user trust, satisfaction, and acceptance of AI-based services. Therefore, it could be helpful to study how the different stakeholder groups, like users, librarians, and technicians, collectively develop the new AI tools in a co-design, co-creative, and inclusive way to ensure the outcomes' relevance and usability.

A fourth research topic could be how AI tools can support the digitisation and translation or contextualisation of the assets of different cultures in the environment of National Libraries, with a special focus on small languages or minority cultures. Small languages and minority cultures often contain cultural heritage with sensitive content. Therefore, it could be worthwhile to elaborate on frameworks for how AI solutions can further discover these culturally sensitive materials and make them accessible to a broader audience.

The fifth area of inquiry could focus on the sustainable usage of AI solutions. The development and maintenance of AI services can be pretty costly and resource-intensive, especially energy-consuming, as also described in the Atlas of AI: Power, Politics, and the Planetary Costs of Artificial Intelligence [5]. Therefore, investigating how AI solutions can be developed and implemented sustainably, for example, concerning the goals of green strategies like the 2030 Agenda for Sustainable Development of the United Nations [6], could be a worthwhile area for future research.

The research on the use of AI in National Libraries revealed various challenges. These issues are, for example, related to the dependency on global players for technology and AI tools developed for specific languages like English. A common and federated approach for the development of AI solutions and AI infrastructures could ensure independence from large vendors, create flexibility, and ensure that the solution will fit the specific needs of the libraries. This could lead to developing generic, reusable, and extensible building blocks. These building blocks could be commonly sandboxed and based on shared AI models and training datasets. To ensure the long-term sustainability of the results, the GOFA (Governance–Operations–Finance–Architecture) model of the European Union [7], as well as the Once-Only Principle defined by the Single Digital Gateway Regulation [8], should be taken into account.

This would help to ensure the development of meta-standards, decentralised data governance models, and ensure their interoperability on the different levels described by the European Interoperability Framework (EIF) [9].

Acknowledgements The work for this chapter was supported by the European Union's Horizon Europe Research and Innovation Programme under Grant Agreement ID 101061516.

References

1. D. Harisanty et al., Is adopting artificial intelligence in libraries urgency or a buzzword? A systematic literature review. J. Inf. Sci. **51**(2), 511–522 (2025)
2. A. Gasparini, H. Kautonen, Understanding artificial intelligence in research libraries—extensive literature review. LIBER. Q. **32**(1) (2022)
3. European Union, Regulation (EU) 2024/1689 of the European Parliament and of the Council of 13 June 2024 laying down harmonised rules on artificial intelligence and amending Regulations (EC) No 300/2008, (EU) No 167/2013, (EU) No 168/2013, (EU) 2018/858, (EU) 2018/1139 and (EU) 2019/2144 and Directives 2014/90/EU, (EU) 2016/797 and (EU) 2020/1828 (Artificial Intelligence Act) (2024)
4. UNESCO, *Recommendation on the ethics of artificial intelligence* (United Nations Educational, Scientific and Cultural Organization, 2021), p. 44
5. K. Crawford, Atlas of AI: power, politics, and the planetary costs of artificial intelligence. Perspect. Sci. Christian Faith **74**, 61–62 (2022)
6. United Nations, *Transforming our World: The 2030 Agenda for Sustainable Development U* (United Nations, 2015)
7. European Commission, Governance, Operations, Financing and Architecture Model (2023), https://ec.europa.eu/digital-building-blocks/sites/display/DIGITAL/4.+Manage+and+maintain+SOC. Accessed 11 May 2025
8. European Union, *Regulation (EU) 2018/1724 of the European Parliament and of the Council of 2 October 2018 Establishing a Single Digital Gateway to Provide Access to Information, to Procedures and to Assistance and Problem-Solving Services and Amending Regulation (EU) No 1024/2012* (European Union, 2018), p. 38
9. European Commission, *New European Interoperability Framework* (European Commission, 2017)

Ines Mergel is a University Professor of Public Administration in the Department of Politics and Public Administration at the University of Konstanz and a Fellow of the National Academy of Public Administration (Class of 2018). After holding positions at the Harvard Kennedy School of Government as a Doctoral Fellow and Postdoctoral Fellow (2002–2008), Professor Mergel was awarded tenure at the Maxwell School of Citizenship and Public Affairs (Syracuse University, NY) in 2014 (2008–2014) and then served as Associate Professor with tenure (2014–2016). Professor Mergel is a member of the supervisory board of the e-Governance Academy (Estonia). Other board memberships can be found here. Professor Mergel is a founding member of the international initiative Teaching Public Service in the Digital Age, which aims to integrate digital skills into the teaching and training of public managers. As part of this initiative, Professor Mergel was appointed a Schmidt Futures Innovation Fellow in 2022.

Justus Kühler is studying for a bachelor's degree in political science and public administration at the University of Konstanz. He is particularly interested in the latest developments in public administration that reflect the trend towards democratisation. He is particularly interested in the application of new forms of participation at the local level. He has already gained initial experience with municipal administration through his involvement in local politics.

Anna-Lea Schumann is currently pursuing a master's degree in Politics and Public Administration at the University of Konstanz. Her research interests focus on applying modern working practices within public administration and their implications for public value creation. In her bachelor's thesis, she explored the use and implementation of design thinking in libraries. She has gained initial practical experience through various internships in public administration, providing her with valuable insights into the operational methods and processes of the public sector.

Carsten Schmidt focuses on concepts and methodologies for e-government in the European Union and the associated countries, as well as the related aspects of digital infrastructure. Particular attention is paid to the areas of the once-only principle, European large-scale pilot projects, and sustainability. Before, he was involved in different positions (Project Director, Work Package Manager, etc.) in European large-scale projects like mGov4EU, TOOP, e-SENS, and e-CODEX. He worked for the Ministry of Justice NRW, Germany, the Technical University of Tallinn (TalTech), and the University of Tartu, Estonia.

Innovating Libraries: The LibrarIN Toolkit for Policy and Practice

Marieke Willems, Marta Anducas, and Elena Silvestrini

Abstract This chapter presents the LibrarIN Toolkit, designed to support the transformation of European libraries to address societal challenges and adapt to the changing needs of their communities through value co-creation and social innovation. The Toolkit addresses the "European innovation paradox" by providing tools and methods that translate research into actionable policy and practice. It comprises three main components: the Library Policy Tracker, the What-Works Database, and the Research Knowledge Base.The Toolkit allows for the benchmarking of National Library policies, fostering the adoption of EU-level recommendations, showcases examples of social innovation practices, and offers a repository of research literature on social innovation in libraries. The Toolkit was developed through a collaborative process involving library experts and policymakers, illustrating the effectiveness of co-creation, evidence-based advocacy, and context-specific innovation.

The chapter provides an example of how each of the tools can be used to support the implementation of AI and digital innovation in library services and operations. By aligning with EU priorities and promoting stakeholder engagement, the LibrarIN Toolkit aims to empower libraries as key pillars of democracy and social cohesion.

Keywords Libraries · Social Innovation · Toolkit · Library Policy Tracker · What-Works Database · Value co-creation · Policymakers · Practitioners

1 Introduction

Libraries underpin vibrant democracies [1]. They play a key role in social inclusion and cohesion and are well-placed to contribute to tackling societal challenges. Under the EU Work Plan for Culture 2023–2026, library experts and policymakers

M. Willems (✉) · M. Anducas · E. Silvestrini
The Lisbon Council, Brussels, Belgium
e-mail: marieke.willems@lisboncouncil.net; marta.anducas@lisboncouncil.net; elena.silvestrini@lisboncouncil.net

I. Mergel, C. Schmidt (eds.), *AI Innovations in Public Services*,
https://doi.org/10.1007/978-3-032-01344-6_15

are called upon to define a roadmap to strengthen the multiple roles of libraries as transmitters of cultural works, skills, and European values [2]. To fulfil these important roles, libraries need to be creative and responsive to change. This requires ongoing innovation and a commitment to changing community needs [3].

There is a need for social innovation in libraries and the participation of communities in the future of libraries, as both trends are increasingly important. Libraries need to perform new functions that can "reposition" them at the core of cultural and socio-economic activity in the neighbourhoods, cities, and regions where they operate, and where they constitute a key part of the innovation ecosystems. Consequently, libraries' immense potential for promoting entrepreneurship, or other public services, may lead to new ways of sustainable development and funding. This requires social innovation and new managerial models where participation and co-creation become possible. Additionally, expectations for increased public value creation to meet today's users' complex demands for public libraries are rising, as well as the pressure to deliver high-quality services in an efficient and accountable manner.

In this context, the transformation of libraries providing public services requires thinking of inclusive ways of citizen engagement to create public value. The traditional view of top-down public administrations, in which citizens can only passively absorb supply-led services, is no longer appropriate. The challenges mentioned above increase the need for a demand-driven design of public library services that incorporate the opportunities provided by new technologies to enable the effective engagement of citizens and organisations "to unlock social assets".

2 The Need for LibrarIN Tools for Library Policymakers and Innovators

In December 1995, the Green Paper on innovation (Com 95/688) [4] introduced a term that framed the debate on innovation policy for decades: the so-called European innovation paradox, which argued that Europe was excellent in research but failed to exploit this knowledge effectively. It is fair to say that this paradox is very much visible in the context of research about public administration—including public libraries—and e-government, which are frequent topics in the New Bauhaus and Green Deal initiatives and where European researchers have been global leaders. However, this impressive body of research (both in quality and quantity) has achieved a limited impact on the practice and policy of European governments. Typically, research projects delivered a substantial review of the state of the art, a set of well-designed pilots, and a well-written, ambitious exploitation plan. While the insights from research were significant, the actual impact on the practice was minimal: the increased attention to openness and co-creation was more the result of institutional isomorphism than of evidence-based policymaking [5].

The LibrarIN project aims to overcome this paradox and dedicates a significant part of the project to achieving policy impact. Rather than focusing on a set of micro-actions, it already includes activities for scaling up public libraries' innovation at a systemic level, by leveraging and learning from the substantial amount of innovation that is already taking place. Too often, public libraries are considered purely resistant to change, when actually they must deal with a complex reality and constantly negotiate their action. LibrarIN recognises this and precisely aims to empower the innovators inside public libraries (policymakers and practitioners) by providing them with the best possible evidence, ambitious policy recommendations and ways to demonstrate progress. This allows them to adapt to the changing needs of their community, contributes to addressing societal challenges, and strengthens their role as vibrant pillars of democracy and social cohesion.

LibrarIN aims to be not only a source of knowledge but a service for change in public libraries. To do so, it creates a set of tools and methods that provide both the knowledge and the incentives to support implementation, sharing some of the most advanced European experiences in social innovation in libraries.

The LibrarIN policy support towards value co-creation and social innovation for a new generation of European libraries is built on three strands of activities. First, LibrarIN research results and insights generate the basis for bold but actionable policy recommendations that provide greater legitimacy and endorsement for libraries' innovators. The LibrarIN evidence-based recommendations are presented in high-impact policy briefs and accompanied by policy roundtables to pave the way for proposed innovation measures. The first LibrarIN policy brief on *Reimagine Libraries: Sparking Collaboration for Innovation to Tackle Libraries' 21st Century Challenges*, provided a first version of the LibrarIN co-creation for library innovation framework and four policy action areas to consider [6]. The evidence-based policy recommendations were rooted in the current policy debate, and expert feedback from library practitioners contributing to the LibrarIN project via its Stakeholder Panel [7]. This collaborative approach linking research results with insights from expert practitioners and policymakers has been key to the delivery and uptake of LibrarIN policy briefs. The second brief *Boosting and Evaluating Collaborative Innovations in Libraries: Managerial Guidelines and Policy Implications* provides practical guidelines for library practitioners to leverage the LibrarIN Research Framework for library innovation [8]. The third and joint TELL and LibrarIN brief, *Collaborative Innovation and Best Practice Diffusion in European Libraries: Adapting for Local Impact*, lists smart library tools and actionable policy recommendations to ensure the effective spread of inspiring and adaptable examples for library innovation in Europe [8, 9]. At the time of writing, additional policy briefs are planned to be published on the new metrics for library transformation, implementing Artificial Intelligence (AI), social entrepreneurship, and living labs to develop innovative public services in ways that enable the co-creation of value.

The second strand of policy support covers the knowledge to implement those recommendations. Co-creation is both an art and a science. LibrarIN provides a structured knowledge base of good practices and open platforms for mutual learning between libraries. It will create a trusted space for honest and direct dialogue between practitioners and researchers, through a set of state-of-the-art online and offline instruments: a database, panel events, and online engagement.

Finally, the third strand of policy support offers a system to track policy progress transparently, intuitively, and appealingly. The LibrarIN policy tracker is a central point of reference to discover who is doing what. The tracker offers incentives for decision-makers to adopt co-creation policy measures by providing a recognition system, again designed to empower innovators inside libraries. Libraries can benchmark National Library policies on a set of "policy indicators": binary variables regarding the implementation of the European Council recommendations on library legislation, corroborated by evidence.

The following sections will focus on the LibrarIN Toolkit, providing policy support via the above-described strands of activities.

3 Description of the Toolkit

This section describes each of the three tools available in the LibrarIN Toolkit and how their collaborative design and implementation with the LibrarIN community of researchers, practitioners, and policymakers ensure alignment with the community needs. Thus, it fosters the adoption of the LibrarIN tools and recommendations grounded in the project research framework to push for a new generation of European libraries well-equipped to adapt to the societal challenges and changing needs of their communities.

Explore the LibrarIN Toolkit here: https://librarin.eu/toolkit/

3.1 The Tools

The Toolkit provides three resources, each operating in a dedicated scope, namely, policy, library, and academic levels. Table 1 outlines each of the tools and their respective scope.

Table 1 Outlines of the tools and respective scope

	Library Policy Tracker	What-Works Database	Research Knowledge Base
Scope	Policy level	Library level	Academic level
Content	Monitors the extent to which national policies align with EU-level recommendations in the LibrarIN research areas	Collects experiences, cases, and good practices that have fostered value co-creation and social innovation in libraries	Repository of papers, studies, and reports on value co-creation and social innovation areas

3.1.1 Library Policy Tracker

The **Library Policy Tracker** systematically assesses the extent to which European Union-level recommendations have been adopted in the national legislation, policies, and strategies of Member States. Focusing specifically on provisions that support or foster the co-creation of value in libraries, the tracker converts these recommendations into an operational checklist of binary (Yes/No) indicators.

The primary reference for the initial set of indicators is the Council of Europe's Recommendation on library legislation and policy in Europe [3]. This document updates the 2000 Council of Europe/EBLIDA Guidelines on Library Legislation and Policy and includes relevant Council of Europe conventions, international legal instruments, and professional standards. It also reaffirms the role of libraries in advancing the United Nations 2030 Agenda for Sustainable Development. Complementary references used are the IFLA-UNESCO Public Library Manifesto 2022 [10, 11] and the New European Bauhaus initiative [12], both aligned with the social innovation and co-creation goals of LibrarIN.

The tracker is designed as a matrix-style dashboard, with EU Member States represented on the horizontal axis, and indicators grouped in five dimensions on the vertical axis:

(a) Participatory management and sustainable growth
(b) Innovation and Artificial Intelligence (AI)
(c) Social innovation
(d) Living labs
(e) Metrics and monitoring

These domains are aligned with the project research framework, policy briefs, and recommendations and allow the tools to interconnect the policy tracker for national alignment with the European policy debate with LibrarIN evidence-based policy recommendations and real-world examples of social innovation in European libraries (Fig. 1).

The matrix uses a colour code for each indicator:

- Green confirms that the EU Member State has a national policy, strategy, or guideline on the topic of the indicator, as recommended on the EU level
- Red indicates their absence
- Blue shows no data have been found

This visual matrix allows for cross-country benchmarking on the adoption of EU-level recommendations in national policies and guidelines and highlights cross-cutting gaps to be considered.

Each bullet is interactive, linking to a country-specific page that presents the indicator statement, the Yes/No/No-data response, supporting documentation for positive responses, and any additional contextual information. These detailed pages serve both as documentation tools and as resources for policymakers and practitioners (Fig. 2).

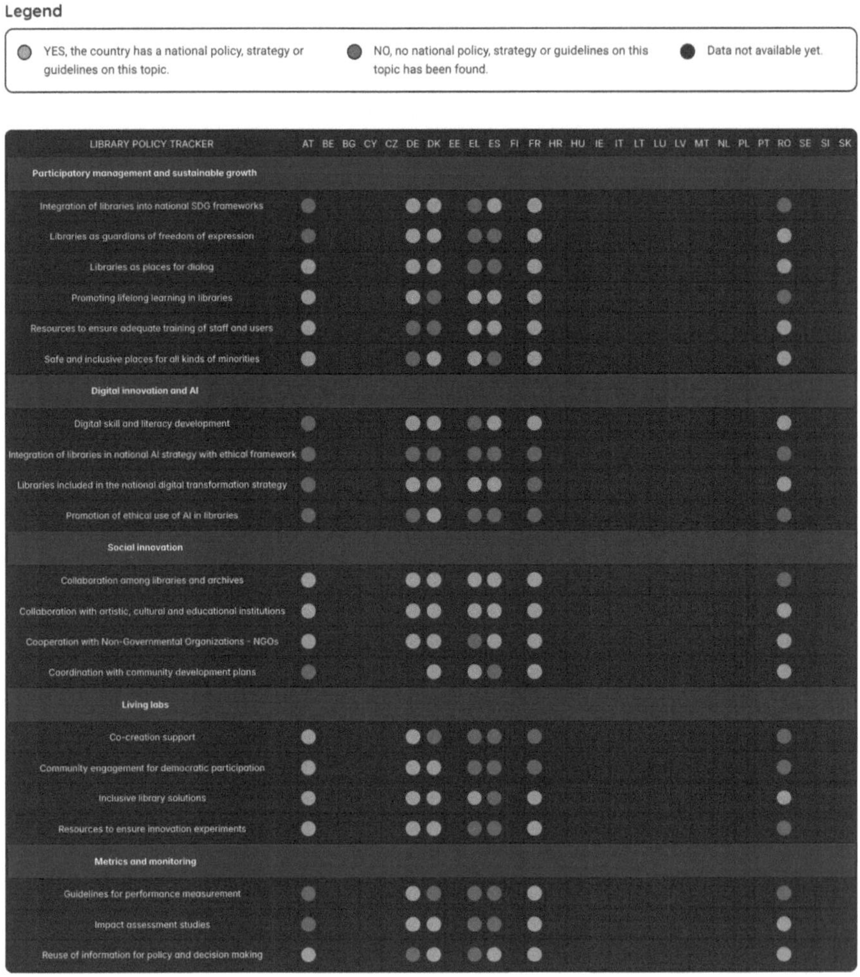

Fig. 1 Screenshot of the Library Policy Tracker with initial data

In addition to evidence sources, they include real-life examples drawn from the project's **What-Works Database**, along with tailored policy recommendations derived from the project's **policy briefs**. This layered structure supports comparative analysis, mutual learning, and policy transfer.

Discover the Library Policy Tracker: https://librarin.eu/toolkit/library-policy-tracker/

3.1.2 What-Works Database

The **What-Works Database** is designed to inspire innovators in libraries by showcasing experiences and proven practices of value co-creation and social innovation from European libraries. It invites library professionals and innovators to explore a

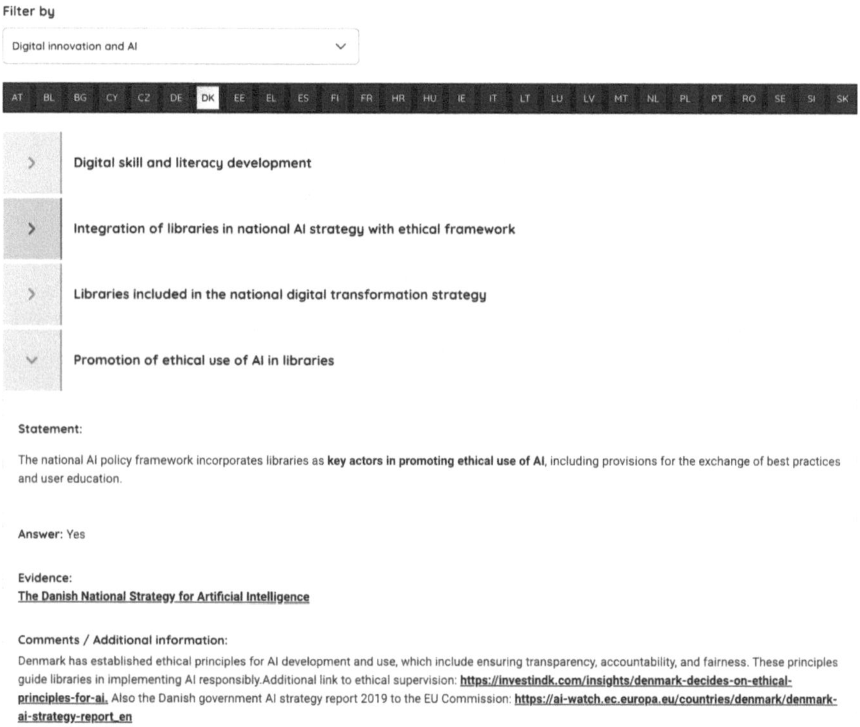

Fig. 2 Detailed page for Denmark for the Digital Innovation and AI dimension

curated collection of initiatives, offering practical methodologies and solutions successfully applied by peers in diverse institutions and national settings (Fig. 3).

The What-Works Database platform features a user-friendly browsing page that is equipped with several filtering options. Users can search by theme (aligned with the dimensions of the Library Policy Tracker), country, type of library, year of launch, and stage of the initiative. An interactive map enables geographic searches, while a free-text search field supports targeted queries.

Search results are presented as a collection of interactive cards. Each initiative is presented as a clickable card displaying the title, subtitle, brief description, library type, and associated tags. Selecting a card opens a dedicated page that provides in-depth information about the initiative, including its summary, stakeholders and beneficiaries, co-creation process, results and outcomes, challenges and bottlenecks, success factors, lessons learned, contributor details, and references. Each entry also has an open comment field, designed as a contact point for questions, guidance, and references for the LibrarIN community.

As the name of the tool implies, initiatives included in the What-Works Database are initiatives that proved successful in a specific library setting at a specific moment in time. To emphasise this, the original title of each of the cases included has

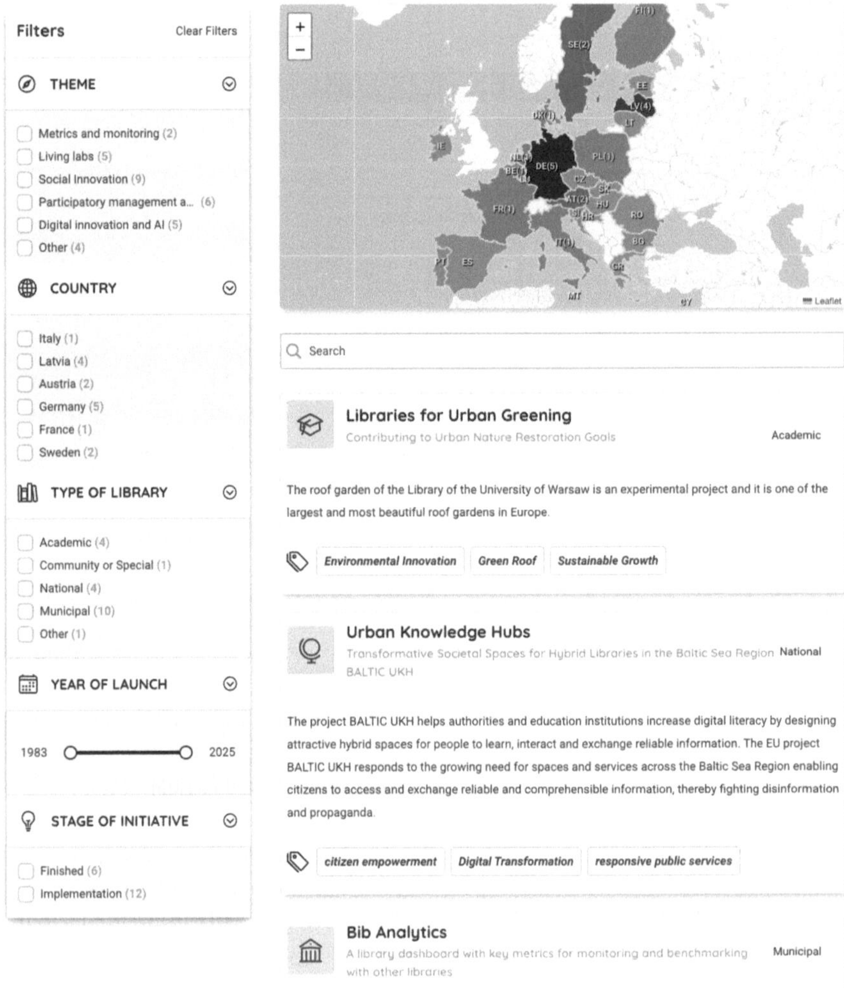

Fig. 3 Screenshot of the What-Works Database main page

remained unchanged while offering a short descriptive text to convey the essence of the initiative, highlighting what worked well.

Navigate the What-Works Database here: https://librarin.eu/toolkit/what-works-db/

3.1.3 Research Knowledge Base

The **Research Knowledge Base** is a curated repository of research articles and publications used in the literature reviews conducted in the project, covering the conceptual and theoretical roots of the LibrarIN research framework. Research articles cover topics such as digital transformation, living labs, co-creation, service

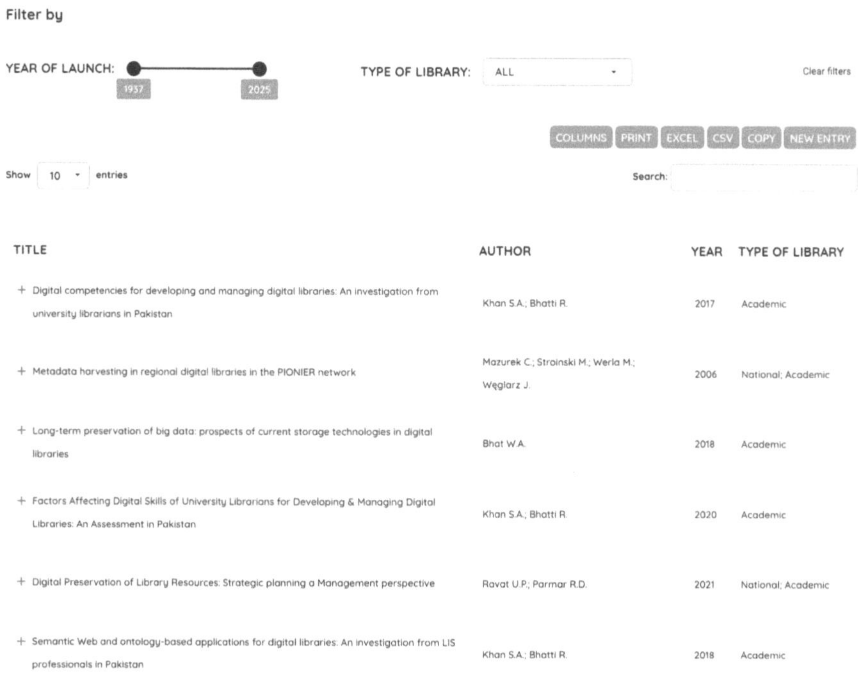

Fig. 4 Screenshot of the Research Knowledge Base

design, and innovation in library contexts. With over 5000 publications from prominent journals and publishers, the database serves as a valuable resource for researchers, policymakers, and library staff who aim to dive deeper into the evolving field of social innovation in libraries (Fig. 4).

The database allows users to filter entries by type of library, year of launch or through free-text searches. Each entry includes the title of the publication, author(s), year of publication, type of library involved, keywords, and abstract. The list of entries can be easily copied, printed, or exported for further analysis or dissemination.

3.2 The Co-creation Process of the Toolkit

Consistent with the co-creation focus of the project, the Toolkit has been designed and populated collaboratively to ensure its future uptake. The process involved project partners, members of the LibrarIN Stakeholders Panel, and a third group of library innovators from the wider network. The LibrarIN Stakeholder Panel comprises a diverse group of 36 experts from 19 European countries with representatives from national, academic, municipal, and community libraries alongside policymakers, international Library organisations, academia, and civil society, each with their extensive, valuable networks.

The design process of the Library Policy Tracker adopts the four-phased approach for effective collaboration in libraries outlined in the LibrarIN policy brief "*Boosting and Evaluating Collaborative Innovations in Libraries: Managerial Guidelines and Policy Implications*". Based on the LibrarIN research framework, this document provides a step-by-step guide for libraries implementing collaborative innovation, emphasising the importance of engaging a broad range of stakeholders, including end-users, other libraries, and organisations (Fig. 5).

3.2.1 Context Analysis

The initial research phase started with a mapping of supranational (international and EU) policies, guiding principles and standards, as well as policies and guidelines by international and EU library associations and civil society organisations. This analysis of the EU policy landscape served to identify key reference points for the initial selection of indicators. Concurrently, project partners engaged in discussions on methodological decisions, considering the project design and research framework. These decisions included the use of binary (Y/N) answers for indicators,

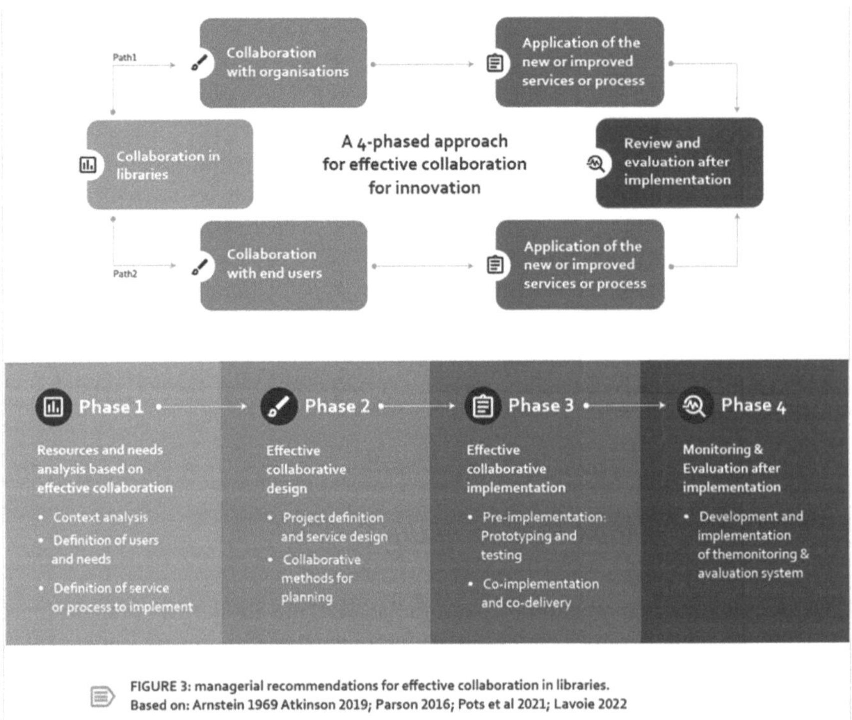

Fig. 5 Four-phased approach for collaboration in libraries described in the upcoming LibrarIN policy brief #2

establishing the analytical scope at the national level and focusing on monitoring the adoption of EU-level policy recommendations in Member States' national policies, leaving specific implementation and local impact to the What-Works Database.

With the context and reference points established, a preliminary list of 19 indicators was developed, focusing on recommendations with direct implications in terms of policy innovation and alignment with the scope of the project. These indicators were clustered into five dimensions, reflecting the LibrarIN conceptual framework and research areas.

3.2.2 Collaborative Design

A co-creation session with stakeholders was held to refine the Library Policy Tracker. Participants engaged in discussions to improve and validate the preliminary list of dimensions and indicators and suggested potential uses of the tool. Their feedback informed the refined list of indicators and helped shape the dashboard. To ensure informed discussions, participants received pre-readings describing the purpose of the Toolkit, the policy tracker, methodological choices, and the preliminary list of indicators. Several techniques were used to encourage participant engagement and participation such as an icebreaker, facilitated breakout rooms, collaborative online boards, and note-taking to collect inputs for further refinement (Fig. 6).

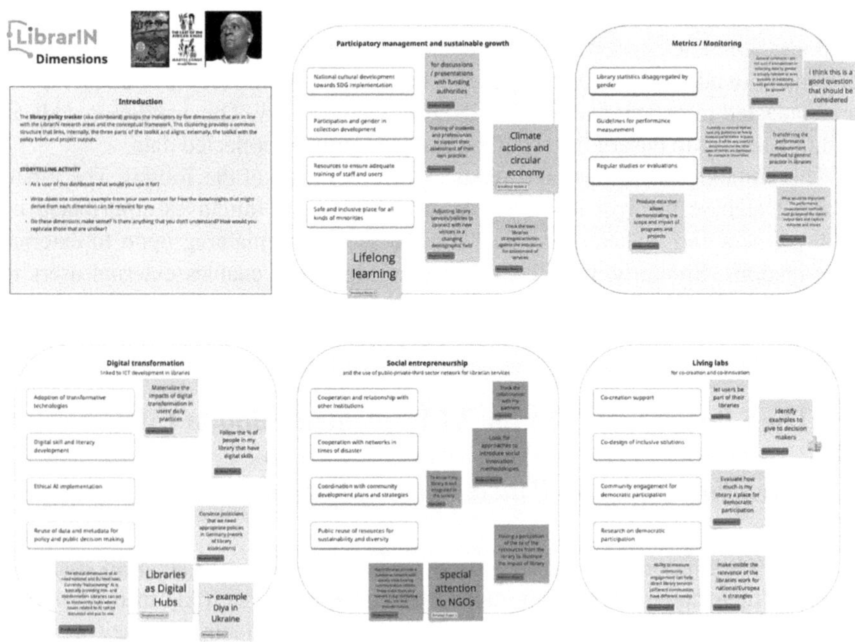

Fig. 6 Online board used during the co-creation session

The integration of feedback from the co-creation session was guided by the relevance of the proposed indicators to potential users. If an indicator lacked meaningful value to the intended audience, retaining it served little purpose and could detract from the effectiveness of the dashboard. Prioritising indicators according to user needs and project goals ensured that the tool remained practical and relevant. Following this approach, four indicators were removed, three were added to the list, and several were rephrased. The refined list of indicators consisted of 18 indicators grouped by the original five dimensions, which remained unchanged.

In the validation phase of the design process, diverse policymakers were consulted to assess the usefulness and relevance of the proposed indicators in supporting their work. Each indicator was evaluated using a four-point scale (Not at all, Slightly, Moderately, and Very well), with an open field for additional comments and suggestions. This feedback led to several adjustments: the addition of two new indicators, the division of one existing indicator, and textual refinements. The final list comprises 21 indicators grouped into five dimensions (Appendix).

3.2.3 Collaborative Data Collection

Accurate and comprehensive data collection from all EU Member States for the Library Policy Tracker requires active collaboration between LibrarIN consortium members, the project stakeholder panel, and country experts from the wider network. Data gathering starts with desk research conducted by partners and stakeholders, who evaluate each indicator for their country by providing a "Yes" or "No" response, a link to supporting evidence for affirmative answers, and any additional comments or clarifications where needed. Following data collection, country experts are contacted to review and validate data for their country. This validation adds an additional layer to ensure the accuracy and reliability of collected data.

This collaborative approach extends to the other tools of the Toolkit. The What-Works Database incorporates multiple experiences and initiatives contributed by both partners and Stakeholder Panel members, while remaining open to external contributions. Similarly, the Research Knowledge Base enables external users to propose new entries through a dedicated submission form.

4 The LibrarIN Toolkit for AI Implementation in Libraries

4.1 *Benchmarking AI Policies Across Europe*

Innovators in libraries looking to address societal challenges or adapt to changing needs of their communities and adopt Artificial Intelligence (AI) in their library services and operations will need to understand the policy landscape they are operating in. The Library Policy Tracker allows them to identify European and national policies and strategies advancing AI for library innovation. In particular, it provides an overview of how EU policies are adopted and evaluated in EU Member States, in addition to evidence of national-level strategies and policies addressing Digital Innovation and AI for libraries.

At the moment of writing, the Library policy tracker contains data on seven EU Member States, namely, Austria (AT), Germany (DE), Denmark (DK), Greece (EL), Spain (ES), France (FR), and Romania (RO) (Fig. 7).

When looking to implement AI in library services and operations, the policy tracker shows the adoption of EU-level recommendations on national level, by providing evidence of existing policies on the topics of (a) digital skill and literacy development, (b) integration of libraries in national AI strategy with ethical framework, (c) libraries included in the national digital transformation strategy, and (d) promotion of ethical use of AI in libraries.

4.1.1 Digital Skill and Literacy Development

When looking at promoting the implementation of effective and tailored media, information and digital literacy programmes for library staff and users in libraries, five out of the seven EU Member State countries currently providing data have national plans or strategies that encourage this.

It is worth highlighting a few country-specific comments on digital skill and literacy development:

- In Spain, although libraries are not specifically mentioned in the National Plan for Digital Skills [12], the IV Strategic Plan of the Library Cooperation Council (CCB) emphasises the importance of "strengthening media and information literacy". This plan highlights the role of libraries as centres of knowledge and learning and includes specific proposals for implementing media and information literacy programmes.

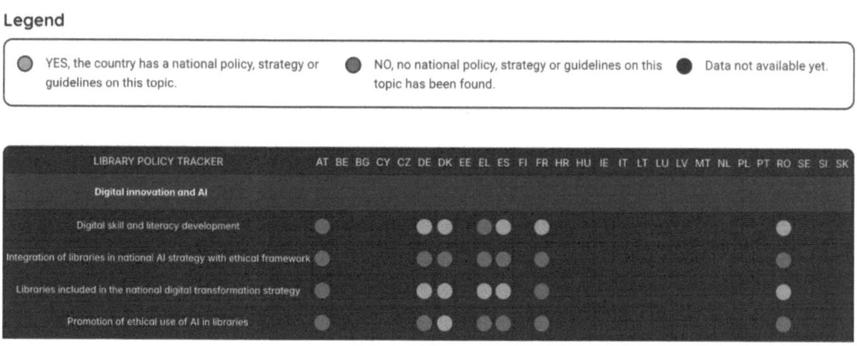

Fig. 7 Screenshot of the Library Policy Tracker with initial data on Digital Innovation and AI from Austria (AT), Germany (DE), Denmark (DK), Greece (EL), Spain (ES), France (FR), and Romania (RO)

- Denmark is the EU's Digital Champion in New Survey [13]. Every year, the European Commission releases the Digital Economy and Society Index (DESI), which measures the level of digitalisation in European Union member states according to four benchmark categories. The four benchmark categories comprise indicators within human capital, connectivity, integration of digital technology, and digital public services, all of which give an overview of EU efforts in digitalisation.
- The "Digital Transformation Bible 2020–2025" [14] sets out the new national strategy for digital transformation. However, there isn't a specific national strategy exclusively dedicated to implementing tailored media, information, and digital literacy programmes for library staff and users.
- The French national strategy to reinforce digital literacy is quite broad, yet libraries are part of this strategy [15, 16].
- In Germany there is no coherent or unique strategy, instead there are several individual initiatives.

4.1.2 Integration of Libraries in National AI Strategy with Ethical Framework

When looking at whether the national AI implementation strategy includes libraries and ensures the enforcement of privacy and equity principles, all of the seven EU Member State countries currently providing data have a national AI strategy, but none of them include libraries.

Important to note is that the French National Library defined and published an AI roadmap [17], but in the French national strategy, libraries aren't at the core of the strategy. And Germany has a national AI strategy, but libraries are not explicitly named in it. However, privacy and equity are core principles of Germany's AI policy. Libraries are also bound by strong data protection and privacy laws (GDPR) and will have to comply with the upcoming EU AI Act.

4.1.3 Libraries Included in the National Digital Transformation Strategy

When looking at provisions to scale up library practices from analogue to digital, five out of the seven EU Member State countries currently providing data have national digital transformation plans that include this.

It is worth highlighting a few country-specific comments on libraries included in the national digital transformation strategy:

- Greece has a national digital transformation plan that includes provisions to scale up library practices from analogue to digital, as outlined in the Digital Transformation Bible 2020–2025.
- The National Digitalisation Strategy 2022–2026 [18] in Spain has been developed by the strategic working group of the Consejo de Cooperación Bibliotecaria

and outlines guidelines for digitising and disseminating bibliographic heritage across various administrations and institutions, including libraries.
- The digital transformation plan related to AI and libraries is hosted by the French National Library [17].
- In Romania, libraries are an important part of digitisation and preserving national cultural and historic heritage and promote this through digital services [19].

4.1.4 Promotion of Ethical Use of AI in Libraries

Out of the seven EU Member States countries currently with data in the policy tracker, only Denmark has a national AI policy framework that incorporates libraries as key actors in promoting ethical use of AI, including provisions for the exchange of best practices and user education. Denmark has established ethical principles for AI development and use, which include ensuring transparency, accountability, and fairness [20]. These principles guide libraries in implementing AI responsibly [21].

It is worth highlighting a few country-specific comments on the absence of promotion of ethical use of AI in libraries in national policies:

- In Austria it is the single libraries, such as the Austrian National Library, which have an AI policy covering the responsible use of AI [22].
- Germany has a national AI policy framework, but libraries are not explicitly named as key actors in it. However, the German Library Association (DBV) identifies AI as a transformative technology for libraries.
- In Spain, the AI Strategy 2024 [23] establishes the Spanish Agency for the Supervision of Artificial Intelligence (AESIA) to ensure the deployment of safe, responsible, and ethical AI systems nationwide. This includes the creation of knowledge, training, and dissemination of ethical AI practices. However, libraries are not specifically mentioned.
- In France, the France 2030 national plan or in the AI national strategy, focus lies more on startups or research than on libraries. Best practices or user education was already part of the missions of libraries. In addition, institutions like the Liaison Centre for Education and Media Information (CLEMI) train people, including children, on AI questions [24].
- In Romania, the National Strategy regarding AI [25], there is no specific mention of ethical use of AI in libraries.

4.1.5 Cross-Country and Cross-Domain Benchmarking

If we compare the country scores on the adoption of EU-level recommendations on Digital Innovation and AI, there is still room for improvement in each of the seven countries currently with data in the Library Policy Tracker, with Denmark scoring three out of four indicators, and Austria adopting none of the EU-level recommendations.

A comparison of domains shows that Digital Innovation and AI have the lowest adoption rate, with only 40% of EU-level recommendations implemented at the national level. In contrast, Social Innovation shows a significantly higher alignment, with 86% of EU recommendations adopted nationally.

Innovators in libraries, both practitioners and policymakers, can adopt and implement the LibrarIN policy recommendations related to the indicators to adapt to the changing needs of their communities and societal challenges. Furthermore, they can source inspiration from the cases related to AI and Digital Innovation directly suggested by the What Works Database (WWD) and adapt it to their specific context.

4.2 What Works? Start Implementing AI in Your Library

The What-Works Database serves as a valuable comparative tool for libraries aiming to adapt to the changing needs of their communities and adopt AI in their services and operations. The taxonomy used in the What-Works Database allows for targeted searches by country, theme, type of library, theme (e.g. Digital Innovation and AI), year of launch of the social innovation initiative, and its current stage.

When looking for inspiration and examples of libraries implementing AI in their services and operations through effective collaboration with their community, the What-Works Database shows six real-life cases at the time of writing. The search indicates cases from municipal and national libraries, from Germany, Latvia, the Netherlands, and Sweden, and two out of six cases have reached their finalisation stage. The structured fields in the individual case pages (such as summary of the case, problem addressed, solution adopted, implementation steps, outcomes, beneficiaries, stakeholders, and challenges) enable library staff to analyse diverse AI initiatives using specific criteria. By examining summaries that highlight key successes and rationales, libraries can understand the motivations behind AI adoption in other libraries and learn what worked well in similar initiatives across different contexts.

Worth highlighting are the following specific fields:

- **Problems addressed and solutions adopted** are particularly useful in identifying recurrent issues and how AI has been leveraged to meet these needs, such as the need for better information retrieval, personalisation of services, or automation of routine tasks.
- The **implementation steps** provide a blueprint for inspiration or replication if possible, offering a chronological view of how other libraries transitioned from concept to execution. Milestones and achievements, when listed, help libraries understand what is realistically feasible at various stages of AI integration.
- The fields detailing **stakeholders and beneficiaries** shed light on the ecosystems involved. Understanding who benefits (be it patrons, researchers, or underserved communities) and who the key actors are (such as librarians, IT

professionals, or external partners) provides useful input for project planning and stakeholder alignment.

- The **co-creation process** field adds further value by illustrating participatory approaches, which can inform more inclusive and sustainable AI implementations.
- The fields on **challenges and bottlenecks** and **outcomes and impacts** help libraries anticipate potential obstacles, such as funding issues or resistance to change, and draw inspiration from how these challenges were addressed or mitigated within other library contexts.

The What-Works Database fields provide structured and comparable information, forming a practical knowledge base that not only showcases innovation but also guides strategic thinking and evidence-based implementation of AI in libraries. As more and more cases are being crowdsourced and uploaded to the What-Works Database, the "AI Parade" [26] case showcases an example of how the information provided can be useful to other libraries as an inspiration for developing AI initiatives (Fig. 8).

The AI Parade case from the KB National Library of the Netherlands in cooperation with the "Dutch AI Coalition" 21 municipal libraries is a travelling exhibition and series of events for municipal libraries with ever-changing activities to introduce the public to the possibilities of AI and to engage in a conversation about it together. The case offers several instructive lessons on the implementation of AI-focused programming within the public library sector to engage the public, raise

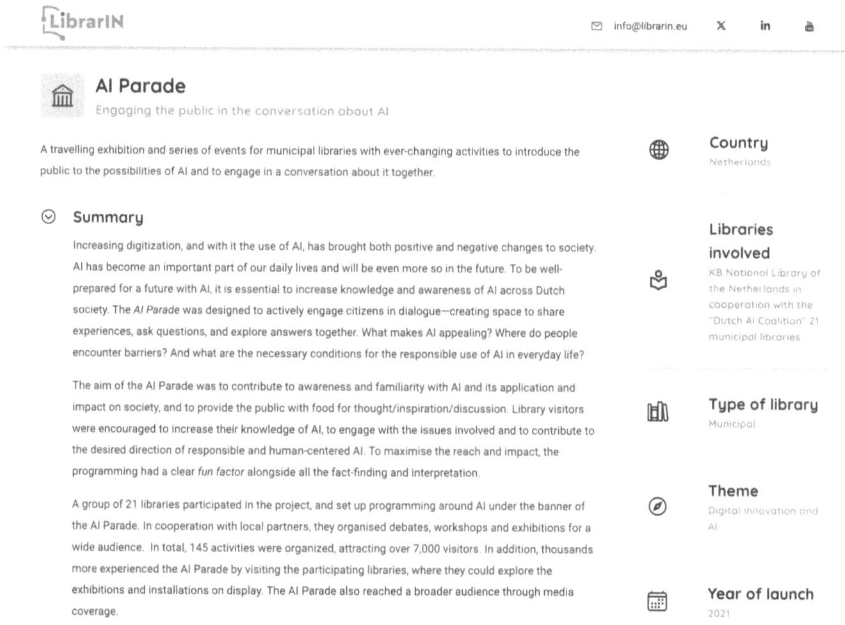

Fig. 8 Screenshot of the What-Works Database with data from the AI Parade case

awareness, and promote responsible AI use. One of the principal lessons emerging from this case shares insights into the necessity of planning adequate preparatory time for such ambitious projects. The originally planned 1-month preparation period proved insufficient for all participating partners; a timeline of at least 6 months was identified as essential for effective planning, stakeholder coordination, and community outreach. Furthermore, the initiative underlined the value of flexible and scalable programme design. The exhibition's initial touring model encountered practical limitations due to the size and transport requirements of physical installations. These challenges were successfully mitigated through the development of modular digital components and the adoption of more adaptable scheduling approaches, allowing libraries to tailor activities to local needs and capacities. The AI Parade also demonstrated the effectiveness of a co-creative and decentralised approach, where libraries operated as both hosts and curators of locally relevant programming within a nationally coordinated structure. This model facilitated meaningful community engagement and addressed the needed contextualisation of AI themes in accordance with local interests and concerns. Importantly, the positive impact of the initiative was significantly strengthened by the prominent societal discourse surrounding AI during the implementation period. The widespread public attention obtained by high-profile generative AI applications—such as ChatGPT and DALL·E—created a favourable cultural climate in which interest in AI-related issues surged. This broader media and societal engagement acted as a catalyst, drawing increased public interest to the library events and amplifying their reach. As a result, the AI Parade initiative was able to capitalise on this momentum, positioning libraries as timely and relevant spaces for informed discussion on the ethical, social, and practical dimensions of AI.

4.3 *Your Evidence-Based Knowledge*

For those wanting to dive deeper into the research literature used in the LibrarIN research frameworks, there is a wealth of information freely accessible via the LibrarIN knowledge repository. It is the corpus of evidence on which the research of LibrarIN is based.

The curated repository shows the academic literature that mapped and formed the basis of the LibrarIN conceptual and measuring framework as well as the theoretical and empirical research conducted. Grounded in this solid research framework, LibrarIN provides a set of actionable recommendations for innovators in libraries, both practitioners and policymakers. At the moment of writing, the first policy brief has been published titled *Reimagine Libraries: Sparking Collaboration for Innovation to Tackle Libraries' 21st Century Challenges* [6] and validated through an open discussion with library policymakers and practitioners. And other policy briefs with recommendations on each of the research areas, and aligned with the policy tracker domains, are planned for the final stage of the LibrarIN project.

5 Lessons Learned, Conclusions, and Future Outlook

"What the LibrarIN project seeks to aggregate is particularly important, precisely because of our desire, as libraries and librarians alike, to know how they are evaluated in the EU Member States, and not only, how libraries could provide new services and what are the optimal directions for this. Being currently president of the National Library Commission and having to report on the state of libraries, filling in the data in the form was revealing for me, from the point of view of the national policies that need to be addressed, in a first phase." (said by one of the libary country experts)

5.1 Lessons Learned

The development and early implementation of the LibrarIN Toolkit confirms that innovation in libraries thrives when built in close collaboration with communities, evidence-based, and fully aware of societal challenges and the current policy debate.

The following lessons learned can be identified:

- **Co-creation fosters relevance and future adoption of the Toolkit**: Involving a diverse group of stakeholders ensures the LibrarIN Toolkit reflects the real needs and goals of the library ecosystem across Europe. This participatory process significantly improves both the usability and uptake of the tools.
- **Tailored innovation is more effective than one-size-fits-all**: The What-Works Database highlights the importance of context-specific and community-based approaches and allows for adaptation to local contexts.
- **Transparency and benchmarking drive policy change**: The Library Policy Tracker encourages national-level reflection and fosters constructive comparison among EU Member States. This approach aims to motivate policy reform and alignment with EU-level recommendations.
- **Evidence-based advocacy**: The curated knowledge base and policy briefs not only inform innovation efforts but also strengthen the advocacy capabilities of libraries, equipping them with data and narratives that resonate with funders and decision-makers.

5.2 Conclusions

The LibrarIN Toolkit has demonstrated the power of structured, collaborative innovation in strengthening the role of libraries as vibrant, cohesive, and forward-looking institutions. Through its three complementary tools, it connects research, policy, and practice. By aligning with the current library policy debate and EU priorities such as the Green Deal and digital transformation, as well as the United Nations Sustainable Development Goals, the Toolkit anchors libraries in broader societal goals, enabling them to strengthen their role as key pillars of vibrant democracies and social cohesion.

In the joint policy brief *Collaborative Innovation and Best Practice Diffusion in European Libraries: Adapting for Local Impact*, TELL and LibrarIN projects address the challenge of effectively sharing groundbreaking best practices across diverse European library systems. They argue that collaboration with the community and smart tools such as the LibrarIN Toolkit can help libraries transform into vital community hubs. The brief concludes with actionable policy recommendations to ensure the effective spread of inspiring and adaptable examples for library innovation across Europe.

5.3 Future Outlook and Topics for Research

For library innovators, both policymakers and practitioners, there is a clear need for a coordinated European effort to bring together the currently fragmented landscape of smart library tools. Such coordination would support libraries in their transformation into vibrant community hubs, helping them to better respond to societal challenges and the evolving needs of their communities. For policymakers, this represents a strategic opportunity to increase the social impact of libraries, ensure a more effective use of innovation investments, and foster cross-border knowledge sharing and capacity building across Europe.

In the remaining months of the LibrarIN project, several steps are planned:

- **Expansion of the policy tracker dataset**: New country-level data will enrich the initial dataset of the Library Policy Tracker, covering all EU Member States, enabling more comprehensive benchmarking.
- **Upcoming evidence-based policy briefs**: Upcoming policy briefs will cover topics such as AI, social entrepreneurship, living labs, and the LibrarIN metrics framework for effective collaboration. Each of the briefs will offer actionable recommendations and will be discussed at policy roundtables with library policymakers and practitioners for further transformation.
- **Final conference and knowledge dissemination**: The Final LibrarIN Conference provided a platform to showcase the LibrarIN Toolkit, share new cases in the What-Works Database, and spark collaboration among innovators in libraries.
- **Sustainability and open contributions**: The Toolkit will remain open to new case submissions and policy data, ensuring that its relevance and impact extend beyond the life of the project. In addition, sustainability conversations are taking place with European library initiatives and associations.

Acknowledgements The work for this chapter was supported by the European Union's Horizon Europe Research and Innovation Programme under Grant Agreement ID 101061516.

Appendix 1: List of Indicators

Below is presented the final list of indicators for the Library Policy Tracker, which are grouped by dimensions and ordered alphabetically (Table 2).

Table 2 List of indicators for the Library Policy Tracker

Participatory management and sustainable growth	
Integration of libraries into national SDG frameworks	**Libraries** or library activities are explicitly **included in official national documents related to the Sustainable Development Goals** (SDGs)
Libraries as guardians of freedom of expression	There is a legal requirement that identifies the **role of libraries as independent meeting places** that contribute to the **freedom of expression and thought** and provide access to a broad range of information **free from censorship**
Libraries as places for dialogue	There are national policies or programmes that **identify and promote libraries as platforms for democratic discussion** among the citizens
Promoting lifelong learning in libraries	There are national policies or programmes that **support and enhance lifelong learning** for library staff and users, ensuring continuous education and skill development
Resources to ensure adequate training of staff and users	There is a dedicated national budget or funding programme **for the training of library staff and users** to ensure that they are able to **make proper use of the new tools and services** now available
Safe and inclusive places for all kinds of minorities	The country provides **guidelines** to all libraries with minimum standards for the **provision of accessible and inclusive services** and promotes, wherever necessary, **special programmes to combat any discriminatory practice**
Digital innovation and AI	
Digital skill and literacy development	There is a **national plan or strategy** that encourages and **promotes** the implementation of effective and tailored **media, information, and digital literacy programmes for library staff and users** in libraries
Integration of libraries in national AI strategy with ethical framework	The country has a **national AI implementation strategy that includes libraries** and ensures the enforcement of privacy and equity principles
Libraries included in the national digital transformation strategy	The country has a **national digital transformation plan including** provisions to scale up **library practices** from analogue to digital
Promotion of ethical use of AI in libraries	The national AI policy framework incorporates libraries as **key actors in promoting ethical use of AI**, including provisions for the exchange of best practices and user education
Social innovation	
Collaboration among libraries and archives	There are regional and/or National Library **and archiving systems** whose members **co-operate on matters of acquisition and circulation of collections**
Collaboration with artistic, cultural, and educational institutions	There are regional and/or National Library **environments** whose members form close **working relationships with other artistic, cultural, and educational institutions**

(continued)

Table 2 (continued)

Cooperation with non-governmental organisations (NGOs)	There are regional and/or national **networks that facilitate partnerships between libraries and NGOs**, enabling collaboration on projects that **address local community needs and social issues**
Coordination with community development plans	The country has mechanisms in place to ensure the **coordination of libraries' activities with the community development plans and strategies**
Living labs	
Co-creation support	The country has a **national plan including** explicitly **the use of co-creation** (active user involvement) to **promote innovation in library services**
Community engagement for democratic participation	There is a national **framework** that supports libraries to **provide platforms for discussion and organise public debates**, engaging communities and fostering a culture of innovation and democratic participation
Inclusive library solutions	The country has established national **strategies that guide libraries in designing inclusive solutions**, incorporating awareness raising, media literacy, broad stakeholder involvement, and cooperation with public authorities
Resources to ensure innovation experiments	There is a **dedicated national budget or funding programme** for the **development of innovation experiments** in libraries
Metrics and monitoring	
Guidelines for performance measurement	The country has **guidelines for quality performance measurement** relating to the different types of **libraries and their missions** in compliance with the SDGs
Impact assessment studies	There are recent **studies or evaluations** within the past 5 years that **analyse the social, educational, cultural, and economic impacts** of different types of libraries in the country, conducted or commissioned by national bodies
Reuse of information for policy and decision-making	There is a **national strategy to exercise control over data and information from library operations** and to **reuse** these **in policymaking and decision-making** processes

References

1. *Manifesto for the 2024 EU Elections* (LIBER Europe), https://libereurope.eu/document/manifesto-for-the-2024-eu-elections/. Accessed 20 Apr 2025
2. Open Method of Coordination (OMC) Group of Member States' experts on Building bridges: strengthen the multiple roles of libraries as gateways to and transmitters of cultural works, skills and European values, https://data.consilium.europa.eu/doc/document/ST-14250-2023-INIT/en/pdf. Accessed 20 Apr 2025
3. Recommendation CM/Rec(2023)3 of the Committee of Ministers to member States on library legislation and policy in Europe, https://rm.coe.int/0900001680aaced6. Accessed 20 Apr 2025
4. European Commission, *Green Paper on Innovation* (Publications Office of the European Union, 1996)

5. D. Osimo, Foreword, in *Case Studies in e-Government 2.0*, ed. by I. Boughzala, M. Janssen, S. Assar, (Springer International Publishing, 2015)
6. L. Rubalcaba, E. Solano, E. Silvestrini, M. Willems, LibrarIN First Policy Brief—Reimagine Libraries: Sparking Collaboration for Innovation to Tackle Libraries' 21st Century Challenges (2024), https://librarin.eu/download/20034/?tmstv=1721386604
7. LibrarIN Stakeholder Panel, https://librarin.eu/who-we-are/stakeholders/. Accessed 20 Apr 2025
8. L. Rubalcaba, E. Solano, M. Willems et al., LibrarIN Second Policy Brief—boosting and evaluating collaborative innovations in libraries: managerial guidelines and policy implications (2025)
9. LibrarIN managerial guidelines and policy implications, https://librarin.eu/download/22759/?tmstv=1747642876 Accessed 13 Jun 2025
10. The IFLA-UNESCO Public Library Manifesto 2022, https://www.ifla.org/public-library-manifesto/. Accessed 20 Apr 2025
11. New European Bauhaus: beautiful, sustainable, together, https://new-european-bauhaus.europa.eu/. Accessed 20 Apr 2025
12. Plan Nacional de Competencias Digitales, https://portal.mineco.gob.es/RecursosNoticia/mineco/prensa/noticias/2021/210127_np_digital.pdf. Accessed 20 Apr 2025
13. Denmark Is the EU's Digital Champion in New Survey, https://en.digst.dk/news/news-archive/2021/november/denmark-is-the-eu-s-digital-champion-in-new-survey/. Accessed 20 Apr 2025
14. Digital Transformation Bible 2020–2025, https://digitalstrategy.gov.gr/website/static/website/assets/uploads/digital_strategy.pdf. Accessed 20 Apr 2025
15. National Strategy for Digital Inclusion: Key Recommendations, https://labo.societenumerique.gouv.fr/en/articles/national-strategy-for-an-inclusive-digital-main-recommendations/. Accessed 20 Apr 2025
16. Libraries on the front line of digital mediation, https://labo.societenumerique.gouv.fr/en/articles/folder-libraries-first-on-line-for-digital-mediation/. Accessed 20 Apr 2025
17. BnF and Artificial intelligence, https://www.bnf.fr/en/artificial-intelligence-bnf. Accessed 20 Apr 2025
18. Estrategia Nacional de Digitalización 2022–2026, https://www.ccbiblio.es/wp-content/uploads/Estrategia-Nacional-de-Digitalizacion-1.pdf. Accessed 20 Apr 2025
19. Strategia Națională privind Agenda Digitală pentru România, https://www.trusted.ro/wp-content/uploads/2014/09/Strategia-Nationala-Agenda-Digitala-8-septembrie-2014.pdf. Accessed 20 Apr 2025
20. Danish ethical supervision, https://investindk.com/insights/denmark-decides-on-ethical-principles-for-ai. Accessed 20 Apr 2025
21. Danish government AI strategy report 2019 to the EU Commission, https://ai-watch.ec.europa.eu/countries/denmark/denmark-ai-strategy-report_en. Accessed 20 Apr 2025
22. Policy Künstliche Intelligenz, https://www.onb.ac.at/mehr/ueber-uns/policy-kuenstliche-intelligenz. Accessed 20 Apr 2025
23. Estrategia de Inteligencia Artificial 2024, https://digital.gob.es/dam/es/portalmtdfp/DigitalizacionIA/Estrategia_IA_2024.pdf. Accessed 20 Apr 2025
24. Experience France 2030, https://experience.france2030.gouv.fr/fr/. Accessed 20 Apr 2025
25. Strategia națională în domeniul inteligenței artificiale 2024–2027, https://www.adr.gov.ro/wp-content/uploads/2024/03/Strategie-Inteligenta-Artificiala-22012024-1.pdf. Accessed 20 Apr 2025
26. LibrarIN What-Works Database details, https://librarin.eu/toolkit/what-works-db/details/22529. Accessed 20 Apr 2025

Marieke Willems is a senior research associate and project manager at the Lisbon Council. She holds a Master of Science in communication science from Radboud University in the Netherlands and a master's in business administration from the Escuela de Alta Dirección y Administración in Barcelona. Willems specialises in the coordination, dissemination, and stakeholder engagement of projects with a focus on democracy and social innovation. Her recent work includes managing diverse European projects and initiatives in the fields of evidence-based policymaking, open science, and research infrastructures.

Marta Anducas is a project manager and research associate at the Lisbon Council. She holds a master's degree from Desarrollo Internacional and a bachelor's degree in computer engineering from Pompeu Fabra University. With field experience studying the customs and traditions of Indigenous communities in the Amazon, Anducas specialises in rural areas policies, social innovation, and cooperation. Her recent work includes designing and implementing collaborative initiatives to drive social innovation at Platoniq, a Spanish non-profit organisation.

Elena Silvestrini is a senior project manager and research associate at the Lisbon Council. Before joining the Lisbon Council, she spent 5 years leading and designing participation initiatives at Platoniq Creatividad y Democracia, a Spanish non-profit, and co-founded Chayn Italia, an organisation committed to fighting gender-based violence. Silvestrini sits on the global steering committee for the design justice network and is an experienced group and process facilitator. She holds a master of science degree in gender, development and globalisation from the London School of Economics and Political Science and a bachelor's degree in political science and international relations from the University of Roma Tre, Italy.

MIX
Papier aus verantwortungsvollen Quellen
Paper from responsible sources
FSC® C105338

If you have any concerns about our products,
you can contact us on
ProductSafety@springernature.com

In case Publisher is established outside the EU,
the EU authorized representative is:
Springer Nature Customer Service Center GmbH
Europaplatz 3, 69115 Heidelberg, Germany

Printed by Libri Plureos GmbH
in Hamburg, Germany